EDUCATING THE PEOPLE

A DOCUMENTARY HISTORY OF ELEMENTARY SCHOOLING IN ENGLAND, 1840–1870

NANCY BALL

MAURICE TEMPLE SMITH · LONDON

First published in Great Britain in 1983
by Maurice Temple Smith Ltd
Gloucester Mansions, Cambridge Circus
London WC2H 8HD

Ball, Nancy
Educating the people
1. Education, Elementary—England—History
—19th century
I. Title
372.942 LA633

ISBN 0-85117-227-X

Typeset by Preface Ltd, Salisbury Wilts
Printed in Great Britain by Billing & Sons, Worcester

CONTENTS

ACKNOWLEDGEMENTS

The author wishes to thank the archivists and librarians without whose help this book could not have been written.

For permission to make quotations in the text: the National Society; the County Record Offices (CRO) of Cheshire, Dorset, Durham, Leicestershire, Staffordshire, Worcestershire; Kent Archives Office; City of Birmingham Libraries; City of Manchester Cultural Services Department; John Murray (Publishers) Ltd (*The Diary of Lady Frederick Cavendish*); the Director, Derby Lonsdale College of Higher Education.

For permission to reproduce unpublished material: the Controller, HMSO (IC); Berkshire RO, on behalf of the depositors (IB, 5H); Cheshire RO (5Lvi, 5Lviii, 7A); Cornwall CRO (5Lv); Derbyshire RO (5Liii); Durham CRO (4Gii); Hampshire RO (6Di); Kent Archives Office (2H); Lancashire RO (5J, 5Li); Leeds City Archives Department (4A); Leicestershire RO (4L, 5Mi); Staffordshire RO (IA, IE); Suffolk RO (5Lvii); Cheltenham Library (IF); Hereford and Worcester County Libraries (2E); Chief Education Officer, Hereford and Worcester (3K, 5Lii, 5Liv, 6Lii); the Governors of Archbishop Michael Ramsey School (5A); the Chairman of Governors, Christ Church School, Streatham (3H); the Vicar, St Chad's Church, Shrewsbury (3Fi, 4D); the Headmaster, CE Primary School, Staveley (3G).

INTRODUCTION

VOLUNTARY SCHOOLING ESTABLISHED

BY 1870 the majority of advanced Western countries had developed a system of national education; but there was an exception. In England schooling for the masses was provided by voluntary groups, almost all professing some religious motive. The role of the public authority was supportive only; it could not control provision or enforce attendance or standards of performance. To advocates of secular education the cause of this sorry situation was obvious: the dead hand of the established Church, 'the ally of tyranny, the organ of social oppression, the champion of intellectual bondage'[1] and, though in terms less abusive than those of John Morley, this has been the verdict of most historians. It has seemed unlikely that schools established under such circumstances could have had much positive significance in educational development and less attention has been paid to them than to the process and influences whereby their monopoly was ended. Nevertheless, their activities are well documented. The purpose of this study is to examine their record.

In most European countries the ancient tradition that education, a work of mercy, was a function of the Churches, helped rather than hindered the establishment of a national system. In eighteenth-century Prussia, for example, a centralising State established control over schools provided by both Catholic and Protestant Churches; whilst in Scotland a dominant Church, through the agency of the old Scottish Parliament, had, in 1696, imposed upon its presbyteries the duty of providing a school in each parish. In England, however, the conflicts of the seventeenth century ensured that no such initiative was possible from either State or Church. Governmental functions were reduced to a minimum in Hanoverian England. Social policy-making was not one of them; and the Anglican Church, deprived of all its coercive powers, was left in a state of privileged impotence, without the machinery to establish schools even if it had wished to do so.

Provision for education, like provision for hospitals, turnpike roads and other improvements, was left to the profit motive ('adventure schools') or to private generosity. The system of voluntary schooling was a natural outcome of the conditions of eighteenth-century English society.

Although wealthy men no longer devoted their fortunes to the founding of great schools, many smaller endowments were still being created, sometimes amounting in the aggregate to very considerable sums.[2] Thus Edward Colston of Bristol, in addition to two major foundations in the city, made bequests to five other schools in Bristol and nineteen elsewhere. Most of these new endowments were unconcerned with 'grammar' or preparation for the universities. Their purpose was to provide such basic education for the poor as would make them good Christians and useful to society, terms which were often treated as synonyms. The desire to attain these ends was not confined to the rich. Pious individuals like Hannah More and her sisters at the end of the century begged from their friends in order to finance schools; and the evolution of the subscription school, maintained by regular annual donations and run by a committee of subscribers, gave persons of modest prosperity an outlet for their charity. The term 'charity school' was commonly used for all three types since, if their origins differed, their policies were similar. They were free schools for the poor of either sex; if their funds allowed, the committees provided clothes for the pupils and arranged apprenticeships for them. Curriculum (the 'literary curriculum') was centred upon religious instruction, with reading, some writing, a little arithmetic for boys and needlework for girls; and, in return for these benefits, both pupils and their parents were expected to submit to a degree of moral supervision.

Anglican charity schools owed much of their success to the activities of the Society for the Promotion of Christian Knowledge. Founded in 1699 to spread the Gospel both at home and overseas, the schools were its primary interest during the first twenty-five years of its existence. It acted as a source of educational propaganda, of advice on organisation, curriculum and discipline and as an employment agency for teachers. The charity-school movement reached its peak in the middle 1720s when Anglican charity schools were educating between 20,000 and 25,000 children; to which total must be added an unspecifiable number in schools established by dissenters. Later the momentum slackened. Individual schools prospered; others survived, to be absorbed, willingly or unwillingly, into the nineteenth-century elementary system. But subscriptions became more difficult to raise; the number of new endowments dwindled (from 235 in the decade 1710–20 to fifty-five between 1770 and 1780); the SPCK increasingly turned its attention to overseas work and the publication of religious literature; and the number of charity-school pupils remained static whilst the child population increased. As a general means of educating the people, the movement had clearly failed.

A major obstacle had been widespread scepticism as to the desirability of educating the poor, even with the aim of their moral improvement. When, towards the end of the century, the interaction of religious revival, the influence of the Enlightenment and a fear of revolutionary upheaval led increasing numbers of the educated classes to feel an obligation to provide schooling for the mass of the people, other difficulties, especially that of finding and supporting competent teachers from the resources available to private individuals, seemed insuperable. Sunday schools, the most fashionable form of educational philanthropy in the latter years of the century,[3] owed their rapid expansion to the fact that they met on the only day of the week on which large numbers of volunteers were free to teach. Without them the schools could not have existed. To those zealots, therefore, who believed that only day schools could achieve educational success, the monitorial system, whereby children were programmed to instruct other children under the supervision of a single teacher, seemed literally providential, answering the needs of education as spinning machinery and the steam engine answered the needs of industry.[4]

Neither Lancaster nor Bell, the two patriarchs of voluntary schooling, was an educational theorist. At the end of the eighteenth century each stumbled upon the monitorial system by accident, in characteristic circumstances. For Lancaster it was an expedient to cope with the hordes of children who flocked to his free school in Southwark; for Bell, when he was superintendent of an orphanage in Madras, a means of breaking a strike of teachers too prejudiced to adopt an Indian method of teaching writing. Both men were gifted teachers whose merits, irrespective of the system, made their schools justly popular and each was convinced that he had found the panacea for all educational ills. Neither believed that the monitorial system should be confined to schools for the poor; but to their followers the system was first and foremost a means of using limited resources to spread a basic education more widely than had hitherto seemed possible.

The natural reaction of any early-nineteenth-century enthusiast was to form a society to disseminate his ideas. The two societies which resulted from the activities of Lancaster and Bell were polarised on the question of religious instruction. Whilst Bell's schools were Anglican, Lancaster, a Quaker, confined religious instruction to the study of passages from the Bible ('scriptural instruction'). The Royal Lancasterian Society, founded in 1808 to keep him out of financial trouble rather than to establish more schools, adopted this restriction as a principle. Lancaster was already under attack as a threat to the established Church. At a time when the Test Act was still on the statute book and when the trust deeds of most endowed schools (both grammar and elementary) prescribed the teaching of the catechism, this principle was unlikely to be acceptable to the Anglican hierarchy. The initiative for the National Society for the Education of the Poor in the Principles of the Established Church came from high-church laymen connected with the SPCK, but it immediately received the support of the whole bench of bishops. Although many Anglicans continued to subscribe to both societies, the polarisation was emphasised when the Lancasterian committee severed its connection with Lancaster. In 1814 it adopted the name of the British and Foreign School Society, thereby aligning itself by implication with the controversial British and Foreign Bible Society, founded in 1804 by an alliance of Anglican evangelicals and nonconformists and abominated by all high churchmen.

Neither society ever controlled more than its own central schools and, later, its own training colleges. Their function was to act as national pressure groups and to assist affiliated schools with advice, facilities for training teachers and, under certain circumstances, money grants. Like other philanthropic societies of the period their structure assumed the existence of local committees or branch societies; but, whereas in the anti-slavery campaign or such bodies as the Church Missionary Society, these were merely fund-raising agencies or, when appropriate, drummers-up of local feeling, National and British committees took permanent responsibility for managing schools or even, in the case of Anglican branch societies, for attempting to develop education in a wide area.[5] Acceptance of prescribed terms of union was a necessary condition for affiliation but, in practice, the societies knew little more about the schools than school promoters chose to tell them and exercised only a minimal amount of control.

Affiliation might be sought by a committee of management, by an individual patron, or by the trustees of an endowment, any of whom might put their own construction on the terms of union.[6] The British terms laid down that pupils should be enjoined to attend a place of worship on Sunday. At Hoddesden British School John Warner, the 'sole proprietor', decided that the boys must assemble in school on Sundays in order to be escorted to the chosen services. The National Society's terms of union prescribed that pupils should, without exception, be taught the liturgy and catechism and attend church on Sundays; but the rules of the branch society in Suffolk gave managers the right to exempt children from Sunday attendance. Even more surprising were instances in which the National Society made grants to schools whose committees had already announced that they did not intend to teach the catechism to children whose parents did not wish them to learn it.[7] Moreover, many school committees were on principle unwilling to affiliate with either society. Evangelicals thought the National Society excessively high church; but the British exclusion of creed and catechism was as unacceptable to them as it was to the Wesleyans in the 1840s. Consequently many Anglican schools never owed even nominal allegiance to either society, just as many nonconformists were not prepared to accept the undenominational stance of the British and Foreign Society. Thus, from the beginning, voluntary-school committees were accustomed to make policy decisions with very little interference and no constant supervision.

Accurate estimates of the number of schools and scholars are therefore lacking. In 1830 the National Society claimed that its supporters were educating about 175,000 children in 2595 daily schools. These figures may have been exaggerated but do not represent the total Anglican effort. The British total was much smaller. The disparity is evident in figures from early nineteenth-century Lancashire.[8] In 1832 there were 139 National schools in the county compared with twelve British schools. There were also schools following Bell's system without being affiliated to the society; in 1839 the number was estimated at nearly 190. By that year the National Society claimed to be educating 29,487 children in Lancashire whilst, on the most generous estimate, the British total cannot have been much more than 12,100. In terms of the effort of individual school committees the figures are impressive; but, as an educational provision for a rapidly increasing population growing up in a society whose traditional structure had been shattered by economic change, they were clearly inadequate.

By 1830, in any case, monitorial schools were losing their reputation. They had begun as free schools, avowedly intended for the poor. In 1859 Mary Carpenter, the philanthropist, nostalgically recalled the days when the first British school in Bristol contained 'the lowest class of children, and the most wretched lanes and alleys were searched for them'.[9] But experience revealed that such children rarely attended regularly and that when they came they drove out the respectable; most schools gave up the attempt to attract them and yet, with some exceptions,[10] failed to modify their approach sufficiently to wean the 'industrious' working class from cheap adventure schools. Few curricula went much beyond the charity-school pattern of the 3Rs and needlework for the girls. Monitors were both inefficient and unreliable since, with most children, the office was unpopular. The merits of Lancaster and Bell, their use of incentives and their mobilisation of pupil opinion in support of their aims, failed to survive in the hands of half-educated teachers with, at best, a few weeks of training. The most that they could be expected to achieve was order and rote learning. To maintain and increase subscriptions in such depressing circumstances was almost impossible. By the late 1820s school committees were struggling against declining resources as well as declining prestige.

Educational enthusiam had not diminished. It flowed into other channels: attacks on the classical curriculum, the reform of higher education, the encouragement of self-improvement amongst working men and, more relevant to elementary schools, three important developments of the middle 1830s. The group of Radical publicists and experts who formed an education lobby founded the Central Society of Education with the utilitarian aim of identifying a rational basis for a State system, 'heaping fact upon fact and argument upon argument, classifying and opposing . . . and drawing a conclusion'.[11] In Scotland, where the monitorial system had never struck deep roots, David Stow developed methods of collective teaching whereby, he claimed, one adult teacher could not only instruct but also educate a large number of children simultaneously. In 1836 the Glasgow Normal Seminary was founded to prepare these 'trainers'.[12] In the same year a group of evangelical enthusiasts for early education formed the Home and Colonial School Society and established a training school in which governesses and teachers in schools for the poor could learn Pestalozzian methods of instructing young children.[13] With these anti-monitorial tides flowing strongly, it might have seemed that National and British schools would be forced into the backwaters occupied by the charity schools. That this did not happen resulted from two factors; a sudden resurgence of activity amongst the Anglicans of the National Society and the excitement generated within all the religious denominations by State intervention in elementary education.[14]

Politicians like Whitbread and Brougham, who in the early years of the century had attempted to carry legislation for public provision of mass education, had been isolated figures; but by 1830 the situation had changed. There was wide agreement amongst politically active members of the governing classes that greater provision for popular education was a necessity. The motives behind this consensus remain a subject of controversy;[15] its existence is illustrated by the almost casual acceptance in a thin House of Commons in 1833 of school building grants, to be paid by the Treasury through the agency of the National Society and the British and Foreign School Society. The grants were not in themselves of great significance. They speeded up the building of schools and they probably slightly strengthened the societies since, to obtain a grant, school promoters had to connect themselves with one or the other. But they were seen as a mere temporary expedient, preliminary to the legislation for which Radicals continued to press. They were therefore regarded with suspicion in some quarters, a suspicion strengthened for many Anglicans by other events. Whatever underlying motives were present it is important to recognise that, at the conscious level, nineteenth-century political disputes about elementary schools were fought over emotive and mutually incompatible ideas of religious freedom: freedom of individual conscience and freedom for the Churches to carry out their divinely ordained duty towards the nation's children without interference from a potentially infidel Parliament. It was no accident that the major conflicts occurred when the position of the established Church in English society was under political attack. By the later 1830s Catholic emancipation, threats of disendowment in Ireland, the ending by the Municipal Corporations Act of Anglican dominance of town councils and, above all, the creation of the Ecclesiastical Commission convinced a group of influential young high churchmen that a godless society was in the making and they determined to awaken the Church of England to her proper function as educator of all classes of people.[16]

As a first measure they induced the National Society to rethink its whole programme through a committee of enquiry which they dominated; they then moved out into the dioceses to arouse enthusiasm and to channel it through the establishment of boards of education. Until recently their importance has been underestimated; yet, although the group disintegrated in the 1840s, as individuals they continued to campaign throughout the mid-Victorian years. The impact upon the elementary system of two of them, Gladstone and Manning, was to be crucial in the next half-century, though in ways which neither could have foreseen in 1838. Many of the group's ideas, the Professorship of Education at King's College, London, the use of cathedral endowments for teacher-training and to provide secondary education for promising elementary-school pupils, the wholesale establishment by the Church of middle-class schools, were visionary. But under their influence the National Society prepared to abandon the monitorial system ten years before the British and Foreign Society was willing to do so. They spread the belief that it was the duty of the clergy to take active responsibility for the running of schools and, because they were concerned with the education of all social classes, they introduced, however tentatively, a liberal element which had hitherto been markedly lacking in the elementary scene.[17] The original curricula of the Anglican teacher-training colleges which they were instrumental in founding[18] were criticised by officials as involving too much higher, and too little elementary, education. Indeed, the concept of a *college* to perform the training function was theirs; governmental preference was for the continental model, the *normal school*. In National schools they were prepared to encourage the mixing of social classes and the teaching of advanced subjects. Finally, their activities ensured the maximum opposition to the plans for education which Lord John Russell presented to Parliament in February 1839.

Compared with foreign systems or with the system established in Ireland in 1831 by the Whigs themselves, Russell's scheme seems tentative and half-hearted.[19] It involved the creation of a department (the Committee of Council) to distribute the education grant, to organise school inspection, to establish and maintain an undenominational normal school, to compile school textbooks and to reward deserving teachers. The secretary to the new committee, Kay-Shuttleworth, believed, optimistically, that these proposals would ultimately lead to control of the voluntary schools by the State. Others thought so too, and a weak government was faced with agitated and almost universal opposition from Anglicans and only partial support from dissenters. The British and Foreign committee cooperated until they learnt the terms of the Concordat of July 1840, but the Wesleyans were hostile to a State-defined undenominational religion, 'adapted to every prevailing variety of religious belief or opinion',[20] and the Congregationalists believed that any State intervention in education was an infringement of civil, as well as religious, liberty. Eventually, after eighteen months of controversy, a compromise (the Concordat) was worked out between the government and the leading bishops. The Committee of Council survived and an inspectorate survived; but the archbishops gained a veto over the appointment of inspectors of Anglican schools (who in practice were always ordained) and drew up their instructions for the inspection of religious education. The proposals for a normal school had already been dropped; the preparation of textbooks was abandoned. In 1843 a veto on the appointment of inspectors of non-Anglican schools, who were to inspect secular instruction only, was conceded to the British and Foreign committee and later extended to the Wesleyans and the Jews. When the Catholics established the Poor School Committee in response to the large-scale immigration of Irish Catholics which followed the famine of 1846, they were given their own inspectorate and a similar right of veto.

It is difficult to see how more could have been salvaged from Russell's original proposals. Since he had justified them by reference to the State's duty to maintain public order and public morality it followed, in the contemporary view, that education *must* be religious; indeed, until 1870, no schools received public money in which the Bible was not read daily. But the State proposed to do no more than give limited assistance to groups prepared to organise and pay for a religious education; it could scarcely expect to determine the form of that education. From the point of view of the religious denominations the claims to intrude a possibly hostile inspector into the schools and to determine the nature of religious instruction in the normal school were the thin end of the wedge, to be resisted at all costs. Whether, had these proposals been accepted, they would have made much difference to the course of events must inevitably remain an open question; as it was, the State, recognising, as Kay-Shuttleworth told the Newcastle Commission, 'the exceeding strength of the religious principle' and 'the exceeding weakness of any other principle; as, for example, of the patriotic or the civil principle – upon which [it] could in any degree rely',[21] accepted the voluntary schools as they had evolved by 1840 as the basis of popular education. For the next twenty-five years the initiative in mass education was increasingly left to voluntary-school promoters.[22] Whilst the first annual grants from the State under the Minutes of 1846 were paid directly to teachers and pupil-teachers, thus bypassing school managers, the latter received the capitation grant of 1853. The Revised Code of 1862, in one sense a tightening of State control, was in another sense an abdication, introducing the policy of leaving the local authority to determine the way in which the grant should be spent.

In 1840, then, the country was committed to an experiment in voluntary initiative aided, but not controlled, by the State. Public, as distinct from profit-making, elementary schools never, of course, swept the board. Small private schools, of which the evidence is probably too scanty ever to permit a connected history, continued to be used by parents from a mixture of independent pride, indifference, personal friendship with the teacher and, as the novelist Charlotte Yonge noted disapprovingly, snobbery:

Mrs Fielding was not a wise woman, and chose to despise Mrs Wright and her [National] school, saying that her child should never go to a charity-school, so . . . she let her go to a little close room, where a person only half taught, and with no guide as to what was the safest kind of learning, kept a little school for the children of a few mothers who, like Mrs Fielding, thought it a disgrace to learn with those a little poorer than themselves. . .[23]

Nevertheless, a steadily increasing number of parents chose to use the voluntary schools whose numbers rose accordingly. For a potential school population estimated by contemporaries at various figures between two and a quarter and nearly five million the Educational Census of 1851 recorded 8571 public elementary schools connected with the Church of England, 1506 of other denominations and 514 British (undenominational) schools in England and Wales. Only 1433 elementary schools received annual government grants in 1851; by the mid-1860s this figure had risen to 6362 and by 1869 there were two million places in inspected schools. The numbers in unaided schools are more difficult to determine. In 1867 60 per cent (about 900,000) of the children on the registers of Anglican schools were under inspection, leaving 600,000 in uninspected schools.[24]

What sort of people 'allowed [themselves]', in West's words, 'to be given an education that was typically connected with religious organizations'?[25] The question is not easily answered. Census returns help little and school admission registers of the period are rare and badly kept. In 1858 the Education Department[26] published lists of the parents of pupils in the six schools which received the largest capitation grants in 1857. Useless as a sample, since the schools were not typical, the lists show certain interesting features. Whilst parental occupations in five of the schools[27] ranged from lawyer to pig-driver, well over 2000 of the 3779 fathers belonged to the white-collar and skilled-artisan classes: shopkeepers, clerks, railwaymen and, above all, skilled tradesmen. In these schools, at least, the dominant group came from the type of household which was to be enfranchised by the Reform Act of 1867.

Anglican predominance in the field of elementary schooling was maintained in mid-Victorian England. In the Anglican revival it became a matter of course that new churches in the towns should be accompanied by new schools;[28] country schools were almost exclusively Anglican unless the landowner was an upper-class Radical or a Catholic squire. British principles showed less capacity for expansion but there was a steady nucleus of support for British schools amongst wealthy Quakers and Unitarians. Some small businessmen and shopkeepers liked them as a means of expressing independence of squire and parson; and they provided an umbrella for the very few large day schools – perhaps twenty, mostly in Lancashire – which were run by committees from working-men's institutions and which sought State aid; the Hull Savings Bank, for instance, or the Ancoats Lyceum in Manchester.

The 1840s and 1850s saw a rapid growth of the schools of non-Anglican denominations. The Wesleyans, having decided that scriptural instruction and the monitorial system were unacceptable, established the Wesleyan Education Committee in 1841 and founded over 600 denominational schools in the next twenty years. The Catholics shouldered the herculean task of establishing confessional schools for the Irish in London and the industrial north. The group, later termed the Voluntaryists, provides an interesting case study. Mainly Congregationalist they had been shocked by the willingness of the British and Foreign committee to reach an accommodation with the State in the early 1840s; led by Edward Baines they finally broke with the society when, by accepting the Minutes of 1846, it accepted State-paid teachers: 'A system of state education', wrote Baines, 'is a vast intellectual police, set to watch over the young . . . to prevent the intrusion of dangerous thoughts and turn their minds into safe channels.'[29]

The Voluntaryists set out to establish a network of schools as free from outside interference as their own congregations. Alone amongst voluntary-school promoters they believed that the working class should be trusted with its own education. Not, perhaps, immediately; but they looked forward to the next generation when their schools would be organised and financed by parents who in their youth had learnt the value of a good education. The failure of Voluntaryism to command sufficient support, acknowledged in 1867 when Baines recanted and advised his followers to accept government aid, is a sad reflection on the fate of educational idealism. Many Voluntaryists drifted reluctantly into support of the National Education League, founded in 1869 by a group of Birmingham Radicals to campaign for a national system of free and compulsory schools. Some of the inconsistencies in the League's programme, notably its demand for unsectarian rather than secular education, resulted from Voluntaryist principles.

Most of the League's founders held the secularist view that the exclusion of religious teaching from the curriculum was the only rational basis for a system of public education. There was no reason why voluntary schools should not have been founded on this principle but, perhaps logically, most secularists preferred to wait for the establishment of a State system. Two exceptions were the much-publicised Manchester Free Secular School, founded in 1854 by the Lancashire-based National Public School Association to demonstrate that their principles were practicable;[30] and the Birkbeck Schools in London, established by William Ellis, secularist and social economist, to show how an advanced education might be provided for the sons of prosperous artisans.[31] These few exceptions, however, only serve to emphasise the extent to which the educational scene was dominated by religious groups.

By the late 1860s thirty years had passed since the State had entered into partnership with these groups. The relationship had never been easy and its success was only partial. Many areas were still without schools; many schools had failed to obtain State aid; the poorest classes scarcely attended school at all. The partnership was thus overdue for reconstruction in circumstances which made the religious commitment of the voluntary groups, and especially the predominant position of the established Church, a liability. Society was changing. It was no longer axiomatic that the duty of government was to support provision for a religious education. Increasing numbers of people (including many Anglicans) now believed that the State should not concern itself with religion at all. Hence the basis for the compromise of 1840 was no longer valid. In education, as elsewhere in national life, the balance shifted against the Churches and in favour of public authority; and of this shift the Education Act of 1870 was one consequence.

Gladstone's Liberal government of 1868–74, which carried the Act, was based on an amalgam of Whigs and Radicals; but the Act took little account of Radical views and received more support from the opposition than from the left of the Liberal party.

Its purpose was only to 'fill the gaps' left by thirty years' expansion, through the agency of rate-aided school boards. Voluntary schools survived and even in 1900 were still educating the majority of elementary schoolchildren. But the best school boards showed what could be achieved with greater resources and greater legal powers than voluntary school managers possessed; and the Act of 1870 has come to be regarded, if not as the origin, at least as the catalyst, of a transformation both in administrative terms and in attitudes towards the education of the people. The contrast is commonly seen as one between obscurantism and enlightenment.

Yet there is little evidence of discontinuity of educational development. The Education Department's power was strengthened, both legally and by the creation of an alternative to voluntary schools, but its organisation, its assumptions and its methods did not change. The Revised Code, gradually modified by a process which had begun in 1867, continued to govern the grant system. Denominational inspection was abolished but the inspectorate did not change; its senior members were all men who had been appointed before 1870. Board schools were staffed from the voluntary schools. The Department created the larger teaching force needed to implement the Act by granting what it had hitherto refused: certificates to serving teachers, without examination, on the recommendation of H.M. Inspectors. Until the advent in 1891 of day training colleges attached to universities the entire elite of trained teachers came from the voluntary colleges. The expertise of many leading members of school boards, Herbert Birley in Manchester, for example, or Titus Salt in Shipley, had been acquired in voluntary schools. Beneath the rhetoric of Parliament and of school-board election campaigns there was a basic continuity of personalities.

How far was there also continuity of purpose? The extent to which the character of English elementary education derived from the experience of voluntary schooling before 1870 can only be assessed when we understand the educational process within mid-nineteenth-century voluntary schools; and there are obstacles in the way of such an understanding. The schools were anarchic in the sense of being subject to less external control than any later schools for the mass of the people; far less than either their sponsoring organisations or the State had originally intended.

The National Society, the British and Foreign School Society and the Committee of Council in its early months had all failed in attempts to prescribe textbooks and teaching methods. Only amongst the Catholics, by the combined authority of the hierarchy and of the orders of nuns who dominated girls' education, was a measure of uniformity achieved.[32] Consequently, valid generalisations about the nature of the voluntary experience can be made only when questions have been raised and answered about what actually happened in individual schools. Who founded them? by whom were they run and how were they financed? to what extent were they influenced by external bodies, voluntary or public? how was the monitorial system superseded and what organisation replaced it? what sort of people were the teachers? what were their relations with parents and pupils? what did they teach, and how, and with what success?

An attempt will made in chapters 1 to 7 to answer some of these questions with the help of documentary evidence from individual schools and school promoters. The educationist Richard Dawes, founder of a famous school at King's Somborne, remarked in 1847 that the real difficulty of the education question lay in 'getting it out of the hands of the talking men, and into those of the practical and working ones'.[33] The real difficulty for the student of educational history is often that the most accessible evidence is that of the talking men. What follows is an attempt to see elementary schooling through the eyes of the 'practical and working ones'.

Notes

(PP. = Parliamentary Papers, q. = question)

1. J. Morley, *The Struggle for National Education* (1873), p. 3.
2. This and the following paragraph derive from M. G. Jones, *The Charity School Movement* (1938), esp. cc. I–V and IX.
3. The view here taken is that Sunday schools were middle class in origin, whatever their later development: see M. Dick, 'The myth of the Working-class Sunday School' in *History of Education*, vol. 9, no. 1 (1980), pp. 27 – 41.
4. As Dr Bell said: A. Bell, *An Experiment in Education* (4th edn. 1808), p. 37.
5. E.g., Hampshire Society for the Education of the Infant Poor (records in Hants. CRO); Suffolk Archidiaconal Society (Suffolk CRO Ipswich); Blackburn Deanery, Dr Whittaker's Coucher Books (Lancs. CRO).

6. The terms of union with the National Society are summarised in H. J. Burgess, *Enterprise in Education* (1958), pp. 27–9; the British terms are printed in D. W. Sylvester, *Educational Documents 800–1816* (1970), p. 288.
7. Hoddesden Boys' British School Minute Book, 2/9/1844 (Herts. CRO); Suffolk Archidiaconal Society Minute Book, 25/2/1812; St James School Clitheroe Minute Book, 23/11/1843, 4/1/44 (Lancs. CRO); Washington National School Minute Book, 10/6/1857 (Durham CRO).
8. Burgess, op. cit., pp. 42–43; M. Sanderson, 'The National and British School Societies in Lancashire 1803–1839' in History of Education Society, *Local Studies and the History of Education* (1972), pp. 1–36.
9. PP. 1861 XXI Part V, p. 115.
10. E.g. Sanderson, op. cit., p. 25.
11. Central Society of Education, *First Publication* (1837), p. 2.
12. M. Cruickshank, 'David Stow, Scottish Pioneer of Teacher Training' in *British Journal of Educational Studies*, vol. XIV, no. 2 (1966), pp. 205–15.
13. Burgess, op. cit., pp. 65–6.
14. The whole sequence of early State involvement is discussed by D. G. Paz, *The Politics of Working Class Education in Britain, 1830–50* (1980).
15. E.g., the long-standing debate on the social-control issue.
16. Described by Paz, op. cit., pp. 62–5; see also Burgess, op. cit., pp. 68–73.
17. E.g., the Winchester Board's rejection, engineered by Samuel Wilberforce, of Keble's proposal that it should prescribe school books: G. H. Sumner, *The Life of C. R. Sumner, Bishop of Winchester* (1876), pp. 261–4.
18. A paper by Gladstone on teacher-training is summarised by J. L. Bradbury, *Chester College and the Training of Teachers* (1975), pp. 33–37.
19. Cf. Paz, op. cit., pp. 82 – 3; R. Aldrich, 'Peel, Politics and Education', p. 13, in *Journal of Educational Administration and History*, vol. XIII, no. 1 (1981).
20. Quoted in D. N. Hempton, 'Wesleyan Methodism and Educational Politics in the Early Nineteenth Century', p. 210, in *History of Education*, vol. 8, no. 3 (1979).
21. PP. 1861 XXI Part VI, q. 2331.
22. See Appendix 2 for the grant structure.
23. C. M. Yonge, *Langley School* (1850), pp. 49–50.
24. Census of Great Britain 1851, *Education. England and Wales* (1854) pp. xxi–xxvii, liii (this figure excludes endowed schools); PP. 1851 XLIV 1, pp. cxli–ccii; 1866 XXVII 117, pp. 495–619; 1870, XXII, p. viii (note); *Statistics of Church of England Schools, 1866–67* (1868).
25. E. G. West, *Education and the Industrial Revolution* (1975), p. 232.
26. The Education Department, i.e., the section of the Privy Council Office which dealt with elementary schools, was officially constituted in 1856.
27. PP. 1857–8 XLVI 261. They were: three National, in London, Derby and Lancaster; one British, in Plymouth; one Catholic, in Liverpool. The sixth, in Devonport, is excluded as all the families were those of seamen, soldiers or naval dockyard workers.
28. E.g., Christ Church, Northam: E. W. Gadd, *Victorian Logs* (1979).

29. E. Baines, *Letters to Lord John Russell on State Education* (1846), p. 72. Voluntaryism is surveyed in J. E. Allen, 'Voluntaryism: a 'Laissez-faire' Movement in Mid-Nineteenth Century Education' in *History of Education*, vol. 10, no. 2 (1981), pp. 111–24; for their concept of education see W. J. Unwin, *The Primary School* (1862).
30. D. K. Jones, 'Socialisation and Social Science', p. 115, in P. McCann (ed.), *Popular Education and Socialisation in the Nineteenth Century* (1977).
31. E. K. Blyth, *The Life of William Ellis* (2nd edn., 1892), pp. 89–109.
32. 'Subordination is the life of a school . . . our schools . . . are subordinate to the clergy' (*The Catholic School*, 7/1849, p. 100).
33. *Hints on an Improved and Self-paying System of National Education* (1847), p. 42.

CHAPTER ONE

SCHOOL PROMOTERS*

THE desire 'that the youth of this Kingdom should be religiously brought up' by which Lord John Russell justified his educational proposals of 1839 had been the express aim of the National Society and the British and Foreign School Society since they were founded at the beginning of the century; and it continued to be the aim of virtually all the groups promoting schools in the 1840s and 1850s. Even the master of the Manchester Secular School felt obliged to point out that 'moral and religious instruction of undoubted excellence, can be given without the introduction of the Bible'.[1] But this unanimity as to the importance of a religiously-based education, to ensure social stability in this world and salvation in the next, was accompanied by the most divergent opinions about its content and extent. Amongst British school promoters, for instance, the managers of one school could declare their aim to be to

> afford the people of Downton . . . an education, as good intellectually, morally, and religiously, as a well-trained master and a well-digested system could present, careful that the subjects taught should be so varied as to adapt the school to all, and that the only limit to the extent of knowledge should be that which would necessarily arise from the brief period during which the children would remain at the school . . .

The committee of High Wycombe Girls' School, on the other hand, congratulated themselves in 1862 'that the Government have come round to their old fashioned notions that "reading, writing, and arithmetic" are the essentials in the education of the class of children for whom schools such as this are intended'.[2] Obviously such different concepts produced schools of very different character. The quality of education in any given locality depended primarily upon the motives and ideas of its school promoters.

Who were the members of this 'charitable and enlightened minority'?[3] Only one social group was largely represented; the majority of clergy of all denominations were actively involved in

* Relevant documents are indicated by asterisks in the text.

school management, most from conviction, others because it was expected of them. Most wealthy families subscribed to schools with varying degrees of generosity or parsimony, but a minority actively patronised education with an influence out of all proportion to their numbers.* The British and Foreign School Society could scarcely have survived without the support of a few Whig magnates and Radical industrialists. But such patrons usually distributed their favours to any schools which they considered deserving. They gave financial security, determined school policy, obtained special concessions from government and, as landlords and employers, could force their dependents to use the school and, indeed, to continue their education after leaving it. Lord Lansdowne, for example, by founding a variety of schools in Calne and by bullying the trustees of the grammar school into reorganising it on modern lines, provided the town with 'a complete system of primary and secondary instruction adequate to the wants of the population'.[4] Some of the squirearchy (like the Sykes family in east Yorkshire or the thirty-one squires in the Archdeaconry of Oxford reported in 1854 to be maintaining their village schools)[5] and some proprietors of mill villages exercised similar control in their smaller domains.

The managers of such schools had no financial problems, provided they deferred to the wishes of the patron. Others had to seek support from the less affluent middle classes. But the lay subscribers, the tradesmen and professional men who played so large a part in charity schools and, indeed, in early National and British schools, were far less prominent in the Victorian era. Although the wealthier dissenting communions – Unitarians, Quakers, Wesleyans – produced some active committees, even these tended to hand over control to single individuals with zeal and leisure enough to attend constantly to the school.† In Anglican and Catholic schools 'the managers' usually meant, in practice, the parson and his curates. Trustees of endowed schools sometimes put up more resistance to clerical control than did committees of subscribers, but in such cases the forces of progress were usually on the side of the clergy.‡

The attitude of many of these school promoters towards mass education was distinctly ambivalent. The moral virtues tradition-

* IA–IE. †IF.
‡IG.

ally inculcated in schools for the poor: subordination, contentment and the like, continued to be emphasised in old-fashioned schools, but there was increasing recognition that they were too simplistic. The virtues necessary for scholastic success, which Titus Salt had in mind when he ornamented the entrance to his school in Saltaire with two stone lions 'emblematical of VIGILANCE and DETERMINATION',[6] were perseverance, self-discipline, punctuality – bourgeois qualities essential to self-help and self-advancement. From belief in these virtues it was a short step to the concept of education as an instrument of social mobility; a step easily taken by industrialists like Salt who remembered their own origins. ' "If you see a number of Irishmen", said one Lancashire mill-owner to the boys of his factory school, "what are they doing?" "They are carrying bricks," was the reply. "And if you see a number of Scotchmen, what are they doing?" "The Scotchmen are telling them where to put them," was the reply. So might he say of those who took care to educate themselves.' A surprising number of Anglican clergy held similar views, although they tended to look for the return of an imagined golden age: 'To educate the working classes would be to restore the old relations of society, by which natural ability and praiseworthy industry may receive their healthy encouragement by the prospect of temporal advancement.'[7] More pragmatically, a school whose pupils succeeded in adult life would attract ambitious parents prepared to pay fees and send their children regularly.* Such attitudes led to advances in curriculum which in turn attracted a new clientele. If mid-Victorian elementary schools were not notably successful in educating the very poor, they increasingly catered for the prosperous tradesmen and artisans who were later the mainstay of the higher-grade schools.

Educationists like Richard Dawes, whose school at King's Somborne served all classes of the village community, often argued that only thus could the school become, in Kay-Shuttleworth's phrase, the 'nursery of the congregation'. If in his stress on the consequent need to provide an advanced curriculum Dawes was not a typical parson, his conviction of the key role of the school in parochial life was wholly characteristic of the Anglican clergy; a conviction which, more than the simple issue of doctrinal teaching, accounted for the hostility which they dis-

*IH.

played towards anything which appeared 'to make the parochial clergyman feel that the parochial school is no longer part of the Church'.[8] In G.F.A. Best's words, 'in lower class parishes . . . *education* was the primary means by which the clergy performed their function as they conceived it'.[9] The school not only Christianised the children; the relationships which it created were the means of reaching many parents for whom the church, as William Rogers of St Thomas, Charterhouse once remarked, was 'the last kind of place they feel disposed to enter'.[10] Elsewhere, the school was seen as a cornerstone, second only to the church, of parochial life;* often part of a network of clubs and organisations; sometimes their focal point. 'The position of a Parochial Minister has led me to the conviction', wrote Samuel Best, 'that the School is the right basis of a parochial system of provident exertion . . . the instrument of the social improvement and renovation of the parish'.[11] This attitude, shared by the Catholics and to some extent by many nonconformist school managers, made schools potentially of great significance in the communities which they served. The potential was not often realised as fully as in Best's parish of Abbott's Ann;† but it goes far to explain the determination with which the Churches clung to the idea of denominational education and the energy which they expended in trying to make it a reality.

Notes

1. B. Templar, *Ten Years' Experience of the Manchester Free School* (1866), p. 9.
2. Downton (Wilts.) British School, *Annual Report* (1852); British and Foreign School Society, *Annual Report* (1862–3), pp. 58–9.
3. PP. 1861 XXI Part I, p. 302.
4. PP. 1864 XLV, p. 157; 1867–8, XXVIII, Part XI, 459, pp. 21–3.
5. T.W. Bamford, *The Evolution of Rural Education, 1850–1964* (1965), pp. 10–11; E. P. Baker (ed.), *Bishop Wilberforce's Visitation Returns for the Archdeaconry of Oxford, 1854* (1954).
6. A. Holroyd, *Saltaire and its Founder* (2nd edn, 1871), p. 19.
7. Report of prizegiving at Zion School, Lees, *Oldham Chronicle*, 7/4/1860; C. H. Bromby, *The Church, the Privy Council, and the Working Classes* (1850), p. 47.
8. E. P. Vaughan, *The Parochial Clergy Turned out of the Parish Schools* (1849), p. 11.
9. G. F. A. Best, *Temporal Pillars* (1964), p. 409.

* IJ. † IK.

10. W. Rogers, *The Educational Prospects of St. Thomas, Charterhouse* (1854), pp. 11–13. For Rogers, see below, 4C.
11. S. Best, *Manual of Parochial Institutions* (2nd edn, 1849), p. 14.

Documents

IA. A SCHOOL REORGANISED BY A PATRON

Rich men who paid the piper by maintaining schools could inevitably, if they so desired, call the tune. Lord Hatherton, a Staffordshire landowner zealous for education, is here seen determining the future of the school at Penkridge, one of several supported by him. An active patron of education in the west midlands, he may have owed his zeal to his second wife, Lady Kay-Shuttleworth's cousin who, as Mrs Caroline Davenport, had been a school promoter in Cheshire (see IC). A(ii) shows that Hatherton's expenditure on this, as on other schools, remained considerable even after the introduction of fees in 1854.

(i) To the Parents of Children in the National School at Penkridge

The Average Annual cost for the last ten years of Maintaining the Penkridge School, including Salaries, Books, School Apparatus, the Rent and Repairs of the Building, has been £150.5s.6d.

This charge has been provided for by

	£	s.	d.
The Annual Amount of Benefactions constituting the Income of the old Charity School.	36	3	0 *
Paid by Lord Hatherton, for Salaries and various School expenses.	61	0	3 *
By Lord Hatherton, for Rent and Repairs of Building (last year, £201.6.6½d.)	53	2	3
	£150	5	6

In consequence of increased attendance at the School, and the improved system of Instruction about to be introduced, which has rendered necessary an Enlargement of the Building, and the appointment of Assistant Teachers, occasioning a great increase of expense, it has been judged desirable that it should cease to be a *Charity* School; and that the Parents of all the Children (except

* [Contemporary note] should be £31.14.6d.; £65.8.9d.

the limited number provided for by benefactors to the original Charity School) should henceforward contribute towards the Education of their Children, by the payment of a small weekly sum.

Another circumstance which has led Lord Hatherton, the Patron of the National School, to require this payment, is the universal testimony borne throughout England to the great advantages resulting from the system of small payments for Education; the Parents of Children having been almost invariably found to value instruction, to the expense of which they have contributed, more highly than that which has been entirely gratuitous.

The Penkridge School has long been one of the very few of the same class remaining in England in which contributions by the Parents of Children have not been made.

In future, therefore, there will be three rates of payment, namely – 2d. a week – 4d. a week – and Six Shillings per Quarter: – all payments to be made in advance.

It will be left to the Parent of each Child to determine which payment he will adopt, reserving to the Patron and the Clergyman, (the Rev. J. Fell) the right of refusing to educate any child, who appears to them not a proper object of Charity, except at one of the higher rates of payment.

They are encouraged to take this course by the knowledge that the plan has been adopted elsewhere; and has been cordially approved and acted upon by the Parents of the Children.

In all future admissions, the Parents will have to state which rate of payment they propose to adopt.

Where there shall be more than two children from one family paying either 2d. or 4d. a week only, some abatement will be made in the charge.

Some portion of the Elder Girls' time will be employed in needlework, for which they will be paid.

Although Lord Hatherton, as Trustee of the old Charity School, is only required "to provide a Master to instruct eight poor boys in reading, writing, and accounts, and to buy them each a blue bonnet" – it is his intention to admit the twelve Head Boys, and the twelve Head Girls, *entirely free*, and furnish them with Caps and Bonnets. If the Parents of any of this number signify their wish not to avail themselves of this charity for their children, others will be selected in their places.

(ii) [*Ms. Note*]

		£	
Cost of School to Ld. H.	1858–59	93	
	59–60	116	
	60–1	157	
	61–2	220	includes interest of School £35 yearly.
	62–3	124	

		£	Ld. H.
1864	Total cost of School	291	155
1865	————	301	150
66	————	344	150
67	————	283	150
68	————	315	150
69	————	303	75
70	————	348	150

(Hatherton Papers, Staffs. CRO D260/M/F/5/120)

IB. A PATRON AND A SCHOOLMASTER

The third Earl of Radnor preserved his correspondence – letters and drafts of his replies – meticulously. Amongst the activities thus recorded was the support of schools on estates scattered throughout the south of England. He subscribed handsomely; distributed improving literature for the pupils to read; and ensured that the managers adopted principles of which he approved. (A former Foxite Whig he would only subscribe to National schools if they operated a conscience clause whereby parents could withdraw their children from doctrinal teaching.) The school at Coleshill, on his own doorstep, he controlled personally. In 1853 an efficient master (Mr Forss) resigned and went to King's College, London, to prepare for ordination. His successor was Mr Joyner, a former student at Battersea College, whose testimonials included one from Kay-Shuttleworth; but by 1856 Radnor had become dissatisfied. These extracts from the correspondence which ensued illustrate the extent of his control of the school and, incidentally, throw light on a number of aspects of mid-nineteenth-century education. It will be noted that if Radnor had reached his final decision in January instead of August, Mr Joyner need never have been dismissed at all!

21/1/56: *Radnor to Joyner* (draft)

As the school, I am sorry to say, does not go on quite to my satisfaction, I should be glad to hear from you that you wish to leave it.

Pray mention when you would wish to go.

21/1/56: *Joyner to Radnor*

I feel very sorry that I have failed to give satisfaction in my school for the first time.

I cannot at present say when I can leave, – unless your Lordship will state if you wish me to leave at any particular time.

I am, of course, not in view of anything at present, and shall therefore feel thankful of a little time to get suited, as I have a wife and family.

Radnor to Joyner (draft)

I do not wish to tye you down to leave on any particular day nor to inconvenience you; but I should wish you not to interpose any unnecessary delay.

24/1/56: *Joyner to Radnor*

I hope your Lordship will pardon my writing again; but having heard that your Lordship does not now leave your rooms, I have thought that I could best state what I have to say in writing.

In thinking over the matter of my leaving Coleshill, there are several considerations which materially affect my future prospects.

I beg therefore to propose three questions, which I hardly dare hope your Lordship will condescend to answer: but which nevertheless contain thoughts which are highly important to me now.

They are as follow.

(1) Am I right in supposing that the defective writing and Arithmetic of the Second Class, together with the low attendance are the sole cause of your Lordship's displeasure?

(2) If your Lordship insist on my removal can I stay till 25th March if I am not suited earlier: – and may I hope for your Lordship's good word when I require it?

(3) Will your Lordship have any objection to my asking the Right Honourable E. P. Bouverie [Radnor's son] for his kind

interest to procure me a writership or other employment in some public office; as I have two brothers who are serving with credit in government offices in London?

I beg now respectfully to submit to your Lordship the following four statements

(1) I have always endeavoured to do my duty honestly, to the best of my ability, and if I have erred, it has been an error of judgement merely, and not at all the result of idleness or inattention.

(2) I find, on referring to the attendance books, kept by Mr Forss, that although he kept up the number on the books, to 70, in some mysterious manner, yet the absentees generally ranged from 30 to 40: – so that often there could not have been present more children than have lately attended: – and I also find that there was a gradual decrease in the number attending the School, up to the time of Mr Forss' leaving.

I mention this, not to implicate Mr Forss, but to clear up a matter, which I had not full opportunity of doing, when your Lordship looked at the books.

(3) If there is any suspicion of my ever having acted wrongly in any matter – I am sorry for it, – but I beg most earnestly to declare that I never wished to act otherwise than in the most straightforward and upright manner. I may have displayed want of caution, but, never, an absence of a deep sense of right, and an earnest desire to do my duty honestly, and to give entire satisfaction.

(4) I shall ever remember with deep gratitude your Lordship's former kindnesses to me.

Begging your Lordship's kind consideration of the above, and once more humbly apologising. . .

25/1/56: *Radnor to Joyner* (draft)

I can assure you that I do not impute to you that you have 'acted wrongly in any matter'. I must decline entering into particulars with respect to my reasons for my giving you the notice which I did – but I repeat generally that it was because I did not think that the school went on satisfactory. [sic]

My son tells me that it is out of his power to assist you in the way you wish.

There will be no difficulty in your continuing till the 25th of

March, but if there should occur unexpectedly any reason for your leaving sooner, I will give you the earliest intimation of it.

[Meanwhile, Radnor had already begun the search for a replacement by consulting the educationist Richard Dawes, then Dean of Hereford.]

21/1/56: *Radnor to Dawes* (draft)

I have to apologise for troubling you – but I think you will pardon me. I have in this place a boys school & I expect to be soon looking after a new master – Can you assist me on procuring one; or can you tell me where I should apply –

This is entirely an agricultural parish. There is in the village a very good infant school – & also a very good girls school; but lately the boys school has not gone on to my satisfaction. I have allowed the master £60 per ann. & the house is large enough to allow the present master to take three or four boarders – and *has kept the children's pence*. Under a former master the attendance was between 60 and 70, but under the present master it has fallen off; this may be to some degree owing to the improvement of other schools in the neighbourhood; but I think is not wholly so. The former master brought the boys so forward that several have gone to situations in London or elsewhere as apprentices – one as assistant to an engineer – another as junior clerk to a Barrister. To this I of course can have no possible objection, but my principal object is to teach the sons of the Agricultural labourers of the place, reading, writing – plain Arithmetic, bible history & Xian doctrine. If to this is added the higher branches of Arithmetic – mensuration & with geography & profane history it is so much the better; & I suppose with the salary I allow this might be expected.

When the school was first established I was averse from any connexion with the National society, disapproving much of the method which they pursued. I believe this is much altered for the better – but I should prefer a connexion with the British & Foreign society. But if you can help me that is what I should like best.

I have to apologise not only for troubling you in this matter; but also for entering into so much of detail. Any hint that you will give me or any advice will be highly acceptable.

* – * probable reading.

24/1/56: *Dawes to Radnor*

It would give me very great pleasure if I could assist you in finding what you are in search of – an efficient master for Coleshill School, but it seldom happens that I know anyone whom I can recommend from personal knowledge.

I have generally applied to the Principal of the Training College at Battersea & through whom I have in two or three instances succeeded very well; I should recommend a master holding a certificate of merit from the Committee of Council on Education & should one be found who had been trained at Battersea, this would not in any way oblige you to place the School in any connexion with the National Society as I have in more instances than one recommended Masters trained at Battersea who are holding Schools in connexion with the British & Foreign Society.

Will your Lordship inform me what the school fees are likely to amount to, & if it is under Inspection of the Committee of Council.

The circumstance of the house being sufficiently large to enable the Master to take three boarders induces me to think of a master who occurs to me, but he is at present an Assistant Master in our Cathedral School here. He was brought up in my Somborne School & was Master of it for many years & came here about three years ago on my recommendation. He is quite the man for a school where both Farmers' & labourers children are united & holds a high certificate from the Committee of Council. . .

Would you kindly let me know when a Master is wanted as I have no doubt in the course of the next three months I might be able to assist you.

[Radnor welcomed this proposal, but Dawes's protégé had other plans. The earl received several direct applications, including one from the schoolmaster of Faringdon workhouse. Dawes enlisted the Principals of Battersea and Highbury and the British and Foreign Secretary, Henry Dunn. After lengthy correspondence, James East from Battersea was appointed temporarily, but in July, after having him vetted by HMI Bowstead, Radnor decided not to make the appointment permanent and resumed his correspondence with Dawes. After an exchange of letters, Dawes produced a new suggestion.]

22/8/56 : *Dawes to Radnor*

. . . About ten days ago or rather more I received a letter from a school-master in Ireland to which I paid little attention but the enclosed letter from the Archbishop of Dublin in which he expresses himself so strongly of a Master under similar circumstances made me think it must be the same, and in writing to Prof[r]. Sullivan in Dublin I find it to be the same . . . tell me whether you would have any inclination to try a Master who is an Irishman and trained in Dublin – of good character but who has changed from the Roman Catholic to the Protestant faith . . . one does not like to see him suffer for it in the way he clearly must do should he remain in Ireland . . . Mr Clive near Hereford had an Irish School-Master since I have been here & altho' he had an Irish accent yet he was one of the most efficient Masters about us. . .

23/8/56 : *Radnor to Dawes* (draft)

I cannot say how much obliged to you I feel for your letter received this morning & the trouble you are taking further about a schoolmaster. . .

Nothing can be more satisfactory than the recommendations of the Archbishop & Professor Sullivan – & it would be a great additional satisfaction to me to have a master from the Irish Model School – But, to tell you the honest truth, I feel a little afraid of the Irish brogue, notwithstanding Mr Clive's experience; & (what is, I fear, more) the fact, that this young man would have to live alone in the school-house; & the domestic arrangements of the Irish are not altogether what would suit me here – At the same time my daughter rather inclines to an Irishman as having a gaiety & liveliness of manner agreeable to children.

It happens that just now the master of the school at our Faringdon Workhouse is thinking of leaving, & of offering himself as relieving officer – I believe he is a superior person, educated, I think, at Kneller Hall* & reported very highly of by the Government Inspector – He leaves the situation on account of his health which he thinks is prejudiced by the confinement of the Workhouse – I know not whether my school would suit him; nor whether he would suit me, but I will endeavour to ascertain

*The government training school for workhouse schoolmasters.

something more about him this afternoon or at latest on Monday. . .

[The reports on him were favourable. Radnor's views had, in fact, changed, for reasons explained in a letter written, but not sent, 'in consequence of E.P.B.'s observations' – who perhaps argued that Dawes might disagree with his father's decision and attempt to reopen the discussion.]

28/8/56 : *Radnor to Dawes* (not sent)

I feel that you will have great reason to find fault with me, as having given you a great deal of unnecessary trouble – but in consequence of a conversation, which I have just had with my steward I am disposed to think that after all it will be best for me *not* to seek for a *first-rate* schoolmaster: but to endeavour to find one of calibre to take little children (boys) when they leave the Infant school, & to go on with them till they go to work: instructing them in reading, writing, arithmetic; perhaps a little geography etc. He tells me that he sees no probability of this school being by any means raised to the point at which it once was (about 100 boys) in consequence of the increase in number & efficiency of schools at the adjoining parishes – at Burcot (the next parish on the North) a very good school with 70 boys, where there was formerly none: at Highworth, the national school very much improved, & a very good British & Foreign established & thriving – at Faringdon a most excellent infant school, with evening classes for lads and a British & Foreign school in *addition* to the National school; – improved attendance also on the other side at Longcot & Shrivenham. Under these circumstances he thinks, & I am disposed to admit, that an inferior (& second-rate) schoolmaster at a smaller salary, would really be more useful.

The schoolmistress at the infant school at Faringdon comes from Cheltenham & I am advised that such a master as I am now thinking of might be heard of there.

This new scheme pleases me in every respect, except that I think you will have good cause to complain of me. . .

[The conclusion of this episode was recorded by Radnor in a memorandum dated 1 September.]

On Saturday Aug. 30 I communicated to East the schoolmaster that I should not continue him here – & I have today told him that he might continue on till the end of November; thus giving him 3 months notice –

On Saturday (or Friday) I had agreed with Mr Kirke at Faringdon that whenever East left me, I would engage him.

(Radnor Papers, Berks. CRO, D/EPb C69)

IC. A REPORT TO A PATRON

The leading members of the very wealthy Leveson-Gower family took a prominent part in promoting education. Earl Granville, the head of one of the younger branches of the clan, was both an active patron and, as Lord President of the Council (1852–4, 1855–8 and 1859–66), the head of the Education Department. He was thus well placed to consult with the Inspectorate. The following extract from a letter written by J. P. Norris, HMI, an unofficial report on an official visit of inspection, describes Granville's schools at the Shelton Iron Works in the Potteries and shows the degree of detailed supervision maintained by a patron who was also a busy politician.

I have been spending today in your schools at Shelton, and on the whole the exam^{n} has been a very satisfactory one, showing more advance than I had anticipated. All three teachers seem to be working industriously & in a right spirit. I was especially struck with Martin's manner, showing more quiet self possession and stability than I gave him credit for last year. His boys passed a better examination in Geography than any boys I have examined except perhaps Lady Hatherton's school at Capesthorne.

In Religious Knowledge there was a marked advance in both Schools. It was of a good quality, showing thoughtfulness.

The writing is decidedly bad in both Schools, & the reading but moderate. But I found a better crop of readers coming on in the junior classes of the girls school.

My impression was that the Teachers had been giving most attention – very naturally – to what they, fresh from their Lecture rooms, take most pleasure in – Geography History etc. & had been rather neglecting the drier part of their work. So I threw my weight into this latter scale, and tried to leave an impression that the Council Office was passionately fond of good reading & good writing.

The needlework seemed much improved.

The discipline is generally improved, but the mistresses are still too saccharine.

(Granville Papers, 29/10/1855: PRO, 30/29 Box 23, Part 2: Crown copyright)

ID. PATRONAGE IN INDUSTRIAL AREAS : 1

This document, like the following one, reflects the extent and limitations of the power of industrialists to promote education. The remarks of Henry M'Connell 'who resides at Cressbrook, and interests himself much in these matters', underline the fact that only where there was no alternative employment could such pressures succeed.

Messrs M'Connell Brothers of Cressbrook Mills, Derbyshire

Regulations for children who want employment.

CRESSBROOK children who wish to be employed in the mills half-time must bring a certificate from the schoolmaster that they know, in arithmetic, simple addition; can read fairly in the Second Irish Book; and can write fairly upon the slate from the Second Book.*

CRESSBROOK children who wish to be employed in the mills full-time must bring a certificate from the schoolmaster that they know, in arithmetic, the first four rules, both simple and compound; in English grammar, the parts of speech and their meanings; can write fairly upon paper, and are able to write well six lines from dictation; and have a fair knowledge of geography.

Mr. M'Connell writes as follows:-

In compliance with your wish, I beg to send you a copy of the rules which you noticed, when last here, requiring from the children resident in my own village, a certain amount of educational progress, before they were admitted into the works either as half-timers or full-timers.

My reason for establishing this rule was that many parents neglected the opportunity which was presented to them of sending their children to a good school. They had various insufficient excuses for this neglect, but the general pretence was that there would be time enough for education during the period the children worked as half-timers, when the law made compulsory pro-

*I.e., the series of readers published by the Irish National Board of Education.

vision for their schooling; as all the cottages are mine and the families all work for me, I had the power of compelling school attendance, but I preferred the less arbitrary mode of declining to receive into my employment children who did not bring the schoolmaster's certificate of the required progress.

You ask me if this scheme has been attended with success. I cannot decide confidently upon this point, it is difficult to trace the working of the parents' minds, but certain it is, that the number of children attending school has materially increased, (indeed, I do not believe there is a single child in the village of sufficient age who is absent,) and the attendance generally has been more constant and regular than before the regulation existed.

I would beg, however, to remark, that though the experiment works satisfactorily with me, circumstanced as I am with my people comparatively dependent on me for employment, and with a good school in the village, it is doubtful whether I could successfully enforce the conditions of admittance into the works upon children who live in the villages two or three miles distant, who have not had the chance of education, and who have other occupations open to them, such as hand-loom weaving, stocking weaving, agricultural labour, and the like. Were I to prevent or retard the admission of such children I should not be extending education, but simply depriving myself of hands, and forcing children to other occupations in which education is not required; and I fear that all factory masters, in towns or districts where other labour is abundant, would be unable to carry out the plan I have succeeded in with the children of my own village. . .

(Report of A. Redgrave, Inspector of Factories, PP. 1859 (Session 1), XII 149, pp. 45–7

IE. PATRONAGE IN INDUSTRIAL AREAS: 2

Attempts to force working boys to continue their education, as in this document, were fairly common. Lord Ellesmere, another member of the Leveson-Gower clan, had inherited the canal and mining interests of the Duke of Bridgewater in south Lancashire, where he was a noted school promoter (see J. S. Leatherbarrow, *Victorian Period Piece*, 1954, pp. 14–19). His plan to send the colliery boys into evening schools, however, was a consequence of the failure, as a result of opposition from the miners, of his attempt to exclude boys under eleven years old from working in the pits (PP. 1857 (Session 2), XXXIII, p. 394).

(i) February 16th 1854

The peculiar nature of Colliery labour requires that the boys intended for it should enter the pits at a very early age; thus withdrawing them much sooner than is desirable from the teaching and the influence of School.

It has for some time been Lord ELLESMERE's wish to establish Evening Schools, accessible to all the lads engaged in his service, by means of which they might, simultaneously with their employment in the pits, retain the advantages of good instruction, and thus preserve and extend the knowledge previously acquired by them.

Arrangements have now been made having this object in view. On and after Monday, the 6th March, Evening Schools will be opened in each of the districts most convenient for the population employed in the Collieries; and Lord ELLESMERE hopes that, through the aid and co-operation of the parents, and with earnestness and attention on the part of the lads, they may be well attended, and that much good will be the result.

It is not Lord ELLESMERE's intention to make this a gratuitous system of education: every boy and lad in the Collieries will be expected to contribute twopence a week from his wages towards the support of the contemplated Schools.

A representation has been made that it would conduce to the convenience of the men employed in working the Collieries, were the existing rule modified, by which boys are at present denied admittance to the pits until after eleven years of age. The operation of this rule has been beneficial, by enabling the children to remain an additional twelvemonth at School. Under the contemplated arrangement, however, which secures to them the opportunity of continued education, and in deference to the wishes of his people, who deserve so well of him, it is Lord ELLESMERE's intention to permit the rule to be relaxed, under proper regulations.

In this paper it is not possible to do more than state, in general terms, that a system of Evening Schools will be brought into operation after the 6th of March.

Means will therefore be taken to explain the details of the plan to the Inhabitants of the several districts, so that the boys may be prepared to attend the Schools when they open.

In affording this opportunity of improvement to the boys employed in the Collieries, it is Lord ELLESMERE's sincere wish that it may be extensively taken advantage of, and that the good sense of the people will render it unnecessary for him to consider any measures of enforcing attendance at the Schools.

(ii) Memorandum: London, February 23rd 1854

The Schools to commence on Monday the 6th March.
Four nights a week – commencing at 6 o'C. in the afternoon, except in the two Districts of Street Gate and Swinton, where the attendance will only be on *three* nights a week:-

No compulsion will be employed to induce attendance, but the lads and their parents will be informed how earnestly Lord and Lady Ellesmere wish them to attend.

Each lad (whether attending or not) employed in the Collieries, will contribute 2$^{d.}$ a week from his wages towards the support of these schools.

These contributions to be carried to a common fund, – which fund will in the first instance be responsible for the necessary expenditure, as stated hereafter, connected with the schools.

This money to be collected, and disbursed by Mr Ridyard, under proper instructions.

In Walkden School to be open *four* nights a week from *6 to 8*
In Dean School to be open *four* nights a week from *6 to 8* at *Morris's Green*
In Farnworth School to be open *four* nights a week from *6 to 8* at *New Bury*
In Ellenbrook School to open *four* nights a week from *6 to 8*
In Worsley School to open *four* nights a week from *6 to 8* at *Roe Green*
In Street Gate Admission to be provided in Mr Whittle's School, *three* nights a week from *6 to 9*
In Swinton Admission to be provided in Mr Saml Dyson's School *three* nights a week from *6 to 8*

The espenses [sic] anticipated are as follows:-

Walkden	say 100 boys –	4 teachers @ 3/– each		12 – 0
Farnworth	,, 50 ,,	– 1 teacher @ 5/– ,,		5 – 0
Dean	,, ,, ,,	,, ,, ,,		5 – 0
Worsley	,, 25 ,,	,, @ 3/6		
		asst. boy 1/–		4 – 6
Ellenbrook	,, 80 ,,	first teacher @ 3/6		
		two assts. @ 2/6 = 5/–		8 – 6
Street Gate	,, 20 boys contract			3 – 0
Swinton	,, ,, ,, ,,			5 – 0
	Probable approximate weekly cost			£2 – 3 – 0

To which must be added expenditure for Books, lights, fires, cleaning, etc., etc.

[Pencil addition]

Mem. The schools are now open three nights each week Dec[r] 3/58.

(Sutherland Papers, Staffs. CRO, D593N/3/11/4)

IF. MANAGEMENT IN A BRITISH SCHOOL

Undenominational committees, since they could not automatically rely upon the clergy to take responsibility for the administration of their schools, were particularly dependent upon the limited number of lay managers who were prepared to give not only their financial support but their time to the task. On the death of one such individual, the treasurer, who was also a magistrate, a Town Commissioner and the Chairman of the Board of Guardians, the master of Cheltenham British School edged his log-book entry with black:

15th January, 1868

Death of Mr Downing, Chairman and Treasurer of the Schools

His connection with them dates as far back as 1847, and it was principally thro' his exertions, and by his personal influence that the present School premises were erected. He was a true lover of children ever foremost to advance their interest. By his death, I have lost a sincere Friend, and the School, one of its warmest supporters.

"He was a man, take him for all in all,
We ne'er shall look upon his like again."

(Log Book, Cheltenham Library, Local Collection)

1G. AN ENDOWED SCHOOL TRUSTEE AND A CLERGYMAN

The strongest resistance to educational change often came from the trustees of old-fashioned endowed elementary schools. The chronicler of events in the Cambridgeshire village of Whittlesford, G. N. Maynard, had attended the village school under 'old Macer', a one-armed sailor, and witnessed the struggle for control of the endowments between a reforming parson and the only surviving trustee, the dissenter Ebenezer Hollick. Whilst he had some sympathy with Hollick's resistance to encroaching clergy, Maynard recognised that the school as reconstituted after Hollick's defeat was a considerable improvement on the old regime.

[Spelling and punctuation as in the original]

Memories of Old Macer, Schoolmaster, 1805–40

. . .The old chap had but one arm, and that was his *left*, but of this he made good use . . . he would hold the boys between his legs, by thier head and neck, and operate most unmercifully upon their hind quarters. Sometimes the boy's would have their revenge by biteing his legs, and repeatedly I have seen his old grey or white stockings saturated with blood . . . but . . . before he left his victim free, he would generally have his revenge. . .

Irrespective of his school he was a sort of factotum for the Village being Church Clerk, Deputy Overseer, and collector of rates and taxes, Parish Clerk etc etc. . .

Note of Developments

In the year 1845 the Rev[d] Thomas Dickes died – he was one of the old school and during the 14 years that he had been Vicar of the parish he was agreeable to the queer and ancient method of training under the care and guardianship of Old Macer with his occasional superintendence in hearing the Chatichism repeated.

[No school had been built by the trustees; Macer had taught in his own house, as had the schoolmistress. The new vicar decided that a school must be provided, as Maynard's father recorded.]

March 28th 1848

Our present minister the Rev[d] P. C. M. Hoskin, – in connection with some of the neighbouring clergymen are making an attempt to take the funds of Westley's Charity to assist in establishing a *National School*.

Mr Hollick . . . says . . . that there should be four Clerical *Managers* and three lay *Trustees* and *Managers*, but that the clerical ones were not to be *trustees*, only *managers*. . .

The decree of the Lord Chancelor always used to be kept in the Church, but our present minister has taken it to Cambridge and refuses to let Mr Hollick have it as he wishes to do. . . He gave Mr Hollick notice that the meeting was to be held at Cambridge, but Mr H. refused to attend, saying the meeting was not lawful unless it was held in the parish. The meeting was however held about a month ago, and the diverting of the funds was agreed upon, but Mr H. protests against it and says he is sure they cannot do it. . .

[Letters from Hollick to the solicitor who managed the endowment]

July 6, 1848

It appears to me that the parsons have nothing to do with the Farm nor the Money nor with the Clothing of the Children nor with the Building of a School these things belong to the Trustees & the Money should be put in the Saving Bank in the Trustees Name where their is an account open in their Name. The parsons have a right to see all moneys paid & attend to the Children & School & to the School Master & Mistress.

The Trustees have a right to all property.

The Managers are concerned with the School Master & Mistress & the Children.

A parson is not allowed to be in any sort of Business.

A parsons Business is the Cure of Peoples Souls.

November 24, 1849

Now at the last Midsummer Meeting you sent by Mr Hoskin the account between you & *me* & 54£ for *me* to pay the Bills with. But how did he act he never gave them to *me* but I caught a glimps of the account & it was refused to *me* but after I ensisted upon them several times as a private account between you and *me* I was allowed to take them the Business went on & after most of the accounts was entered he handed to me a paper & asked me if I would sign it I said yes after I had received the £54 from him then he paid me a Memorandum saying I received of him from you 54£.

Now these Parsons . . . have several times said they ought to have the Ballance put in their hands They want to get the Money into their hands as they have in Most cases all over England But in this School it belongs to the Trustees to hold and to lay out.

[Hoskin nevertheless managed to provide a school building of sorts, which served until a new school was built in 1859 after Hollick's death.]

Note of Events

Tinworth carried on the Boys School in the House of Macers from the time of his election, his wife also had the girls School at her own house in the Village up to the same period viz. 1849 when a change was effected by . . . Rev[d] P. C. M. Hoskin . . . he had prevailed upon the lady of the Manor Miss Hollick to let him the building standing upon the Village green for the purpose of converting it into Schools for the children. This was done and the place altered for the purpose.

(CRO, Cambridge, R58/5/6)

IH. EDUCATION AND ADVANCEMENT

Successful schools liked to call attention to their ex-pupils' prosperity as a proof of the quality of the education they had received. The following lists are summaries of information from two village schools published by J. P. Norris, HMI for the north-west midlands, in his final report. The first probably refers to Lilleshall, a school maintained by the Duke of Sutherland, the head of the Leveson-Gower family; the second is from Acton in south Cheshire, a school founded by the Tomkinson family, the local squires, in imitation of Dawes's school at King's Somborne. It is interesting to note the extent to which the railways promoted social as well as physical mobility.

A Parish School in Shropshire

The following are all sons of labourers:
Carpenter at Stafford
Carpenter at Wolverhampton
Engineer in Stoke

At service in London
Carpenter and sawyer (head man in the choir)
Carpenter and Sunday School teacher
Groom and gardener (bass in the choir)
Under station-master at Bedford – £60 p.a.; age 22, got by examination
Three certificated schoolmasters
At Cape Town; teacher and lay missionary, preparing for holy orders
Groom
Collecting agent for LNW Railway at Ludlow
Railway guard, S. Wales
Foreman in goods warehouse, Hereford
Copying clerk, Shrewsbury station
Ticket collector
Guard on the LNW Railway – won by examination
Carpenter in Manchester with excellent wages
Butcher doing well in Lilleshall
Engineer, Woolwich, £2 per week; married a captain's daughter
Fusileer Guard – became a sergeant in two years
Position in the Post Office, London
Two carpenters in Liverpool
Farmer in America

Acton

Porter in Wolverhampton
Began as labourer; saved and took smallholding; now has farm of 160 acres
Farmer and hotel-keeper, Worsley, Lancs.
Roller in Mersey Steel Co. – 50s. per week
Deformed boy – clerk, LNW Railway – £65 p.a.
Coachman – has shares in a lead mine
Clerk – Secretary of the Provident Club and collector of tithes – highly respected in the neighbourhood
Head Carpenter at Dorfold Hall
Carpenter – married master's daughter
Keeps large shop (ironmongery, drapery and grocery) near Malpas
Porter, LNW Railway; about to be promoted guard
Porter, Mold; 18s. per week

Hand at steam mills, Chester; £1 per week
Solicitor's clerk; £65 p.a.
Keeps shop (drapery and grocery) at Peckforton
In telegraph office, Birmingham, 1 guinea per week; and keeps 7 cows
Butler
Farmer
Solicitor's clerk; £70 p.a. and rising
Pointsman, Birmingham; £1 per week
Has large business as provision dealer
Carpenter, running his own business
Village shoemaker; employs two men and an apprentice
Certificated schoolmaster in London
Engine-driver, Crewe, 4s. per day

(Summarised from PP. 1864 XLV, pp. 122–5)

IJ. THE ROLE OF THE ANGLICAN SCHOOLMASTER

Rev. Sanderson Robins, the rector of various parishes in Dorset and Kent between 1826 and 1862, was one of many clerical writers on education. His book *The Church Schoolmaster*, the source of this extract, gives a particularly clear, if somewhat wordy statement of the clerical concept of the function of Anglican schools and the role of their teachers.

There is no reason why the schoolmaster should not undertake his charge, in the same spirit in which another gives himself to labour among the heathen. . . .While we render all due honour to those who make great sacrifices, and endure heavy trial for extending the kingdom of Christ in the wilderness of Paganism, we must not overlook those who, in the heart of a Christian land, are Pagans in all but the name. . . The same work is to be done nearer home. . . There are myriads in our populous towns, and forgotten multitudes scattered through the villages of our land, who are perishing in their ignorance, and who plead with us, by their very helplessness, for moral and mental training. Those who are in authority are doubtless bound to use their influence, and those who are affluent to contribute their money, for the advancement of education among their countrymen. The responsibility which clings to them is undeniably very great; but . . . No liberality will avail any thing, nor any system, however carefully improved, nor any books of instruction, however well prepared, unless there be the voice and the mind of a well-qualified teacher, to put a soul into this mute machinery. We cannot easily overrate the importance of his work, or form too high an expectation of its results, if only it be followed with a single eye and a devoted heart; above all, if it be carried out in the spirit of that Blessed Teacher, who was content to spend years in the midst of a hard and self-willed generation, correcting their mistakes, bearing with their perverseness, and leading them patiently in the way of truth and holiness.

There is no one to whom the influence of the school is more important than the clergyman. It is of all the aids to his ministry that which tells the most. He cannot dispense with it, because it is here that the people of his charge must be early formed for receiving with intelligence the great lessons of Christian doctrine which it is his business to deliver; and it is here that the tokens of amendment may be first expected, the promise of benefits which will be gradually diffused through the whole population. If there be neglect in this department, the traces of it will be seen elsewhere. Religion is generally at a low ebb in families, whose children are left without education.

It is a great matter for the well-being of a parish, that the clergyman and the schoolmaster should be united in affection and interest. . . The school-house lying, as it ought, under the shadow of the church, is the visible witness and emblem of the relation in which they stand to each other. Partners they are, and fellow-labourers. Their duties, though different, are connected throughout. The one indeed has been called to a higher ministry and service; but, among his lay helpers, there is none so important as the schoolmaster. . . There is no one who has a better claim upon his hearty cooperation and support, for there is no one who does more in making ready to his hand the materials of his spiritual work, or to whom he is more indebted for putting impediments out of his way. . . We have no right to expect that a man will receive the influence of religious truth into his heart, unless he is at least able to understand the terms in which it is stated to him. For this ability we must, in a great degree, depend upon previous preparation; and there is no aspect of the schoolmaster's office which has a deeper interest, than that which connects it in this way with the ultimate object of life. This union in purpose and labour, secures to him a great increase of authority. The pastor, who is set to watch over the welfare of the people, delegates to him a portion of the trust which he cannot, through the pressure of other claims, fulfil in his own person. Encouragement, and counsel, and daily help, he is able to give, but the duty of systematic teaching in the school, with the responsibility which belongs to it, he confides to another, and with it, the sanction derived from the spiritual community to which they both belong.

But this is not all. Parents are bound to provide education for their children, just as much as food and clothing. They may be unable to do any thing in this respect themselves. Their condition is straitened, and their time and care all bespoken by the labour of the day;. . . or they are so disqualified, morally and mentally, for teaching any thing, that they cannot even make the attempt; and yet they are not unwilling that their children should be taught. When they send them to school, they tacitly commit to the master, as much authority as is needful for their training. Hence he has a right to their obedience, not merely on the ground of being wiser and more experienced than they are, but because, for the time, he stands in the place of those whom, by the law of nature and of God, they are bound to obey.

The schoolmaster bears a very weighty and beneficent charge, and it is thus maintained by a twofold sanction. . .

(Sanderson Robins, *The Church Schoolmaster* (1850), pp. 7–13)

IK. WELFARE AND THE SCHOOL

In a manual written for the use of his parishioners Samuel Best explained the way in which schooling in Abbott's Ann was linked with welfare. The school had a reputation nearly equal to that of King's Somborne for the quality of education provided in it. At this time the curriculum included, in addition to the normal elementary subjects, linear drawing, book-keeping, and the elements of geometry, mensuration, algebra, mechanics and agricultural chemistry. The fees varied from 1d. to 1s. weekly, according to social class; children of widows were admitted free.

In the *Infant School* the children are received at three years of age. Now let it not be supposed that it is to get them out of your way, but that . . . they may be accustomed, even through their games and amusements instilling knowledge, to that association in classes which shall hereafter be of the greatest utility. . .

Into the *Day-School*, at six years of age, the children are received from the Infant School. . . Here they will be kept, if they are so long permitted to remain, until their education in secular knowledge at least is complete; that is, complete according to the standard we are compelled to adopt.

There are few, I need not remind you, who stay with us in the Daily-School over their tenth or eleventh year. With those only who do remain beyond that age can we talk of carrying forward any education in the useful and practical branches of science, of the philosophy of nature, or of the chemistry of agriculture. . . To all who do so stay with us the advantages . . . are equally and unconditionally offered. Without reference to class or circumstances, the same education is offered to all, for the smallest payment that its cost will allow. Yours, therefore, is the responsibility if your children do not participate in the advantages offered them. . .

It is a trite but true saying, that the way to the soul is through the body. . . The means which contemplate our temporal improvement now claim our consideration.

First among these, and connected immediately with the School, the burden of which it is intended to relieve, is the *School Coal and Rice Fund*.

Before we enter on the provisions of this fund, let me say a word to you on the *School Card*. This is the instrument by which these provisions are carried out. By these cards the contributions to the fund are regulated. Each card records weekly for the information of the parent – first, the number of attendances; secondly, the result of the weekly examination, in the number of good marks which are given at the repetition of lessons on the Saturday; and, thirdly, the place of the child in his class. It records, also, in separate columns, on the last Saturday of every month, what is due for books, School payments, or payments to the Provident Society required under the School Rules. Under the regulations of the Fund a premium is given on all sums contributed, the amount of the contribution depending . . . on the regular attendance and good conduct of the child.*

The reasons for the assignment of this premium are as follows. The object of all funds of this sort . . . is to aid those who in the largest and heaviest families have the greatest burden to bear . . . but who are those who most require it? Why those who, conscious of their duty as parents, are making the greatest sacrifices to fulfil those duties in the education of their children. The School Card points these out, and thus accomplishes in itself what the nicest discrimination in such matters has great difficulty in determining . . . each child from his first entrance into the School is required by the School rules to pay 1d. at least weekly, or more at the option of the parent, into the Provident Society to provide, so run the rules, "for sickness and old age, for the settlement or advancement of the subscriber in life, or for such other purposes as conduce to his permanent comfort." With this, or part of it (according to our agreement with the medical man, at present 1s. 3d. a-year for each child), provision is first made for medical attendance. This is secured to every child in the School. If the parent choose to subscribe more weekly, one-half of the sum so subscribed, at the option of the parent, may be repaid at the end of each year in clothes, such an addition having been first made by way of benefaction . . . as the donations . . . and Savings' Bank interest will permit.

An effort still earlier than the time of the child's entrance into School has been encouraged . . . by the appropriation of the churching fee to the child in the books of the Society. An account, as it were, even from the cradle, is thus commenced. . . When the first payment is taken up and continued by the parent, as in most cases it is, inasmuch as a very small addition secures the very evident benefit of medical attendance for the first year of its life, it will amount often to a considerable sum by the time that the child comes into School. Our object, that of raising the character by prudence and thoughtfulness, thus very happily falls in with the provision of a fund for each educated scholar. As he leaves the School, this gives him a fairer chance of carrying out

*By regular attendance and good conduct a child earned ½d. per week (with ¼d. for Sunday School attendance) which went to reduce the price of coal for his family.

into practice the instructions he has there secured. It removes some of those temptations and embarrassments that beset the path of one who is without means or resources. . .

(S. Best, *A Manual of Parochial Institutions*, 2nd edn (1849), pp. 14,24–8)

CHAPTER TWO

DENOMINATIONAL INFLUENCES

VOLUNTARY school promoters were, in theory, supported by a whole network of agencies. The two oldest, the British and Foreign School Society and the National Society, had been from 1834 to 1839 the exclusive channels for the distribution of State building grants. But the dualism implied by this policy and apparently confirmed by the division of HM Inspectorate into Anglican and undenominational branches after the Concordat, was already obsolete by the 1840s. Low churchmen continued to dislike the high-church leanings of the National Society, preferring evangelical pressure groups like the Home and Colonial School Society or the Church of England Education Society, established as an alternative to the National Society in 1853.[1] The British and Foreign School Society, even in its most prosperous days numerically small compared with the National Society, was nearly destroyed by internal conflicts over the Minutes of 1846 and survived to act only cautiously and conservatively for the rest of the century.

But already it had lost ground to groups which held that mere 'scriptural instruction' failed to achieve a truly religious education. *'Legitimate denominational objects', wrote John Scott, the Wesleyan, 'require that education, because religious, shall be denominational'.[2] The foundation of the Wesleyan Education Committee was followed in 1843 by that of the Congregational Board of Education, later the chief organ of the Voluntaryists, to 'promote the extension of primary education imbued with evangelical truth'.[3] The 'undenominational' members of HM Inspectorate in practice spent much of their time in the denominational schools of the Wesleyans, the Presbyterians, the Congregationalists (after 1867), minor groups like the Swedenborgians and the Jews, and in ostensibly British schools which were intimately associated with the chapels of particular denominations.[4] The Catholics entered the field with the foundation of the Poor School Committee in 1847 and achieved State recognition within a year. At the national level, therefore, there were not two

* 2A.

but many bodies involved in advising and supporting individual schools.

Faced with similar problems, they adopted broadly similar policies. All non-Anglican teacher-training (except for that of the nuns at Mount Pleasant and St Leonard's) came from these sources: Borough Road and Stockwell (British); Westminster (Wesleyan); Homerton (Congregational); and Hammersmith (Catholic).* The National Society maintained three colleges in London (St Mark's, Battersea and Whitelands); whilst, in addition to the Home and Colonial College in Gray's Inn Road, the evangelicals established Highbury and Cheltenham. Apart from the subsidised books of the Irish National Board, most pre-Revised Code school books were produced or at least sponsored by these organisations.[5] The provision of depositories from which books and equipment could be bought at reduced prices increased their influence over the schools and was, of course, very useful to impecunious managers. The National Society's depository, for instance, increased its turnover from about £9000 in 1851 to £29,960 in 1867.[6] Periodicals not only disseminated the views of those bodies which could afford to publish them, but by their advertisements provided a means whereby managers could recruit teachers.[7]

Grants of money or materials for building and equipment were made by most groups; the Congregational Board, for instance, spent a total of £120,000 in this way.[8] Only the National Society, however, had the resources to work on a large scale. A determined manager could get considerable help from this source. Robert Gregory (later to become the Society's treasurer) obtained for his schools in Lambeth a grant of 2s.6d. per child (the standard rate) in 1859; an additional £150 in 1860, to enable him to complete the building before the government's new building-grant restrictions came into force; £5 for fittings in 1861, £25 for new classrooms four years later; and in 1865–6 a total of £90 towards another new schoolroom.[9] However, perhaps fortunately for the Society's funds, few managers were as persistent as Gregory!

The Church of England Education Society concentrated on maintenance grants, arguing that '*the pressing* educational want'

*2B.

was a reliable source of income.[10] The National Society preferred to earmark most of its recurring grants for specific purposes: for example, a grant payable for three years to enable rural schools to employ certificated teachers and thereby qualify for government aid. Other groups, notably the Catholics and the Congregationalists, tried to enter the field of maintenance but found the drain on their resources too great.

Throughout the period the British and Foreign Society employed inspectors – usually five or six; until 1865 the Wesleyans had one. In 1859 the Home and Colonial Society decided to appoint 'visitors' to inspect its old students; these 'teachers of experience, well acquainted with the principles and practice of the system, and of decided piety'[11] were perhaps the first professional women inspectors in England.* The National Society, on the other hand, left inspection to the localities and employed 'organizing masters' who were sent to a district to hold vacation courses (harvest schools) for teachers† and to advise on the improvement of individual schools. They were paid between £120 and £150 a year. After 1848 they were normally holders of first-class certificates and in 1857 the Education Department agreed to pay augmentation grants as if they had been teaching in inspected schools. Until the early 1860s there were usually three or four; later the Society ceased to employ them directly but contributed towards the salaries of some still working in remote areas – the diocese of Carlisle, for example.[12]

The activities of organizing masters illustrate a major advantage possessed by the Anglicans – the existence of local agencies larger than individual school committees. The movement to establish diocesan boards of education, deriving their authority from the bishop, began in 1838 and gained momentum from the dispute between Church and State in 1839–40. By the middle 1840s boards existed in most dioceses, having superseded or absorbed the branch societies created in the early days of the National Society. In 1843, for example, the Hampshire Society for the Education of the Infant Poor handed over to the Winchester Diocesan Board all its functions except the running of the Winchester Central School.[13] Thus the Church had, to all appearances, constructed a network not unlike the county boards pro-

* 2C. † 2D.

posed by the Newcastle Commission, to organise provision in each area and to act as pressure groups at both national and local level.*

Each board had its own quirks so that there were few proposed remedies for educational problems which were not tried somewhere. Only on one point was there near-unanimity – the importance of teacher-training, to improve education and to ensure that teachers would be 'persons who will aid and abet us in our religious and moral work'.[14] Outside London almost all teacher-training was provided for the rest of the century in colleges founded by diocesan boards, some of which put nearly all their resources into training.† Otherwise their activities were wholly uncoordinated.[15] Many employed the organizing masters and organised harvest schools. Most made building and maintenance grants of varying amounts and upon various conditions. Some established teachers' libraries and depositories where managers could select books and equipment, or employed book-hawkers to tour the schools. Later, many became involved in the prize schemes which proliferated in the 1850s and 1860s in an attempt to improve attendance.

Some boards made direct attempts to fill the gaps in State activity by financing a measure of training for teachers below certificate level‡ or by paying 'diocesan' monitors who had been tested to see that they had attained a minimum standard of education. Others sought to assist the recruitment of pupil-teachers by giving bursaries to promising eleven and twelve-year-olds to support them until they were old enough to be apprenticed; other bursaries, in the lean years after the Revised Code, maintained selected students in training colleges. In a notable instance the London Diocesan Board virtually provided a pilot scheme for the pupil-teacher minute of 1846.[16]

Some form of inspection, deriving from the bishop's ancient authority over schoolmasters, was ultimately established in almost all dioceses. Its efficiency varied according to whether the inspector was a paid, full-time official (as in the dioceses of London and Canterbury);§ selected for his interest in education (as in the Oxford diocese); or simply the rural dean, as most bishops apparently felt was demanded by church discipline. A

* 2E. † 2F. ‡ 2G.

§ 2H.

few boards reinforced their inspectors by appointing ex-teachers as assistants.[17]

The achievements, however, of these denominational bodies were less impressive than is suggested by a catalogue of their activities. Certainly they were led by enthusiasts. Apart from the Church of England Education Society, which saw itself as a bulwark against the wiles of papists and tractarians, they did not waste much energy fighting each other until the conscience-clause controversy in the late 1860s. They could even collaborate, as in 1861–2 against the original version of the Revised Code. But their administration was amateurish; they had few sanctions to enforce their policies; and, above all, their resources were wholly inadequate to their aims. Diocesan and national organisations alike suffered from a general difficulty in raising money for anything but strictly local educational activities. Except for the National Society, comparatively affluent with the resources of the established Church behind it, their subscription lists were pitifully short and they all had to curtail their programmes through lack of funds. Schools might get advice and information from these sources; persistent managers might get money, but not financial security. For that, many of them looked to the State.

Notes

1. See Burgess op. cit., pp. 142–4; R. Aldrich's note on its origin, in History of Education Society *Bulletin*, 18 (1976), pp. 41–3.
2. Wesleyan Education Committee, *Annual Report* (1860), p. 39.
3. *The Congregational Board of Education – its Origin, Constitution, Past Operations, and Proposed Measures* (undated), p. 1.
4. E.g., Leamington British School, in which the Baptist minister and his family filled roles identical with those of the parson's family in an Anglican school – Log Book (Warwicks. CRO).
5. J. M. Goldstrom, *The Social Content of Education, 1808–1870* (1972), pp. 64–152.
6. Figures in National Society, *Annual Reports*.
7. *Monthly Paper* (National Society), *Educational Record* (British and Foreign School Society), *The Educator* (Congregational Board of Education), *Educational Paper* (Home and Colonial School Society), *The Catholic School* (Poor School Committee)
8. H. B. Binns, *A Century of Education* (1908), p. 152.
9. National Society Files, St. Mary's, Lambeth.
10. Church of England Education Society, *Annual Report* (1854–5), p. 13.

11. Home and Colonial School Society, *Annual Report* (1858–9), p. 14.
12. PP. 1857–58 XLV, pp. 32–5; 1866 VII 115, q. 1402; National Society, *Annual Report* (1861), p. ix.
13. Hampshire Society, *Annual Report* (1843).
14. PP. 1865 VI, q. 3363 (statement by Rev. R. B. Girdlestone).
15. The records of diocesan boards are scattered and incomplete. The National Society has a collection of their annual reports, which is drawn on here.
16. Bursaries of £10 rising to £15 for assistants (thirteen to seventeen years old) in selected schools, to be instructed by the teacher and the clergyman and at seventeen to compete for exhibitions to the National Society's Training Colleges (PP. 1844 XXXVIII 219, pp. 146–8).
17. E.g., Flint, formerly a National Society organizing master, author of *Plain Hints for Organising and Teaching a Church School* (1856), was assistant inspector in the Lichfield diocese.

Documents

2A. DENOMINATIONALISM IN THE 1860s

When the Voluntaryists admitted defeat and began to bring their schools within the government system, the inspector who saw the most of them was Joshua Fitch, HM Inspector in Baines's home ground, the West Riding. As a former pupil and teacher at Borough Road, he disapproved of denominational schools; so his unexpected evidence as to the strength of grass-roots sectarianism as late as 1867 is interesting, even if the statement in his second sentence is historically incorrect in the case of areas in which nonconformity was strong.

. . . I am much struck with the fact that the new schools which promise to multiply around me here are not as a rule to be on a comprehensive basis, but distinctively sectarian. Independents, Baptists, and Wesleyans twenty years ago were accustomed to combine in establishing "British" schools, in which the Bible was read and diligently taught, but in which no attempt was made to teach a catechism or to influence the discretion of the parents as to the Sunday school or place of worship chosen. *Now* each of these bodies desires to have its separate schools; and I know of several Yorkshire villages, already possessing a Church and a Wesleyan school, which will shortly be supplied with a third under the care of the Congregationalists, the Baptists, or the "Free Church". All three will be competing for pupils; all three will receive Government aid; and between them the work of instruction will be done less economically, if not less efficiently than by one united school. Parents will "patronize" each school in turn, not on educational or religious grounds, but whenever an unreasonable request is denied, or when there is any wish to flatter the managers of one school at the expense of the others.

(PP. 1867–8 XXV, pp. 345–6)

2B. TEACHER-TRAINING AND THE VOLUNTARY SOCIETIES

All the voluntary bodies had extreme difficulty in raising funds to support their training colleges and therefore sought government aid even before it was offered (see N. Ball, *H.M. Inspectorate 1839–1849* (1963), c. 9). This financial dependence and the contol of Queen's Scholarship and Certificate examinations by HM Inspectorate made teacher-training the one area successfully dominated by the policy of the Education Department. Consequently the elite minority of trained teachers experienced an almost uniform programme of training. The 'method' syllabus which follows, that of the Catholic Poor School Committee's college for men at Hammersmith, might have been drawn up, except for the appearance of Jacotot and Girard in point 18, for use in any of the Protestant colleges.

First Year's Course: On Methods

1. On method in general, and its fundamental laws.
2. On special methods:
   (a) analytic and synthetic;
   (b) interrogative, elliptical, and expository;
   (c) individual and simultaneous.
3. On the comparative advantages of oral and book instruction.
4. On the art of questioning.
5. On the means of securing attention.
6. On the use and abuse of illustration and apparatus.
7. On notes of lessons.
8. On the *relative* importance of the various branches of elementary instruction.
9. On the use and abuse of object lessons.
10. On the manner of conducting a class.

Second Year's Course: On School Management

1. On school organisation in general; its object, its characteristics, the principles on which it is based.
2. On systems of teaching:
   (a) individual. (b) collective. (c) mutual and monitorial.
3. On the plans of organization proper to each of the above systems, illustrated by diagrams.
4. On classification; its true basis, the number, shape, and arrangement of the classes.
5. On time-tables.
6. On the economical distribution of teaching power, and the personal contact of the master with each child daily.
7. On the manner of arranging, by anticipation, the amount of work to be done weekly and quarterly.
8. On school apparatus.
9. On school registers.
10. On the playground, and its uses.
11. On securing regular and punctual attendance.
12. On the government, teaching and training of pupil-teachers.
13. On the master's duties towards managers and parents.
14. On the means of perpetuating relations with the children after they have left school.
15. On school libraries.
16. On industrial schools.
17. On night schools.
18. On the systems of instruction followed by –
    Jacotot, Pestalozzi,
    Père Girard, Stow.

(PP. 1860 LIV, p. 416)

2C. INSPECTION BY THE HOME AND COLONIAL SCHOOL SOCIETY

The reports of inspectors from the voluntary bodies provide an interesting supplement to the reports of HMIs. The Home and Colonial Society had always attempted to keep control of ex-students of Gray's Inn Road, expecting them to write to the college within three months of taking a post, sending timetables and sample lesson notes, and subsequently to write annually.

Visitors were appointed when this means of control was seen to be inadequate. The women involved appear (to judge from log-book records of their visits) to have spent one or more days observing the routine of a school and then, after giving advice, to have revisited it quickly to see if that advice had been carried out. They seem to have been efficient; one of them, Miss Jones, was sent to the USA in 1861 to organise infant training at Oswego (*Educational Paper of the Home and Colonial Society* (1861), pp. 19–21).

The following summary of the experience of one visitor throws a good deal of light upon conditions in schools for young children, a subject on which many HMIs had little to say, and upon details which they were unable to discuss when the length of their reports was restricted by the Education Department in the 1850s.

One of the Visitors of the Society having been asked to point out what has struck her most in her visits to schools, has kindly written to us at considerable length on the subject. Our limits do not permit the insertion of all that she has sent; but we think the following brief hints may be useful, it being understood that they by no means relate to schools *generally*, – they are rather the exceptions than the rule.

SCHOOLROOM. – The Visitor finds that when schoolrooms are plastered, parts of the plaster is continually broken away by nails or by accident and left unmended. The walls are sometimes of yellow and other sombre colours, instead of being light and cheerful. Both in plastered and unplastered schoolrooms dust and cobwebs are too often allowed to accumulate. In some cases the windows were not cleaned sufficiently often. In others attention was not paid to the floors; they were not scrubbed with sufficient frequency, and when scrubbed proper care was not taken to keep them clean. From her experience she strongly recommends scrapers and mats, not only as useful in themselves, but as important means of training children into good habits. The Visitor mentions with approval two schools where plants were placed on the window-sills, the windows opening from the top.

SCHOOL FURNITURE, ETC. – The Visitor thinks that more taste might sometimes be displayed in the arrangement of school furniture, whilst at the same time greater convenience would be obtained. She recommends teachers to give more attention to the subject, and not consider it necessary that an article once placed in a position should always remain there. Sunday-school forms are, she says, not unfrequently huddled up on one side, and occasionally broken chairs and stools are placed on them, giving rooms a very untidy appearance.

Maps and reading-boards were too often hung by a single string, and therefore on one side, having a very unpleasant appearance. She thinks that pictures, &c., &c., when hung on the walls, should either be pasted on wood, or on very stiff pasteboard, or in wooden frames, so as not to warp. Loose sheets, pictures, &c., should be put into a portfolio and kept in a cupboard, and not left about the room. She thinks slates far better than black-boards, and that the latter are too often left uncleaned. She advises lesson stands for reading-boards, the pegs to be fastened to them by a string, and suggests that every easel for placing slates or black-boards upon, should have fastened to it a pointer, a chalk box, and bag with a duster, in order that there "may be no racing about and losing time when a lesson is about to be given, and such things are wanted." She greatly prefers cupboards to boxes for books, &c., and thinks these cupboards ought not only to be put right once a week, but always kept right, by placing things in them in an orderly way, and by the teacher's inspection at the close of each day. This will also enable the teacher to satisfy herself that nothing is left about.

VENTILATION. – The Visitor complains, as every one does who has anything to do with schools, and none more loudly than Her Majesty's Inspectors, of the great and constant want of ventilation; she recommends that no school should be without a thermometer, and the more strongly as they can now be procured for one shilling, – this thermometer to be frequently examined. If no proper means of ventilation exists, she suggests that one or more windows should always be open at the top, and all windows regularly opened at play-time; on these two points she found many omissions.

DINNER HOUR. – In several schools she found a great want of comfortable arrangements for those children who remained during dinner; often no convenience for washing, and even where the necessary apparatus existed, she has frequently been told by a child, when asked why she had not washed, "There was no water, or no basin, or no towel, or no soap." She thinks the practice of the elder children dining in the baby-room, to keep the large one clean, a bad one, and laments that the children so seldom have a tablecloth or knives and forks – sometimes indeed she found them even without drinking-cups; some of these articles, she says, if provided, might be useful in the babies' school for lessons. At all events she considers them essential to the right and orderly training of children. In some good schools for older children, where arrangements for washing existed, children with dirty hands were not allowed to use books, but sent to a class having a reading board. An intelligent teacher told her that she had often obtained cleanliness among the babies, by appealing to the sympathies of the mothers, pointing out, for example, that visitors had admired and praised some little ones, whilst theirs had been neglected, and begging them, for the sake of their dear children's feelings, to send them clean.

PUPIL-TEACHERS. – She thinks a right employment of pupil-teachers during school hours is not sufficiently attended to, that they are often kept too long at one gallery or class. She mentions a case where a teacher, who had not been trained at the Home and Colonial, gave to a pupil-teacher in her third year the constant charge of the babies, and that her health suffered in consequence. Another in which the pupil-teachers changed their sections of children every gallery lesson, and their classes weekly. This was erring on the side of too much variety. Pupil-teachers, she says, are often allowed to touch children, and even to push them into the line, &c. This, she thinks, ought never to be done. The pupil-teachers should only speak to them. If pupil-teachers and monitors are employed in a school, she suggests that the former should have the largest class, but not always the upper division of it.

GIVING OUT BOOKS, ETC. – Some teachers give out books, move about the forms, &c., work which ought invariably to be done by pupil-teachers or children. Teachers should remember that excellent rule, "Do nothing in their schools which others can do as well for them." Their business is to *teach*.

MARCHING. – In a great many schools marching is not well done. The children are not required to keep their knees straight. They stamp and make much noise, without any real improvement in the carriage of the body.

DISMISSING A SCHOOL. – The Visitor recommends that the children should bow and curtsey together, and bid the clergyman (if there) "Good morning or afternoon;" then the mistress, then the pupil-teachers, and not bow or curtsey separately as they go out.

HATS, BONNETS, ETC. – The pegs for hanging these, she thinks, should be of iron; and she says that even then they need to be frequently replaced. Broken hat-pegs have an untidy appearance. In some schools there are clothes-horses for the hats and bonnets, and these are drawn up to the ceiling. This, when the ceilings are arched and lofty, she thinks, answers very well; but she prefers placing them on castors, and taking them to the lobby. She thinks clothes-horses better than baskets, though she has never heard any objections to the latter, except that they require the hats, &c., to be taken out in wet weather, and they are cheaper. In some schools she has seen the pegs numbered, and each child having its own number; and is inclined to recommend it.

PLAYGROUNDS. – She has found these not unfrequently neglected; draining often required. She strongly recommends a covered shed in every playground for wet and hot weather. This shed may be, she thinks, used occasionally for lessons; more general attention on the part of teachers to the appearance and cleanliness of their playgrounds and offices she says is very desirable.

BABIES' ROOM. – She thinks the babies often require more attention than they receive – the value of the seed which may be sown here is too often forgotten. She says the children should not be kept too long in one position; sometimes their hands should be behind, and sometimes before; that if arms are folded too tightly the back grows round. She thinks babies should always be sent out to play twice in the morning, from twenty to twenty-five minutes each time; and if one gallery lesson must follow another – the necessity of which she greatly doubts – there should be plenty of drill between. When giving lessons to infants she thinks they should always have something to look at, and as often as possible, something to handle.

TEACHING – ORDER OF SUBJECTS. – The Visitor has often found a want of systematic order in the teaching, particularly in the religious lessons. She strongly recommends teachers to follow the course pointed out in Miss Mayo's "Religious Instruction," until they have worked out a course for themselves. She thinks a systematic course on Natural History, Objects, &c. . . . would be very desirable in girls' or mixed schools, and avoid much unnecessary repetition.

TEXTS OF SCRIPTURE. – She sometimes found that texts were not repeated sufficiently often for the children to say them correctly; and suggests either more frequent repetition, or to have the same text more than once.

GALLERY, OR SECTIONAL LESSONS. – She thinks that often one head of the lesson is not made sufficiently clear before going on to another, and that distinct heads might often have a summary, so as to have two or three short summaries in a lesson, instead of one long one at the end.

ANSWERS OF CHILDREN. – She has sometimes found teachers satisfied with very meagre answers, often merely yes or no. She recommends that children should be required to answer in a sentence, as this would enable teachers to judge how far the child understood the question, and at the same time be very beneficial to the other children. She often finds a want of attention to enunciation and pronunciation, and that the teachers get so accustomed to provincialisms as to forget to check them.

CLASS TEACHING – Her impression is that teachers of schools generally devote too much of their time to the highest class; and she strongly recommends more attention to the lower classes, and to the teaching of the pupil-teachers. In infant-schools, she thinks, more time might be given to the highest class, as many children leave those schools without going to any other.

READING. – Reading with proper expression and intelligence, she says, is not made a sufficient point of; and she thinks children require as much questioning at reading as at other exercises.

WRITING. – The Visitor says, letter writing among the older children is not sufficiently general; and that all children are not required to read the copies they write. When the teaching power is not strong, she recommends copy-books where the copies are set.

ARITHMETIC. – She has frequently found notation not sufficiently attended to. . . She thinks more sums with fewer figures in them would be far better than the long sums now too often set. She thinks, also, that young girls might very well learn to make out bills of parcels as well as boys, and that entering sums in a ciphering book is useful, though now somewhat out of fashion. She would however confine it to practical questions, and their solution.

NOTE-BOOK. – The Visitor strongly recommends teachers to keep notebooks to record, not only the courses of lessons given on each subject, but the substance of every lesson. She is satisfied that, by doing this, even for a single year, they will greatly lighten their labours, and improve their teaching.

(Home and Colonial School Society, *Educational Paper* (1861), pp. 22–4)

2D. IN-SERVICE TRAINING

Harvest schools, or meetings, the precursors of modern vacation courses, were begun by Rev. William Fry of Leicester in 1842, with the purpose of improving the standards of existing teachers by bringing them together during the summer holidays for instruction and for the exchange of ideas. They quickly became common, at least in the midlands, and the National Society's organizing masters usually spent part of the summer months running them. The following passage is an unusually detailed report on one such meeting at Ludlow, written by the organizing master involved. At least one HMI, W.J. Kennedy (anticipating the duties of his successors), believed that the Education Department should run such schools annually (PP. 1851 XLIV 401, p. 443).

The Harvest meeting was held this year at Ludlow, under the superintendence of Mr. Lomax, assisted by Mr. Wath, of the Blue School, Hereford,* whose lectures on practical science were greatly appreciated by the teachers. The following extracts from Mr. Lomax's reports will possess general interest:-

The number of teachers present this year was 51. 18 masters and 18 mistresses were from the Archdeaconry of Salop, 9 masters and 6 mistresses from the Archdeaconry of Hereford. One out of this number already possesses a Government certificate; ten have been more or less previously trained; and twelve are in schools under inspection, in six of which it is Government inspection, and in the others Diocesan.

The aggregate number of children brought under the influence of the instruction given at the meeting is upwards 2,500.

I was glad to observe that all the masters belonging to the Salop Archdeaconry who had previously attended the Harvest

* The Bluecoat School, managed by Richard Dawes, then Dean of Hereford.

meeting at Hereford, (with the exception of two who have left the County) were present again on this occasion.

You will be pleased to learn that I can speak with great satisfaction respecting all the arrangements of the meeting. At the same time I cannot forbear urging upon the Board the desirableness and great advantage, still to be gained over anything we have yet attained to, that would accrue from providing accommodation for the teachers in a body – the masters together in one house and the mistresses in another.

A programme of the course of lessons was issued prior to the Harvest meeting, and each teacher was requested to select for himself the subject upon which he was most anxious to obtain information.

Our meeting was commenced every morning at 9 a.m. with prayers, taken from the book of Common Prayer, one of the Canticles, and the lesson for the day. In the afternoon at 5, it was closed in the same way. The evenings were spent either in visiting places in the neighbourhood possessing interest, or by the masters in practical land surveying, or in attending lectures at the rooms.

The following will show the selection made as well as the course pursued:-

Number	*Subject*
21 masters and 14 mistresses	English Grammar
17 ,, ,, 8 ,,	Geography
8 ,, ,, 18 ,,	Arithmetic
12 ,, —	Euclid
13 ,, ,, 10 ,,	Vocal music

The following is a list of the points brought before the attention of the meeting:-

First. In the practising school – The mode of opening and closing the business of the day; of registering attendance and absence; of securing cleanliness and dealing with latecomers; method of imparting instruction in the Bible, Liturgy, and Catechism of the Church of England; Reading; and of teaching the following subjects: Writing, Dictation, Composition, Singing; also the method of using the following books and apparatus authorised by the Society – Scripture and other prints and illustrations, maps and black boards, pointers and parallel desks, the Third, Sequel, and Second reading books, and the National Society's excellent series of small books, in Geography, Grammar, Arithmetic, History, and Arithmetical tables.

Second. In Normal and conversational lectures, the following points were discussed with great interest:-
How to secure the attention of a number of children.
The rules to be observed in questioning.
How to cure *extempore bad grammar* in schools.
The want of point observable in much of the instruction given at school, and the value of making children prepare lessons in the evening at home.
The necessity for a *defined* and *consecutive* course of Bible instruction for both the elder and younger scholars.
The analysis of the Fourth Book of the Dublin series;* for the purpose of laying down some definite *method of using it as a text and class book* in our schools, and for developing a method of teaching best suited to the matter contained in each section.
The value of Fables and Poetry as a means of School teaching.

The construction of time tables and necessity of making provision for *household instruction as well as needle work* for the girls, and for instructing the boys in practical matters, such as Mensuration and the subjects contained in the Agricultural Class Book – the importance also of setting apart half an hour weekly for imparting information upon current events of a national, local or otherwise interesting character, likely to be of use to them now or hereafter – such as a new discovery, an improved invention, a remarkable occurrence, an act of greatness, an offence, a voyage, a journey, in short, anything calculated to awaken intelligence, truthfulnesss, courage, reverence, morality, and impart a bias for good to the mind – subjects which, at present, find no room for direct teaching in most of our schools, but are left to chance to exert what influence they may. One other point occupied our particular attention, that of the "management of children"; and the importance of a good system of *games and amusements* as well as rewards and punishments. Under this head was considered the great importance of marking the difference between incapacity and idleness, children's offences and parents' faults, offences against

* I.e., the series published by the Irish National Board, as was the Agricultural Class Book (below).

order and those against morality, the objects of punishments and the impression to be made by their infliction. Games also occupied our attention as an antidote to want of punctuality, by offering an inducement to the children to appear for a quarter of an hour before school in the play ground.

It is rarely that any game – save the circular swing and the leaping bar – is introduced for the children's amusement, whereas the trap ball, and cricket, the skipping rope, and battle-dore are *games of skill* which might be easily introduced into every school, and may be employed not only in addition to, but in place of the former, which for several reasons are not always to be had.

In no one present was the knowledge of the Scriptures actually deficient.

One way in which the usefulness of the Board's exertions in this respect has manifested itself, is that two of the pupils of last year (one master and one mistress) have since obtained certificates of merit from the Privy Council. The mistress (who had previously received no training whatever) obtained *a first division of the second class*. The master *a first of the third*.

(Hereford Diocesan Board, *Annual Report* (1853), pp. 13–16)

2E. A DIOCESAN BOARD AND NATIONAL POLICY

The Hereford Diocesan Board was concerned with an area of scattered rural communities and little wealth. This memorial, drafted in 1856 by William Poole, the Board's secretary, and with the exception of the passage in brackets adopted by the Board, was an attempt to influence public policy by analysing an undoubted weakness of the Education Department's centralised system. It was rejected by the Department but may have had some influence in bringing about a minor concession in 1858, whereby capitation grant was payable in schools (for young children) which served as feeders for a central school under a certificated teacher (PP. 1857 (Sess. 2) XXXIII, pp. 17–25; 1857–8 XLV, p. 40).

Memorial of the Hereford Diocesan Board of Education, & of the Diocesan Inspectors of the County of Hereford

Considerable experience of the practical working of the present System has convinced your memorialists that one main obstacle to the more rapid spread of Education has arisen from the attempt to deal with all Schools upon one uniform & unvaried plan. In the frequent efforts which the Hereford Board has made to obtain from the Committee of Council some recognition of the needs of smaller Parishes, this has ever been the objection, an unwillingness to lower the Standard of Education, a fear of precedents which might be insisted on by larger & richer districts. It was denied that any district could fairly be called destitute, it was maintained that all could easily come up to the requirements demanded of all.

Experience has proved that this is not the case – there are in fact *four* Classes of Districts needing Schools, in many respects unlike each other,

1st Rich Town Parishes inhabited by a mixture of Classes, containing a considerable amount of wealth, as well as a large poor population –

2nd Rich Country Parishes, of a population sufficient to furnish a School of from 50 to 100 children, inhabited by several wealthy residents, or landowners able and willing to assist the Schools.

3rd Poor Town Districts inhabited solely by artisans & labourers, a shifting population often out of work, often mixed up with a large infusion of a degraded class who care nothing for the Education of their children.

4. Very small or poor Country Parishes. Where the land is either in the ownership of non resident proprietors, who consider that their duty is fulfilled by aiding the Schools in their own neighbourhood – or in the hands of poor free holders who make a hard living out of it & the labour of their own families – or where the land is heavily mortgaged, the interests eating up all profit – or in chancery, or otherwise so hampered that it is hopeless to expect any considerable sum to be raised for School purposes.

To treat these four classes alike is evidently unreasonable. If the two rich Districts should be taken as the standard of help required, the two poorer ones will be starved. If the poorer are sufficiently aided, the richer will be wastefully supplied.

If, however, Schools seeking aid were distributed into four classes, & the regulation of aid varied according to the class in which the School may be placed this difficulty would be met. The distribution of schools into their proper classes might be the work of an officer or a small Commission, appointed for the purpose & would be neither a difficult nor a lengthy operation. The same authority could also point out the districts where Schools ought to be erected.

It would needlessly occupy time to go into the regulations suitable to each class – But your memorialists believe that if some such distribution of Schools were adopted, there would be found no insuperable difficulty in the other questions which surround this subject.

E.g. (In the poor town districts where degraded parents suffer their children to spend their days in the streets, & where police regulations are already in force, it might not be impossible to insist on compulsory attendance at something equivalent to "Ragged Schools, without interfering with the liberty, or injuring the revenues of other Classes of Schools)* – & in districts where very small Parishes lie together, or some accidental conditions of Property offer reasonable hindrances, it might be possible to sanction dames Schools, or so to vary the regulation, or the Report of the proper authority, as to suit the circumstances of the case, without establishing a precedent for the schools in the other classes.

And believing that even after the most exact regulations and definitions, the working of any Conscience Clause must in a great measure be a matter of mutual confidence, they see no reason to doubt, that if such a disposition should be manifested on both sides – on the part of those who impose as well as of those who receive it, there would be no serious difficulty in satisfying the reasonable requirements of Managers, Parents & the Central Authority.

It would be, however, needless and probably impossible without unduly occupying your time to enter into the many details and facts with which these views may be illustrated & confirmed.

Your memorialists would therefore venture to express a hope, that in any future legislation on this subject this great variety of condition in School Districts may not be lost sight of.

(Poole MSS., vol XVI, Hereford Library)

2F. TEACHER-TRAINING IN THE DIOCESES

The uniform pattern of training noted above (2B) meant that there were few essential differences between institutions, whether

* Passage in brackets deleted by Diocesan Board.

national or diocesan. The following instructions on preparing an oral lesson, which might, indeed, have been given at any time between 1850 and 1950, were part of the method course at the York and Ripon Diocesan Board's college for men in York during the late 1850s.

How Should a Lesson be Prepared?

1. Textbook.
   Should be used to obtain matter,
   But not for *method*, *arrangement*, *language*.
   Should be as *full* and *elaborate* as possible.
   More than one author should be read.
2. Matter.
   Read more widely and thoroughly than an individual lesson needs.
   Digest the matter and interweave it with illustration.
   Let the matter be *graphic*, *interesting*, *suitable*.
   Guard against *too much* and irrelevant matter.
3. Illustration.
   Procure *more than one illustration* for the same difficulty.
   The *real object* is generally preferable to the picture.
   The *picture* to the verbal description.
   A diagram drawn on the Board during the lesson to one previously prepared.
   Decide as to what apparatus will be required.
   Decide as to how specimens may be most profitably introduced.
4. Object.
   (1) Should be determined by the *subject*.
   (2) Should be determined by the *condition of class*.
   (3) Should be chosen with a view to giving the lesson *force*, *definiteness*, *consistency*.
   (4) Guard against it being *fanciful, indefinite*.
   (5) Keep it in view throughout the lesson.
5. Plan.
   (1) *a* The beginning of the Lesson should
   introduce the subject;
   arouse attention;
   enlist sympathy;
   it should therefore consist of

a bold picture or
searching examination.

b The Middle contains the new matter and is properly *the lesson.* This should consist of a number of stages or divisions following each other naturally and logically. It is a great art to give clearness and system to the body of the lesson without obtruding the divisions too nakedly.

c The end should *apply what is learnt,*
test the success of the lesson;
it should therefore be *short, clear, testing.*

(2) Notes

a Should consist of *Chief Heads.*

b Should consist of *Condensation of matter* arranged as intended to be given.

c The method by which the lesson is to be taught.

d Should bear – The title of the lesson.
The object of the lesson.
The class to be taught.
Time to be occupied in delivering it.

(PP. 1860 LIV. pp. 352–3)

2G. TRAINING FOR UNCERTIFICATED TEACHERS

Most diocesan boards sought some means of raising standards of teaching in schools outside the government system. In 1847, when it was dominated by Archdeacon Denison, the Bath and Wells Diocesan Board devised the following scheme as an alternative to the Minutes of 1846. The training led to a Bishop's Certificate of Competency, awarded on the results of an examination. The scheme was continued after the Board had ceased to oppose the Minutes, as a means of establishing an identifiable standard of efficiency in small rural schools.

The work of the district inspectors of this diocese was coordinated and regulated by a diocesan inspector who was paid an honorarium of £50 p.a. (Bath and Wells Diocesan Board, *Annual Report* (1854–5), pp. 13–14)

Grants for Training Pupils within the Diocese

The Board offer a certain number of Grants, for the purpose of training promising pupils at schools within the Diocese.

RULES

1. The Grants shall be made for training pupils in any schools within the diocese, certified by the Diocesan Inspector as suitable for that purpose.
2. Grants shall be tenable for three years, and the candidates shall not be less than 15 years of age.
3. The amount of grant shall not exceed £15 a year for males, and £12 for females; of which £3 shall be paid, in each case, for instruction.
4. Candidates shall be elected by the Diocesan Board, on the report of the Diocesan Inspector, assisted by two District Inspectors to be named by him, after an examination held in such place as the Diocesan Inspector shall elect.
5. In every case the exhibitions shall be paid half-yearly, on the production of a certificate of having received proper instruction from the master, and of regular attendance and good conduct – to be sent by the clergyman or manager through the District Inspector.

Certificates will be required before the examination –

(a) Of baptism.
(b) From the clergyman of the parish, of good character.
(c) From the District Inspector, of qualifications and fitness to teach.

The Diocesan Inspector will act on the following general principles in giving Certificates that schools are suitable to receive the Training Pupils.

1. The master or mistress must hold the Bishop's certificate of merit.
2. The District Inspector's report of the school, to the Bishop, for the last two years, must have been a favourable one as to instruction, discipline, and the general apparatus of the school room.
3. In the case of female training pupils there must always be a mistress, and not merely a female to teach needle-work in the afternoon; and if there be a master in the school, or in the adjoining boys' school, he must be a married man.
4. The parochial clergyman must certify that there are respectable persons with whom the training pupil can lodge, and that the rooms intended for them are airy and comfortable.
5. The school, if a mixed one, must have at least 50 children in

attendance on an average. If a boys' or girls' school only, not less than 40.

(PP. 1865 VI, p. 476)

2H. DIOCESAN INSPECTION

Inspection under the bishop's authority extended in theory to all Anglican schools but varied greatly in efficiency; and much evidence survives to show how easily part-time inspectors could undermine their own usefulness by offending their fellow-clergy with criticism. However, in the few dioceses which appointed a paid professional, their position was stronger. Rev. B.F. Smith of Canterbury was paid £200 p.a. and visited about 200 schools annually (see his evidence to the Select Committee on Education, 1866: PP. 1866 VII 115). His published reports were mere lists of statistics; but in his reports on individual schools he no more minced words than did HM Inspectors.

Report of Chevening Boys' and Girls' School
Inspected April 29th 1851

Girls'. – The demeanour of the girls bespeaks a good moral tone; though better discipline and more methodical action might be introduced with advantage. The attainments in Arithmetic are considerable, in other things fair. But more pains should be taken in developing intelligence, for want of which the religious knowledge, though considerable, is not wholly satisfactory. The writing also should be improved.

Boys'. – In consequence of the School being under the government of a Mistress, a spirit of rebellion is generated among the boys, which her husband vainly endeavours to restrain by physical force. To this circumstance, unfavourable to the formation of character, may also be attributed their want of intelligence and of activity in school work. The religious knowledge however is, fair. But in every thing greater exactness should be insisted on. Arithmetic alone forms an exception to the general mediocrity of attainment in the subjects of secular instruction.

(Kent Archives, P 88/25/11)

CHAPTER THREE

THE GOVERNMENT GRANT*

GOVERMENT grants were rarely the major source of a school's income;† their importance was that they could make the difference between solvency and debt. But, apart from the fact that lethargy or prejudice prevented some managers from applying for them, the terms on which they were offered excluded many schools. The number of annual grants certainly increased more than fourfold between 1850 and the middle 1860s;[1] but even then the majority of parishes were without grant-aided schools.[2] Some had no schools, some only bad ones and in a few cases managers were so secure financially that they were indifferent to the grant. Others were too poor or too remote to have any chance of meeting the required conditions.‡ Hence in any discussion of the system administered by the Education Department[3] it must be remembered that many schools, from choice or necessity, remained outside it.

Many of these had received building grants, made on a pound for pound basis, on condition that the school should be open to inspection. This by itself meant little, since after 1846 the inspectorate was too busy with annual-grant schools to make regular visits to others. The annual grants established by the Minutes of 1846 with the aim of simultaneously providing financial assistance to schools and improving the quality of teaching were generally welcomed except by a small minority of high Anglicans who regarded them as Erastian and a larger minority of nonconformists who saw them as an attack on the freedom of the individual.[4] HM Inspectorate which, through its reports on schools and its examination of teachers and pupil-teachers, was the linchpin of the sytem, had already won a large measure of acceptance amongst school managers;§ and the initial enthusiasm for the Minutes was so great¶ as to alarm the Education Department about their financial and administrative implications even before Kay-Shuttleworth resigned in 1849.[5] The administrative burden which they created was immense. All the examining for

* Appendix 2 should be consulted in connection with this chapter.
† 3A. ‡ 3B. § 3C. ¶ 3D.

Queen's scholarships and certificates of merit was carried out by Department officials. All the grants – augmentation, gratuities for instructing pupil-teachers, pupil-teachers' stipends – were paid directly to the individuals concerned. Managers received no money but the Department had to communicate with them constantly over inspection, staffing and the state of their schools. Not surprisingly the system was generally unpopular with the overworked officials who had to administer it.

The intention of this astoundingly centralised policy was that managers who wanted aid should be forced to establish in their schools standards of pay, organisation and teaching which they did not determine and which they therefore could not lower. But the conclusion which some certificated teachers tried to draw, that they were servants of the State rather than of the managers, was never admitted by the Department. The position of a schoolmaster, as defined by Kay-Shuttleworth's successor, Lingen, in 1852 was 'that of a public servant acting under a public body (the Managers of his School). In that relation his duties are executive only'.[6] The only major addition to the grant system between 1846 and 1862, the capitation grant of 1853, was paid directly to the managers.

This grant was introduced to meet the criticism that the Minutes of 1846 benefitted only those schools, mainly urban, which were already wealthy enough to pay the salaries required and large enough to employ pupil-teachers. Originally confined to rural schools it was extended to all because of the impossibility of drawing a valid distinction between rural and urbanised communities. Lingen opposed it, and even more its extension, on grounds which illustrate the dilemma fundamental to the Department's policy. Public money was granted, he said, 'not to pay for the Education of the Country as it has been, but to pay for its improvement'.[7] Yet the purpose of the grant was to encourage efforts to improve; and to attempt to raise standards by refusing recognition to genuine effort was to ensure that the system would never become universal and that it would arouse resentment. Any manager who just failed to meet the conditions for a grant, knowing his school's problems and his own efforts, could plead with perfect sincerity that his was a case deserving of special treatment. The administrator saw things differently: 'The central authority struggles to guard its trust by rules which are right on the whole, but tyrannical in detail – and dares not relax those rules when they ought to be relaxed, because experience proves to demonstration that one justifiable relaxation inevitably admits a hundred unjustifiable.' Not surprisingly the author of these words, the future Archbishop Frederick Temple, saw proposals to base the grant upon examination results as 'a means of escape from what I considered to be a vicious system'.[8]

In one respect this rigidity was already causing a breakdown in the later 1850s; there is abundant evidence that the pupil-teacher system had reached crisis point.* The stipends bore no relation to the wages obtainable by young people generally; they did not differentiate between boys and girls; since they were paid at the end of each year, after examination, no account was taken of how the pupil-teacher was to live in the meantime. As a result, according to HM Inspectors of all denominations, both the quantity and quality of male pupil-teachers was declining. Of 661 male candidates for Queen's scholarships in 1861, for instance, only 468 reached scholarship standard, although there were 615 vacancies in the colleges.[9] The Revised Code's remedy, to abolish the stipend and leave payment to be determined by the managers, was admittedly draconian; but the more flexible structure which eventually emerged, if less than generous, nevertheless gave the pupil-teacher system a better chance of survival.†

Unsuccessful attempts at legislation and the appointment of the Newcastle Commission in 1858 delayed change in the grant system until 1862. Given the desire to make it simpler and more flexible and the Victorian belief in examinations as the best means of testing worth, the Revised Code's solution of a unified grant payable to managers on the results of examination was probably inevitable. But it removed the security hitherto enjoyed by managers who could forecast their income on the basis of their teacher's class of certificate, their pupil-teacher's year of apprenticeship and the number of children likely to attend for 176 days; and the original proposals for the examination were so unrealistic as to justify the fierce attack which was immediately mounted by almost all the voluntary bodies involved in elementary education. The concessions which they extorted – that one-third of the grant was to be paid on attendance, that infants were exempt from

* 3E. † 3F.

examination and that examination according to age was abandoned – made the Code more workable; but the publicity resulting from the struggle increased the panic with which it was greeted.

Inept administration during the first months of the system worsened still further the relations between schools and the Department.* In December 1863, for instance, Christ Church Schools, Crewe, were suddenly deprived of £167.2s. of their grant on the grounds that the subvention from the LNW Railway Company was not a subscription; only to have it restored, as suddenly, a few weeks later. Article 52d, which reduced a school's grant by the amount of its endowments was applied, not at Faversham where the schools received £500 annually from the town charities, but to poverty-stricken schools receiving £5 a year from Betton's Charity.[10] Such incidents contributed to the explosion of hostility towards the Education Department in 1864, which led to Lowe's resignation and a series of select committees.

By this time, however, the new system was settling into a routine which lasted for thirty years. Some teachers suffered a cut in salary, although in many cases managers made up the amount of the lost augmentation grant.† For a few years there were cuts in staffing, especially of pupil-teachers who were replaced by monitors or sometimes by adult assistants whose appointment did not involve a five-year commitment. The Code was generally, though possibly inaccurately, believed to have caused a decline in the teaching of advanced subjects and advanced children;[11] hence the beginning in 1867 of the move towards Standard VII and the examination of the'higher subjects', a process accelerated in the 1870s.

Whatever its weaknesses, few people wholly endorsed Matthew Arnold's sweeping condemnation of the Code. A more typical view was that of C.H. Alderson, HMI, who described it as: '. . . a very good test of a bad school, and a very indifferent one of a good school. It runs like a sword through a mass of half-acquired, ill-digested knowledge, and lays bare the shortcomings of an incompetent teacher with striking effect. But it is too mechanical, monotonous, and inelastic to be an adequate test of the school work of a conscientious and vigorous teacher.'[12]

* 3G. † 3H.

In practice, those which seem to have suffered most were mediocre schools under timid teachers who were too frightened to spend time on anything beyond the 3Rs. Good schools were largely unaffected since their pupils passed the examinations without difficulty.* Some even benefitted financially, like the Cheltenham British Schools, which received a total grant of £262.9s. in the last year of the old Code. Next year the amount rose to £292.15s.2d. and remained at that level throughout the 1860s.[13]

The major weapon against bad schools which the Department acquired by the Revised Code was in Article 52. Hitherto the grant could only be given or withheld in its entirety. By authorising reductions of between a tenth and a half for listed deficiencies, the article enabled the Department to penalise schools without driving them out of business. Reductions of one-tenth were fairly frequent and certainly caused some managers to make improvements. Article 52 was, in Lingen's words, 'one of the keystones on which the Code rests'.[14] But even so, the Department's power was very limited.† Managers could withdraw from the system if they chose; moreover, if they were prepared to forego part of the grant, they could take the rest and ignore criticism with impunity. The Department was a significant factor in educational development but, lacking the power to close schools and lacking both the resources and the desire to take major responsibility for their maintenance, it could not be decisive.

Notes

1. See above, p. 19.
2. In 1863 only Lancs., Herts. and Surrey had grant-aided schools in over 50 per cent of parishes with over 200 inhabitants; in Cambs., Lincs., Norfolk, Northants. and Suffolk the figure was 25 per cent or under (see PP. 1864 XLV, p. lxx).
3. The term was in common use long before it was officially constituted (see Ball, op. cit., p. 197) and will therefore be used of the period before, as well as after, 1856.
4. The followers of Archdeacon Denison and Baines respectively.
5. E.g., the permitted ratio of pupil teachers to scholars was cut from 1:25 to 1:40 (PRO, Edn 11/31, 4/10/1849 et seq.).
6. PRO, Edn 9/12, p. 278.
7. PRO, Edn 9/12, p. 312; PRO, 30/29, Box 23, part 1, 19/4/1854.

* 3J. † 3K.

8. *Oxford Essays* (1856), p. 270; PP. 1865 VI, qq. 8246–7.
9. PP. 1862 XLII, p. 22.
10. Christ Church Boys Log Book, 7/12/1864, 9/12/64, 24/1/65 (Ches. CRO); Faversham Boys Log Book, Report, 1865 (Kent Archives); for Betton's Charity see 3A.
11. The evidence in school records does not altogether confirm this view – cf. 6, note 10.
12. PP. 1866 XXVII 117, p. 245.
13. Log Book, 7/5/1863, 26/6/64, etc.
14. PRO, Edn 9/4, p. 223.

Documents

3A. INCOME AND EXPENDITURE IN A STATE-AIDED SCHOOL

Schools aided by government grant could not normally hope to receive more than about one-third of their income from public funds. These accounts, from a village school in Cheshire in the last year of the old Code, show less than 25 per cent from this source; but that was because an energetic clergyman tapped all possible sources in order (almost) to balance his books.

The tea party was the Victorian equivalent of a coffee morning. Betton's Charity, administered by the Ironmongers' Company, distributed about £5000 a year in grants to impecunious schools (PP. 1865 VI, qq. 2617–24).

Accounts of Haslington Church of England School

DR	£	s	d	CR	£	s	d
Subscriptions (local)	14	11	0	Master	83	0	0
,, (Friends at a distance)	14	7	0	Infant mistress	43	0	0
School pence	45	0	4	Sewing ,,	10	0	0
Tea party (farmers' wives)	13	15	0	Fuel, books etc.	30	6	11
Collections	13	0	0				
Betton's Charity	5	0	0				
C. of E. Education Society	10	0	0				
Diocesan Board	10	0	0				
Capitation Grant	8	17	0				
Augmentation Grants	31	0	0				
Deficit		16	7				
	166	6	11		166	6	11

(PP. 1863 XLVII, p. 60)

3B. EXCLUSION FROM STATE AID

Whilst it was natural for officials to argue that only inefficiency or obstinacy prevented managers from bringing their schools within the government system, a variety of factors in practice hindered its spread. Two such factors are illustrated below.

(i) *Poverty*

The Factory Inspectors were empowered to distribute the money collected in fines for infringement of the Factory Acts to assist education in factory districts. In this passage Leonard Horner justified a grant of £25 to the school at Lumb in Rossendale:

The last-named school . . . is one of those numerous cases in which the rule of the Committee of Privy Council on Education, that they give no money except in aid of subscriptions raised on the spot, operates with great severity . . . I cannot give so good a description of the condition of this district as that contained in the following letter which I received from Mr Kinder:-

Lumb, Rossendale, Rochdale,
July 14, 1849

SIR

WHEN you were lately in this neighbourhood, you kindly seemed somewhat interested in the new parish of Lumb, as to its means and facilities for promoting education.

Permit me then to take the liberty of further troubling you with an outline of our position.

When appointed to the district about three years ago, I found that there was a great deficiency in school accommodation, as well as a want of a good schoolmaster, there being, in fact, at that time, no public school in the district.

My first object, therefore, was to procure as large a room as possible in a central situation, which was opened as a daily and Sunday school; and although we had at first some opposition to encounter, our numbers have kept increasing, and at the present time the average attendance in the day school is about 100.

Having nothing to offer as salary but the pence of the children, it was some time before I could meet with a competent person to undertake the duties of the school at so small a remuneration, and

I have occasionally been obliged to teach in it myself without any assistance in order to prevent its failing altogether.

Now, however, and for the last twelve months, we have had a master and mistress, whose services I hope to retain.

Our only resource for the support of the schools is an annual collection, which has hitherto averaged about £16, and is entirely expended in rent, books, cleaning, and repairs, without providing us so amply as could be wished with the necessary apparatus for instruction. . .

My hope was to build a school and master's house; but of this there is now no probability for some years to come, as the church which has recently been erected is about £500 in debt, and the parish so poor that in the whole resident population (amounting to about 2000) there were but three individuals who subscribed upwards of twenty shillings towards its erection.

Such is our position, and having no one here to second my endeavours, I trust to a kind Providence to raise up friends among strangers.

Praying your Christian sympathy, and, if possible, your aid in promoting the cause of education in a district which is at present so inadequately provided for,

I remain, etc.,

RALPH KINDER, *Incumbent of Lumb*

Leonard Horner, Esq.

Scanty and imperfect as the education given in such circumstances must be, had it not been for the exertions of this good man these poor children would have been left in the same state of neglect, as far as school-education is concerned, that all previous generations in Lumb had been. . . There are many places in my district as badly off as Lumb is, where, as the children are employed in factories, it is obligatory on them to attend day-schools; and I, therefore, feel myself specially called upon urgently to plead for them, and to entreat that you [the Home Secretary], as a member of the Committee of Council on Education, will use your influence to get this rule relaxed, and apply a large portion of the annual grant in such neglected spots.

(PP. 1850 XXIII 181, pp. 18–19)

(ii) *Remoteness*

Augustus Smith, the Proprietor of Scilly, enforced school attendance and insisted that HM Inspector visit all the schools in his domain; but, as there were certificated teachers only on the main island, St Mary's, the other schools received no government grant. In an unusually open attack upon Department policy the Inspector concerned, the Anglican E.P. Arnold (Matthew Arnold's brother), described in his report for 1869 the uncertificated teacher of St Martin's and urged a change which the Department was forced to adopt in 1871 (see above, p. 22).

. . .an excellent and industrious man, and the school . . . not only educates all the children on the island, but educates them at least as well as any of the schools under certificated teachers on the other islands. When I visit this little school to which I have seen the children late on a summer's afternoon bounding down like wild deer through the long fern all eager for their examination, and then a few minutes later answering questions from the Bible with thoughtfulness and intelligence, and doing arithmetic and dictation with neatness and accuracy, I cannot but think that there is some flaw in a system which sends me as a Government Inspector into that school and yet refuses to make a grant to it. . . What . . . must the master of St. Martin's school in the Scilly Islands do before he can gain a certificate? He must first take a voyage of four or five hours (over a very stormy sea) in the depth of winter to Penzance, he must then travel 133 miles to Exeter, which will occupy if he travels third class about seven hours, and oblige him to sleep on the road either at Penzance or Plymouth. As the examinations begin on a Monday he must leave home on the previous Friday, and as they last five days he will not be able to reach home again till Saturday evening, having thus been compelled to travel 346 miles and to be absent nine days from home. To a poor man with a family, it is mockery under such circumstances to talk about his going up to sit for a certificate. Of course the Scilly Islands are an exceptional case, but the distance from the west of Cornwall, and from many places on the north coast to Exeter is at least 100 miles; long distances have often to be travelled by cross roads before the railway is reached; and for a large part of my district I may say that practically schoolmasters are debarred from attaining certificates even if they wish to do so. I can only repeat the suggestions which I made in my last report.

1. That the inspector should have the power to recommend for a certificate without examination teachers above a certain age, and who had served for a certain number of years, if in his judgment they appeared to deserve it.
2. That there should be several local centres in each district at which teachers could offer themselves for examination. My own district on the mainland is more than 120 miles in length, yet there is *not one place in it* where a master can be examined for a certificate. In a county like Cornwall there ought to be several centres at which teachers might be examined by the inspector of the district with the help, if they would consent to give it, of the Local Board of Education, and the examinations ought at the longest not to occupy more than two days.

(PP. 1870 XXII, pp. 36–8)

3C. ATTITUDES TO HM INSPECTORATE

Whatever its limitations, the system established by Kay-Shuttleworth during the 1840s gave, ultimately, thousands of schools an opportunity for unprecedented development. The speed with which the inspectorate won acceptance is reflected in the following quotation from the Bishop of Winchester's Charge of 1850. In an attempt to persuade all his clergy to apply for grants, Bishop C.R. Sumner publicised the favourable opinions of those who had already done so.

I submitted the following queries to all the clergy (of the diocese of Winchester) whose schools are on the list of inspection in the last Report, about 70 in number.
1. Have you experienced any inconvenience from the government inspection of your school, and, if any, what? Answered in the negative by 66. Four stated objections, but none, except in a single instance, which bear upon the system.
2. Have you experienced any advantage, exclusive of the grants to pupil-teachers, and the certificates of merit to masters and mistresses? – Answered in the affirmative by 55. "Stimulus;" "suggestions," "shows where there is deficiency," "increased interest in the parish," "example of pupil-teachers has a happy influence," "discipline improved," "increased exertions of masters and children," and the like. One writes, "no interference with religious teaching, except for good." Another, "they," the Inspectors,

"have appeared to me anxious to do their duty in a fair and considerate spirit; and as regards religious instruction, while studiously seeking to give the clergyman the chief place in this part of the examination, they have not failed to let it be seen by the children how much importance is attached to it."

(PP. 1851 XLIV 401, p. 378)

3D. THE CERTIFICATE OF MERIT

For teachers the introduction of the Certificate in 1846 seemed to point the way to new prosperity and new status. The atmosphere of devoted optimism thus generated is obvious in HMI Frederick Watkins's account of the first Certificate examination held by him in April 1848, in Wakefield. He began the day with prayers:

For this purpose the masters, with very few exceptions, cheerfully attended at a quarter before eight in the morning and remained for a quarter of an hour after eight in the evening, when the eight hours of the day's work were at an end. All seemed to join heartily in the prayers of the church, and chanted with great spirit the "Venite" or "Te Deum" in the morning, and the "Magnificat" or "Nunc Dimittis" in the evening. This devotional exercise was not, I believe, without its effects on the hearts of those who were assembled for so important a purpose. The work of each day then proceeded with the greatest regularity and order. All the candidates were strictly punctual in attendance, and scrupulously attentive to the directions given to them.

I had very rarely occasion to enforce the rule of absolute silence, nor had I, except in one doubtful case, in the whole number of 85 masters, any reason to suspect an attempt at copying a neighbour's paper, or a desire to obtain illicit information. Their courteous conduct to each other, and kind sympathy with each other, were very pleasing. Of the latter I may mention an instance. One of the schoolmasters lost his purse, containing about 30s., of which sum £1 was intended to convey him to his home, in the county of Durham. It was requested by some of the number that I would mention the loss to his fellow teachers. In a few minutes, the amount was contributed by them, with a surplus of 10s.6d.: which latter sum was, after a moment's thought, devoted by them towards the funds of St. Andrew's schools, in Wakefield, for which a sermon was to be preached on the following Sunday.

No captious complaints of the difficulties of the examination were made, though in several instances the papers were returned to me without answers. I did not mark anything like impatience or envy at another's greater success. In several instances, the candidates declared their intention, if unsuccessful on this occasion, to persevere till their efforts were successful. One or two of them announced, that they would not cease till they had obtained your Lordships' highest certificate of merit.

I cannot at present give any opinion as to the probability of their success or failure on this occasion, but I can gladly testify to the excellence of their conduct and their right feelings, their brotherly spirit towards each other, and their ready obedience to myself.

(PP. 1847–8 L, p. 143)

3E. THE PUPIL-TEACHER SYSTEM BEFORE 1862

The Minutes of 1846 had prescribed the stipends of pupil-teachers; but increased economic prosperity in the 1850s made them steadily less attractive. The partial collapse of the system in the early 1860s, which had little to do with the Revised Code, was forecast by most members of the inspectorate in the later 1850s. The following letter was sent to D.J. Stewart, HMI for the eastern counties (not one of the worst affected areas), by the manager of 'one of the most useful schools this district can produce'.

I have been led to think the stipend offered to pupil-teachers too small, from having observed that of the children who have left our school, those who have gone to day labour, or into service, are far better off, in a money point of view, than those who have become pupil-teachers.

From instances that have come to my knowledge, I believe, that in consequence of the smallness of the pay of the pupil-teachers, especially during the early years of their apprenticeship, we lose every year many promising boys and girls who would otherwise become pupil-teachers. I can speak of some cases, in which *I know this to be so*. Parents have said, "We cannot afford to advance any money, nor can we meet those expenses which the stipend will not defray".

In all cases of pupil-teachers with whom I have had anything to do, the same difficulty has existed, of finding money to support them during the first years of their apprenticeship. The parents, generally, cannot advance the money. School managers frequently find it inconvenient to do so.

I think the stipend too small, from the fact that £10 for the first year, or 3s. 10d. per week, and £12. 10s. for the second year, or 4s.9½d. per week, is a sum inadequate to the maintenance of a pupil-teacher, which must include lodging, board, clothes, washing, and books.

Pupil-teachers are not apprenticed till the age of thirteen or fourteen, and probably the parents have made some sacrifice to keep their children at school so long. At day labour or in service, children earn more at the age of thirteen or fourteen than 3s. 10d. or 4s.9½d. per week, and less is required of them both in attainments and qualifications.

I subjoin a few facts; first, about pupil-teachers whose circumstances I know; secondly, about scholars who have left our school. The latter instances are taken quite at random, for of many children I have lost sight, and many are well provided for, though I cannot state exact particulars.

1st. – PUPIL-TEACHERS. Ages from 13 to 18.

A.L. About £7 given to him by a friend.	His stipend advanced by school manager.
W.P. £2 paid by a poor mother, £5 lent to him by school manager.	His stipend advanced by school manager.
S.J. Hard struggle to live on her stipend with a little help.	Her stipend advanced by school managers.
E.K. £7. 10s. given by her father, a labourer.	Her stipend advanced by school managers.
W.V. From £10 to £15 lent to him by a widow mother, being savings on wages, and withdrawn from a savings' bank.	The master boards the boy, and waits a year, therefore, for the money.
C.R. Hard struggle to live on his stipend, with a little help from parents.	Tradespeople with whom he boards give him credit for a year.
S.W. £6. 10s. lent to her by the rector.	Rector advances her stipend.
M.A.F. £7. 10s. laid by in weekly deposits by her parents. Farm bailiff.	School managers advance the stipend.

Of the above, four of these pupil-teachers were educated at our school.

2nd – SCHOLARS who have left —— SCHOOL for labour or service.

J.H. aged 13, Page in a large house, clothes, lodging, food, etc., and £5 wages.
M.L. ,, 15, Under housemaid, food, lodging, etc., and £4 wages.
S.B. ,, 15, 9s. per week. Letter carrier.
G.B. ,, 12, Day labour, 4s. per week.
B.F. ,, 15, Day labour, 11s. per week.
B.S. ,, 16, Stable lad, 8s. per week.
J.K. ,, 14, Page, well provided for.
S.S. ,, 16, Nursery maid, everything provided, and £5 or £6 wages.
T.M. ,, 8, Labourer, 4s. per week.
W.F. ,, 11, Labourer, 6s. per week.
D.M. ,, 9, Labourer, 3s. per week.
G.S. ,, 12, Labourer, 4s. per week.
M.A.M. ,, 13, Teacher in a Girls' National School (well qualified to pass as pupil-teacher, but is too poor), has lodging, good food, washing, tuition, and books, and 1s. per week is to be added the second year.

The Council Office arrangements are very good, but, if apprentices could have £15 every year, or rather begin with £15 and go on to £20, we should not lose so many of the well-qualified young people who are now carried off into other callings, not so much because of the higher pay they then obtain, but, because they cannot *maintain themselves on their stipends*.

(PP. 1857 Sess. 2 XXXIII, pp. 432–4)

3F. THE PUPIL-TEACHER SYSTEM IN THE 1860s

Uniform payment of pupil-teachers disappeared with the old Code. Neither the Department nor, when it came to the point, many managers were prepared to pay increased stipends in the first years of apprenticeship; but all recognised the need for greater flexibility, as the managers of St. Chad's School, Shrewsbury, found when they asked the advice of their HMI, Mr Bonner (i) and the majority of managers recognised that it was unwise to make pupil-teachers wait twelve months before they were paid. F (ii), a summary of the methods of payment to the reduced number of pupil-teachers at the end of the 1860s, shows the greater flexibility achieved and, to some extent, reflects the class distinctions between British, Anglican and Catholic schools. The high proportion of Catholic girls paid annually is explained by the fact that many of them were boarded by the nuns to whom they were apprenticed.

(i) *Proposed for St Chad's Schools*

	Males			Females			Old Code
	per week	per year		per week	per year		
	s. d.	£. s. d.		s. d.			£. s. d.
1st year	1 6	3 18 0	(1)	1 0	2 12 0	(1)	10 0 0
2nd year	3 0	7 16 0	(2)	2 6	6 10 0	(2)	12 10 0
3rd year	4 6	11 14 0	(3)	4 0	10 18 0	(3)	15 0 0
4th year	6 0	15 12 0	(4)	5 6	14 6 0	(4)	17 10 0
5th year	7 6	19 10 0	(5)	7 0	18 4 0	(5)	20 0 0
		58 10 0					75 0 0

Mr Bonner recommends the following for *male* Pupil Teachers:-

	£. s. d.
1st year	4 0 0
2nd year	6 0 0
3rd year	15 0 0
4th year	17 10 0
5th year	20 0 0
	£62 10 0

But "it must always depend on the rate of wages given in the neighbourhood, and the advantages of any particular school, wherein to learn the business of a Teacher".

(undated, but evidently 1862–3: Records of St Chad's Church, Salop CRO, 1048/4579–83)

(ii) *Payments to Pupil-teachers, 1869*

	Church schools		British schools		Catholic schools	
Wages begin at	Male	Female	Male	Female	Male	Female
Under £5	9.7%	16%	11.2%	21.7%	4.5%	4.5%
£5–£10	79.9%	80.3%	80.8%	74%	86.4%	83.6%
Over £10	10.4%	3.7%	8%	4.3%	9.1%	11.9%
Wages rise to						
Under £10	4.1%	6.2%	2.4%	2.8%	2.7%	2.5%
£10–£15	13.5%	21.9%	9.7%	25.4%	8.2%	16.6%
£15–20	72.3%	69.7%	72.8%	67.1%	84.6%	79.8%
Over £20	10.1%	2.2%	15.1%	4.7%	4.5%	1%

	Church schools		British schools		Catholic schools	
Wages paid	Male	Female	Male	Female	Male	Female
Yearly	39.6%	35.6%	46%	43.8%	34.6%	49.3%
Half yearly	6%	5.7%	6.2%	6.1%	1.8%	0.7%
Quarterly	46.4%	52%	36.9%	41.8%	40%	40.1%
Monthly	4.6%	5%	7.8%	6.6%	19.1%	6.7%
Weekly	3.4%	1.7%	3.1%	1.7%	4.5%	3.2%

(PP. 1870 XXII, p. xxiv)

3G. A REACTION TO THE REVISED CODE

The complaints of witnesses to the Select Committtee on Education of 1865 and 1866 show that once the Revised Code was in operation its continued unpopularity resulted not only, or even mainly, from its major provisions, but from the Education Department's apparent determination to see that it produced the maximum possible savings in the grant. The reduction under Article 52d was one instance. It bore particularly hard, as the vicar of Kirkby Stephen pointed out (PP. 1866 VII 115, qq. 48–55), on a group of north-country schools which, at the time of enclosure, had been endowed with land in lieu of subscriptions, by agreement amongst small freeholders. One of these was Staveley School in Westmorland whose managers, refused grant under Article 52d, found themselves without funds to pay the pupil-teacher and wrote to Lingen as follows:

Staveley Parsonage
August 1st 1865.

Sir, I should have acknowledged the receipt of the report on our school much earlier had I been able to give a definite account of the Pupil Teacher, Robert Taylor. Finding that there is not a penny to pay his stipend, it was folly to continue his services. Government have completely broken faith; there is no reliance to be placed upon their word. We were induced to apprentice the lad with a guarantee that his stipend would be paid.

I am thankful to say I have obtained a situation for Robert Taylor, so that we may be preserved for the future, from such base and disgraceful treatment. We have not a penny to pay the salary in arrear. You can, therefore, remove the name of Robert Taylor from our list. Our case should be cited to show how badly the R.C. works. A population exclusively of the manufacturing class. Not a single wealthy resident. No support to the school but the bare endowment,* which is, of itself, insufficient to pay the master a good salary. Money is lavishly wasted in wealthy neighbourhoods, but where poverty is the general misfortune, there this unjust and iniquitous arrangement called the R.C. increases the pressure. Surely my lords might make grants to pay arrears when pupil teachers are engaged upon their offers of help and but now dismissed so that they can no longer prove a burden?

(Extracts from the Log Book of Staveley School . . . 1859–1902, CRO, Kendal, WDY/12)

3H. DISTRIBUTING THE GRANT UNDER THE REVISED CODE

Under the Old Code only the capitation grant was at the disposal of managers; all other public money was distributed by the Department. After 1862 managers had to determine for themselves how the grant was to be used. At Christ Church, Streatham Hill, a sub-committee was set up to consider the question and produced the following report which was accepted in December 1863.

Report of the Sub Committee appointed 1st July 1863 "to consider what pecuniary arrangements should be made with the Teachers in consequence of the Revised Code coming into operation."

The following Statement has been received from the Master & Mistresses of the Schools of the sum received from Government under the former system of payment and the probable amount that would be received under the provisions of the "New Code".

Amount of the last years grant under the Old Code	
Payment to Master Mistresses & Pupil Teachers	£105
Capitation Grant to School Funds	38
	£143

Estimated Grant under New Code £98.18.

This reduction is to be attributed partly to the altered mode of payment by the Government & in some measure to the falling off

*£60 p.a. (PP. 1867–8 XXVIII Part XVI, p. 411)

in the number of Scholars in the Upper School since the opening of the Schools on Tulse Hill in January last.

The average number in daily attendance being now only 93 while in 1861 it was 118 & in 1862 it was 132.

The Sub Committee therefore begs to recommend as a present arrangement that the whole amount of the Government Grant under the provisions of the "New Code" be applied as far as it goes

1st To the payment of the Pupil Teachers.

2nd To the payment of the usual Gratuities to the Master & Infant School Mistress for the Instruction of the Pupil Teachers.

3rd To the making up proportionably to the Master and Mistresses a sum not greater than the Augmentation Grant they would have received if the Old Code had remained in force.

4th The Balance if any after the above payments are made to be placed to the Credit of the School funds.

The Sub Committee further recommends

That in consequence of the diminished number of the Scholars in the Upper School, the number of the Pupil Teachers in that School be reduced to two and that as it appears Josiah Creagh has the opportunity of an engagement as a Pupil Teacher in the School of St. Peters Pimlico that his Indentures be cancelled on the payment of whatever portion of his Stipend may be due to him in addition to the sum of £6.5/- as provided by the Terms of the Indentures themselves.

[The grant for 1864, £94.14s.6d., was divided according to this arrangement: £47.10s. to four pupil-teachers (three at £12.10s., one at £10); £9 each to Mr Jones and Miss Lee for their instruction; £19.18s. augmentation grant to Mr and Mrs Jones and £9.6s.6d. to Miss Lee.]

(Minute Book, 1860–70, pp. 58–61, GLCRO, P95/CTCI/35)

3J. EXAMINATION UNDER THE REVISED CODE

Managers awaited the first examination under the Code with trepidation and it was carefully monitored by the voluntary organisations. The National Society published this description which scarcely suggests that the examination made unreasonable demands upon a school of ordinary efficiency though, as Matthew Arnold complained, the process must have been tedious for HM Inspector (Cf. J.E. Dunford, *H.M. Inspectorate of Schools, 1860–70* (1980), pp. 25–34).

The Inspection of a School under the Revised Code

The following was the plan which one of HM Inspectors adopted in examining the children in each standard in a school in Wiltshire. It should first be stated, however, that he very carefully examined all the classes assembled in two groups in religious knowledge, he commencing the examination and the mistress finishing it.

STANDARD I

1. *Reading*. The children came up to the Inspector one by one, and read from a page in the "First Book" (New Series). The Inspector held the book on his knee, and pointed to each word. Not more than two or three blunders over easy words were passed.

2. *Writing*. Four letters were dictated to them by the Inspector, – a capital and small one alternately, – to be written one underneath the other. Three out of the four letters had to be done right for the child to pass.

3. *Arithmetic*. An addition sum, a subtraction sum, a number between 10 and 20, were written down by the children on their slates, at the Inspector's dictation, and then worked out. The addition sum was 4+2+3, the children being made to put the numbers under one another; the subtraction sum, 7−5; and the number for notation, 17. A child doing two out of the three things given right was passed.

Results. Presented, 37; passed, 21, 35, and 35, in reading, writing, and arithmetic respectively.

STANDARD II

1. *Reading*. Standing in the desks, each child read from the "Second Book" (New Series), page 61, about a sentence a-piece. Hesitation or blunders in two or three common, easy words were marked as failures

2. *Writing*. The children had to transcribe from the "Second Reading-Book" (New Series) a passage of about twelve lines. Legible and fairly regular writing was passed.

3. *Arithmetic*. Two sums were dictated to them: (1) an addition sum, 406+18+390+7; (2) a subtraction sum, 342−89. In the multiplication-table they were told to write out 8 times. Two things right out of the three given passed a child.

Results. Presented, 17; passed 10, 17, and 3, in reading, writing, and arithmetic respectively.

STANDARD III

1. *Reading*. Each child read about a paragraph from "First Sequel to Second Reading-Book," p. 45.

2. *Writing*. Dictation on slates. A passage from the "Second Reading-Book," p. 12, was chosen by the Inspector. First read through, and then dictated by a teacher, a word at a time. Not more than three mistakes, and those not in very common words, were allowed to pass.

3. *Arithmetic*. Three sums were dictated by the Inspector, to be worked on slates. (1) An addition sum, 2416+305+7049+4003; (2) a subtraction sum, 3418−349; and (3) a division sum 4672÷9. Two out of the three were required to be done right.

Results. Presented, 17; passed 17, 16, and 12, in reading, writing, and arithmetic respectively.

STANDARD IV

(1) *Reading*. The children, standing in a semicircular class, read a paragraph each from the "Third Reading Book," p. 72.

(2) *Writing*. Dictation on paper. A passage of about nine lines was selected from the "Third Reading-Book," p. 25. First read through, and then dictated to them, a few words at a time. Not more than two or three mistakes in spelling, and those not in very common words, were allowed to pass.

(3) *Arithmetic*. The following sums were dictated to them:

(1)	£	s.	d.	(2)	£	s.	d.	(3)		£	s.	d.
	24,108	5	11		78,416	2	$5\frac{1}{2}$		8	81,763	14	$9\frac{3}{4}$
	1,919	12	$11\frac{1}{2}$				8					

These were first to be worked on slates, then copied on paper. As in the other standards, two out of the three were required to be done right to pass a child.

Results. Presented, 5; passes, 5, 3, and 4, in reading, writing, and arithmetic respectively.

Results for the whole School. Presented, 76; passed, 53, 71, and 54 in reading, writing, and arithmetic respectively; or very nearly four-fifths of the school.

(National Society, *Monthly Paper* (1864), pp. 16–17)

3K. THE REVISED CODE IN OPERATION, 1863–73

The following extracts from a log book show the fortunes of one school over the first ten years of the Code. It is included to illustrate both the depths which even an inspected school could plumb and the comparative impotence of the Education Department, for Clifton-on-Teme School was saved not by official action but by natural causes.

Frederick Noad had been appointed to the school in 1847 and was a registered teacher (see Appendix 2) who became entitled by the Revised Code to a 4th Class Certificate. His wife was the schoolmistress and his daughter the monitress. The inspector throughout was Rev. W. Hernaman; the chairman of the managers, Rev. Slade Baker, entered the reports in the log book and also occasionally used it to record his visits. Otherwise the entries were made by the master, whose punctuation is retained.

1864–4

30/11. [Inspection: report recorded 16/2]

The Religious knowledge is pretty good and the discipline fair, but the general state of the School is unsatisfactory. The reading is very monotonous. Proper attention has not been paid to notation in teaching Arithmetic to the second and third standards. The children in the first Standard are very backward in writing. More specimens of plain needlework should be exhibited on the day of Inspection.

Remarks by the Secretary of the P.C. [Privy Council]

My Lords are by no means satisfied with the report of HM Inspector.

Only one child in the first Standard has passed in writing, whilst not a single child of the twenty-six presented in the second and third standards passed in Arithmetic.

This unusual display of ignorance in the lower classes of the School indicates a thoroughly unsound state of instruction; and my Lords have ordered a reduction by one-tenth under Article 52,a, in the Revised Code.

The issue of Mr Noad's certificate (under Article 134 in the same Code) cannot be allowed till his school is more favourably reported on.

R.R.W.L.*

The Grant actually received amounted to £22.10.7.

17/2. The foregoing is the sweet comfort and consolation to a Schoolmaster, after a year,s [sic] devoted zeal, and decided hard work, with about 70 children, many of them, for intelligence, or even common sense, is but one remove above the brute creation, which could be proved on examination the first day of their entrance into the School, and ought to be done.

The whole of this so called Inspection for 62 children in 5 Standards for Reading, Writing, Arithmetic, Dictation, Catechism and Religious Knowledge, including all hindrances, was hurried over in one hour and a quarter, the Inspector entering the Room at 12.30 and leaving it at 1.45, any person knowing the children of this locality, can judge whether the Report is a fair one under the circumstances.

[In margin]

N.B. July 23 1865 I have only just discovered this entry. Slade Baker, Chairman of Committee of Management.

1865

12/6. [Inspection: report recorded 23/7]

The school has improved since my last visit, and is in a fair state of efficiency. The discipline is fair. The Religious Knowledge and Geography are fair; the reading is not sufficiently loud and distinct; the Dictation is pretty good; the Arithmetic is better than it was, but is still faulty in the fourth Standard, the notation especially; the supply of needle work is inadequate.

Remarks upon the Report

Looking to the improvement reported by HM Inspector My Lords have allowed the Grant without reduction, but they are not

* I.e., Lingen's personal endorsement.

disposed to issue Mr. Noad's certificate, until the Arithmetic of the older children has been raised to a satisfactory standard.

26/7. With respect to the paltry Certificate, it being of no money value whatever, it is a matter of perfect indifference to me if "My Lords" never send it, but in justice to myself I must here state, that if a Committee were called together unawares to me, before the vacation takes place, I could prove to them notwithstanding what the Inspector thinks proper to state, that many of the 1st Class can work sums in the Rule of Three Vulgar Fractions, including the Square Root, correctly, and without my being near them, which I should suppose far enough for plough boys.

I must here state however in fairness to the Inspector, that both the people and the children are so highly nervous, when a stranger questions them, that what they can do ordinarily, they appear to be quite bewildered at when wanted,

11/8. Examined the various classes of the School in most of the different branches of their education, and was satisfied with their progress.

Slade Baker.

1866

11/6. [Inspection: report recorded 15/7]

The improvement in the state of this school which I noticed last year, has not been maintained. There is a great falling off in Arithmetic, in which only twenty per cent of the children passed. The Religious Knowledge is deficient in thoroughness and accuracy; and the Reading is indistinct and without expression. The discipline is fair on the whole; but there were too many cases of copying to justify me in speaking favourably of the general moral tone.

Remarks by the Secretary of P.C.

My Lords regret to learn that notwithstanding the caution given to the Master last year, the children have passed such a bad examination in Arithmetic. A deduction of two-tenths has been made from their Lordships grant on account of imperfect instruction: and the issue of the certificate to the Master has been again deferred. . .

As the total grant would have amounted to £22.15s.8d, and, as the deduction (2/10) will amount to £4.11s.2d. – the sum to be received will be £18.4s.6d.

1867

24/6. [Inspection: report recorded 26/7]

I regret that I cannot report any marked improvement in the state of this school during the past year. The discipline is fair on the whole, but cases of copying are still frequent. The Religious Knowledge in the upper classes is better than it was. The Reading, Writing, & Spelling are fair. The Arithmetic is hardly more satisfactory than it was a year ago. The needlework & geography are good.

Remarks of the Secretary of P.C.

My Lords have ordered the grant to be reduced by two tenths (Article 52a) on account of HM Inspector's report of the low state of the knowledge of Arithmetic, and of the prevalence of copying. The Master's certificate must be still withheld.

Amount of grant actually received £16.16.11.

29/7. Children never will do the sums correctly, while the Inspector adopts the method of giving out three different sums at once, for the simple reason, that one sum confuses another, to prove this, let a stranger try this in one,s own family, he will find the results the same.

1868

22/6. [Inspection: report recorded 22/7]

The condition of the School is only moderate, much the same as it was at my last visit; the Discipline is fair on the whole. The Attainments in the several subjects of Instruction are as follows:- Religious Knowledge, pretty fair; Reading drawling and without expression; spelling imperfect; writing good; needlework fair; Arithmetic bad.

Remarks of the Secretary of P.C.

My Lords regret that in view of the very unsatisfactory report that the school has again received, they are under the necessity of reducing the grant by three-tenths. The Master's certificate cannot be issued until his School receives a satisfactory report. . .

Amount of Grant 12.8.3

23/6. [July is meant] There are 8 absent to day, if this continues, there must be some alteration made, as the master cannot afford to be the loser, for their non-attendance, he being the loser of a shilling a week for the next year, through this cause, (in this way,) whatever the grant is less than £15 is to be deducted from his salary, but when it is more than £15 he is not to have the overplus rather one sided I call this.

29/7. There are 14 absent today some are leaving, others are gone to a picnic, two are ill, it is a thing impossible for any Schoolmaster to get them up to the requirements of the Inspector while such a state of things are allowed to exist, for after having their own way so often, there is no aptitude for learning lessons, such is my experience.

1869

31/5. [Inspection: report recorded 8/7]

The condition of the School continues to be only moderate. The children have no knowledge of notation, and the failures in arithmetic are consequently almost universal. The Spelling is unequal, good in the third and sixth, imperfect in the fourth and fifth standards. The Religious Knowledge and writing are pretty good; the reading fluent, but sing-song; the needlework fair. . .

Remarks made by the Secretary of P.C. on Education

My Lords impose with regret the continued reductions which these unfavourable reports necessitate.

The gross total of claim was £17.4s.4d. . . . and the deduction being 3/10 i.e. 5.3.4. – the net sum payable is 12.1.0.

1870

1/6. [Inspection: report recorded 12/7]

The condition of the School is rather better than it was at my last visit. The Religious Knowledge is pretty good, and the Reading, writing, spelling, Geography, and needlework are fair. There are fewer failures in Arithmetic, but the notation is still very defective in the second and third standards, and must have much more attention.

Remarks upon the Report

It is not without hesitation that my Lords have refrained from making a reduction under Article 52(a) on account of the defective instruction in the Arithmetic. A more favourable report upon this subject will be looked for as the condition of an unreduced grant next year. The issue of Mr Noad's certificate must be deferred.

Amount of Grant to be received 28.8.0.

1871

14/6. The time taken up by the Inspection was from 11.30 to 1.30, but unfortunately, for the School in general all the Standards were risen, consequently the children had to do the work of two stages higher instead of one. . .

[Report recorded 1/8]

This school has been so very unsuccessful under the present master and continues to be in such an inefficient state, that I cannot but recommend the Managers to part with him, and to appoint a more competent person in his place. . .

Remarks upon the Report

My Lords regret to have received so unfavourable a report of this school; two tenths have been deducted for faults of instruction in arithmetic and spelling.

The issue of Mr Noad's certificate must be deferred for the present.

The Balance of grant payable after deduction is £21.4s.0d.

23/10. A private meeting of the Committee held this day at the Vicarage, to consider the late recommendation of the Inspector with respect to parting with the present Master. Decision arrived at, the Master to go on as usual, and do his best.

1872

27/5. The master too ill to appear in the School at all to day.

28/5. . . . the Master still too ill to attend, but the Rev[d] S. Baker has kindly taken a Class each day, the Monitress doing the rest of the work.

24/6. In consequence of the death of the late Master the school will be carried on by the Mistress, and Monitress, for 3 months. . .

2/7. [Inspection: report recorded 2/8]

The school is in a rather better condition than it was at my last visit. The children read creditably, and write and sew fairly but they do not spell well, and are, as heretofore, very deficient in arithmetic.

Remarks of Educ^n Department

My Lords will expect to find great improvement in this subject next year as the condition of an unreduced grant.

Amount of Grant £23.8s.0d.

[Charles Millage, 2nd Class Certificate, appointed from Michaelmas.]

4/10. By examination I find that the Reading throughout the School is monotonical – the Writing in the II & III classes is only moderate – Dictation with many misspellings, and the Arithmetic is very deficient.

11/10. I find that the boys and girls in the Second Class cannot set down hundreds correctly.

1873

23/4. . . .After the School had undergone a most searching examination – Her Majesty's Inspector was pleased to find that the scholars had made considerable progress since my appointment. He was gratified to find the improvement generally of the School. I assured him that I hoped to give him greater satisfaction upon his next visit and he expressed confidence that I should.

(Log Book, Worcs. CRO, 250.6 BA4434)

CHAPTER FOUR

SCHOOL ADMINISTRATION

EXCEPT in very small communities managers were normally responsible for two or three schools. If they were Wesleyans or Evangelicals there might be an infant and a juvenile school, both mixed. Otherwise there were two single-sex schools and perhaps a separate mixed-infant school. The infants, if they had no school of their own, were almost invariably housed with the girls.

Scottish influence produced the mixed Wesleyan and Evangelical schools; the English tradition favoured segregation. Moral arguments were reinforced by practical considerations. It was axiomatic that boys' and girls' education should be different, since they were being prepared for different roles. In particular, adequate provision for sewing was difficult in a mixed school without the employment of an extra teacher. The Education Department strengthened the case for segregation in annual-grant schools by its refusal, on moral grounds, to accept the apprenticeship of a girl to a master. As for the separate infant school, there is little evidence of influence from Owenites or the followers of Wilderspin. Although a minority of managers justified special provision for infants as 'sheltering them from the baneful influence of bad habits, and guarding the opening faculties from receiving a wrong bias', the majority shared the views of the British committee in Derby who, when forced by lack of funds to consider closing one of their schools, decided that the infant school was the least important and the most easily restored.[1]

The primary motive for founding an infant school was often to remove from schoolrooms in which older pupils were taught the disturbing influence of children as young as eighteen months or two years. There was never any difficulty in filling infant schools; they provided safe keeping for children too old to be immobile and too young to be of use. Managers who, out of consideration for their teachers, attempted to exclude the under-threes, could soon be brought to heel by parental threats to keep their elder children away to 'nurse' – one of the commonest causes of absence. Hence, whatever the underlying theory, an infant school served several useful purposes and, at a time when working life began for many before they were nine years old, it was difficult to refute the argument that education should begin as soon as possible.

Early monitorial schools, like the charity schools, were, in nineteenth-century terminology, 'eleemosinary'. Committees charged no fees; they often provided clothes for their pupils; and they expected to exercise considerable control over the appearance and conduct of both the objects of their charity and their parents, frequently summoning the backsliders to be reproved. But from the late 1820s onwards they were increasingly driven by lack of funds to abandon charity and introduce fees. New foundations of the 1840s were generally fee-paying from the start. The charges varied. Wesleyan and Congregationalist fees were on average the highest, Catholic, predictably, the lowest. The Anglicans, again predictably, occupied the middle ground. 'A National school', said William Rogers, 'is a twopenny school.'[2] Good educational and moral arguments for fees were easily found. They improved attendance, it was held, inspired confidence and removed the stigma of 'charity'; parents and children valued education the more if it cost them an effort. The Education Department encouraged the trend; the capitation grant could not be claimed on children admitted free. Fees rose steadily;* they were a much more important source of funds than the government grant. In Lancashire and Yorkshire they formed over half the total income of Anglican schools.[3] More surprising, in view of rural wage levels, is their importance in country schools – over £45 at Haslington,[4] for instance, compared with under £40 from government and £55 in subscriptions and collections.

Graded fees were common. The old practice of varying the fee according to the number of subjects learnt was frowned on as uneducational, but increased charges in the higher classes were frequent.[5] Fees graduated according to parental income or status, as advocated by Dawes (and imposed in a simple form by Lord Hatherton at Penkridge) were surprisingly successful, provided that the school was good. The attitude of managers who followed this practice was explained by Samuel Best to the Taunton Commission: 'We think the education is worth a shilling a week, and

* 4A.

if we choose to give it to the poorer classes at a much cheaper rate, we have a right to do so.'[6]

The transformation of virtual charity schools into schools which drew a significant proportion of their income from parents had important effects on curriculum and on the social classes represented in the schools. In the country the success of a school designed, like King's Somborne, to serve the whole village community depended on the willingness of farmers to allow their children to associate with those of labourers, and this varied not only from district to district but from village to village. The Cheshire imitation of King's Somborne at Acton succeeded. A similar attempt eight miles away at Audlem was defeated by resistance from the farmers.[7] In towns the natural tendency of managers and teachers to prefer respectable children who washed, attended and brought their pence was strengthened by the determination of their parents that they should not be contaminated by the dirt, disease and depravity of the slums.* Many town schools avoided all contact with the really poor; Patrick Cumin noted with disapproval a British schoolmaster's remark that 'one great advantage of the ragged school is that it relieves him of the dirty boys'.[8]

On the other hand, zeal for evangelisation through education led some slum parsons to create school complexes of surprising sophistication. Gregory's schools in Lambeth were one instance, but the best known were in the disreputable district of St Thomas, Charterhouse.† The incumbent, William Rogers, believing that 'this stronghold of Satan and hell must not be attacked with a pop-gun'[9] established day and evening schools of such excellence that they were immediately invaded by prosperous families living outside the district who drove out the costers for whom they were intended. Rogers, a pragmatist, then used the profits from these schools to maintain another, as well staffed and equipped, for his own parishioners, which was subsequently publicised as living proof that the 'ragged' class of child need not be fobbed off with inferior provision in ragged schools.[10] But despite such exceptions as St Thomas, Charterhouse, the general failure of voluntary schools to serve the disreputable as well as the respectable was perhaps their most serious weakness.

Managers were forced to recognise, often reluctantly, that their

* 4B. † 4C.

attitude to parents had to be modified. Policemen, skilled artisans, railwaymen, farm bailiffs and the like could not easily be bullied and resented any suggestion of a charity-school approach. Consequently many of the restrictions designed to emphasise the subordination of the poor were gradually abandoned, often in the face of opposition from subscribers who failed to realise the extent of the school's dependence upon fee-paying parents.* Except in Congregationalist schools parents were not allowed a share in school management, but there is evidence that some of them were prepared to make active contributions to the welfare of a good school. The workmen who formed a committee and raised £280 for the building fund of St Paul's School, Hull, by working overtime, are an example, whilst in 1856 the ratepayers of King's Somborne decided to levy a sixpenny rate to pay for extensions to the school and an annual rate of 2d. in the pound towards its maintenance.[11]†

Dependence upon fees led to a more systematic recording of attendance than had hitherto been customary; and, simultaneously, the State began to take an interest in registration. Where the Factory Acts operated, the half-timers' 'Mill Books' had to be completed, whilst the introduction of the capitation grant caused the Education Department to begin an energetic drive to improve standards of accuracy.‡ It was an uphill task. The lady manager who told HM Inspector that she knew the registers were inaccurate but as 'the errors were as often *against* as in *favour of* the school, she had not thought the matter of any consequence . . .'[12] was not alone in her levity. But the Department persevered; the characteristic elementary school preoccupation with registers dates from this period.

More accurate registration revealed the full extent of the attendance problem.§ There was general agreement amongst managers and teachers that frequent absence and almost-as-frequent changes of school were the greatest obstacles to educational progress. The short stay of pupils in school, cited by so many commentators, did not normally imply as short an education. It resulted from migrations, often as much for the sake of variety as for any other reason. For instance the Church of England School at Wordsley, with an average attendance of about 125 and,

* 4D. † 4E. ‡ 4F.

§ 4G.

according to HM Inspector, 'considerable mental life and activity', lost fifty-three pupils to a new private school between 16 October 1865 and 19 January 1866, when the weekly average dropped below seventy. Forty-four boys returned between March 1866 and 13 February 1867 when, not surprisingly, the curate 'addressed the scholars . . . pointing out especially the evils of changing schools, illustrated by the most evident retrogression of those who have lately been re-admitted only three of whom are really fit for the classes they were formerly in . . .'[13]

Constant efforts were made to improve attendance. Enquiries or threats did little save cause annoyance. ('She is quite tired of sending him', complained one mother, 'because the Master makes so much bother when he is absent.'[14]) Prizes, treats and certificates for good attenders were common; in many schools part of the capitation grant was given to the children who had earned it. Some educationists argued that a more practical or more advanced curriculum was the answer to the problem. Others demanded the extension of half-time as a means of keeping pupils in school until the age of thirteen. Although the half-time system was much criticised for reducing education to a mere adjunct of employment, there was no doubt that some schools made it work;* the education of the fifty ex-half-timers serving their apprenticeships in seventeen schools circularised by Leonard Horner in 1857 had clearly been successful.[15] Factory legislation was extended beyond the textile industries in the 1860s; but since the late 1840s there had been experiments in voluntary half-time, which were encouraged by the Education Department to the extent that eighty-eight days' attendance under such a scheme qualified for the capitation grant.† At best, however, these were only palliatives; the attendance problem remained.

School buildings became increasingly uniform during this period.[16] The plans published in the Minutes of the Committee of Council were available for all to use; so the semi-ecclesiastical style favoured by government architects appeared in buildings of all denominations. Department regulations demanded that the school include a teacher's house. In practice, following the endowed-school tradition, it was normally provided and maintained as an effective supplement to the teacher's salary.

* 4H. † 4J.

A similar tendency towards uniformity affected internal organisation, so that by 1860 pupils could move between schools of various denominations without encountering any marked differences. In the early 1840s this had not been the case. The first inspectors of schools, sent out by Kay-Shuttleworth as anti-monitorial missionaries, found every variety of practice. The Wesleyans were committed followers of Stow who trained their teachers until the opening of Westminster College. Some Evangelicals were Pestalozzians. Although most National schools were still monitorial, the society itself regarded the system as, at best, a necessary evil. The British and Foreign Society was more reluctant to abandon it, but accepted the inevitable later in the decade. By the early 1850s, though monitors remained, the system, which interposed the monitor as instructor between the supervising teacher and the learner, was dead. There was increasing consensus about the new structure, encouraged by the uniformity of practice imposed by the Department upon teacher-training. Object lessons, remotely derived from Pestalozzi, became standard for young children. National and British schools adopted collective teaching but in units smaller than those favoured by Stow; whilst the Wesleyans gradually recognised that the vast and crowded galleries of the Glasgow system were too much for the lungs and discipline of the ordinary teacher.

The typical elementary school of the 1860s consisted of four, or multiples of four, classes. (The upper standards of the Revised Code were usually combined in the first class.) There was no class teaching in the later sense of the term, whereby each class was an entity for which one teacher was responsible. Since educational theory demanded provision for interaction between adult teacher and child, pupils were supposed to alternate between instruction in large groups with the master or mistress, in classes with pupil-teachers or senior monitors and in sub-divisions of classes supervised by ordinary monitors. This arrangement had been popularised originally by Henry Moseley, HMI, under the name of the 'tripartite system'.* Success depended upon relatively generous staffing and the possession of at least one classroom in addition to the schoolroom. In many schools all that could be attempted was to see that each child came under an adult once a day, that difficult subjects like arithmetic were not left to junior

* 4K.

monitors and that the classes were subdivided into small groups for reading. But even this degree of apparent flexibility could only be achieved with the aid of a rigid timetable which now became an accepted part of school organisation.*

Administratively as well as socially the period 1840–70 was one of rapid change in the schools. Still by official standards woefully unbusinesslike – in the later 1860s the Department conducted a brisk campaign to improve their accounting – they nevertheless achieved a complexity of structure previously unknown.

Notes

1. Bridport Industrial School papers: *Address to Bridport* (Dorset CRO, D43/C49); Minute Book, Derby British Schools, 7/10/1852 (Derby Library).
2. PP. 1867–8 XXVIII Part IV, q. 13693.
3. Lancs. 53 per cent, Yorks. 55 per cent: F. Watkins, *Letter . . . on the State of Education in the Church Schools in Yorkshire* (1860), p. 27.
4. See 3A.
5. See 4C.
6. PP. 1867–8 XXVIII Part III, q. 7221; for Hatherton, see IA.
7. See IH.; PP. 1867–8 XXVIII Part XIV, p. 18.
8. PP. 1861 VII 395, q. 3406.
9. W. Rogers, op. cit., p. 35.
10. PP. 1861 VII 395, qq. 3806, 3928.
11. PP. 1857 (Sess. 2) XXXIII, p. 471; 1861 XXI Part III, p. 224.
12. PP. 1867 XXII, p. 276.
13. Log Book, *passim* (Staffs. CRO, D227/4). For a fuller study of attendance see N. Ball, "Elementary School Attendance and Voluntary Effort before 1870", *History of Education*, vol. 2, no. 1 (1973), pp. 19–34.
14. Log Book, Bexley Heath National School, 28/9/1865 (Kent Archives, C/ES 23/2/1).
15. PP. 1857 (Sess. 2) XVI 201, pp. 19–25.
16. See A. C. O. Ellis, 'The Structure and Organization of Victorian Elementary Schools' in History of Education Society, *Victorian Education* (1976), pp. 2–13.

Documents

4A. FEEPAYING IN ELEMENTARY SCHOOLS

The annual 'Abstract of Returns of National Schools Aided by Charity School Funds' of Leeds Parish Church records the growth

* 4L.

of a group of urban schools over a long period of time. The extracts given below show that in no case had fees been lowered between 1850 and 1862 and that in some cases their increase had been very considerable. They are a sample of the abundant evidence that the rise in fees of the 1860s, often blamed exclusively on the Revised Code, was merely a continuation of a process already well established in the 1850s.

Fees and Attendance in Leeds: 1850, and 1862

School	Pence		Average Attendance	
	1850	*1862*	*1850*	*1862*
St. Peter	£70	£340.16s.	340	518
St. Peter's Sq.	£39	£52.15s.	100	115
St. James	£68	£88.4s.8d.	210	222
St. Thomas	£42.17s.9d.	£72.10s.2d.	144	150
St. Mark	£75	£101.17s.7d.	250	364
Christ Church	£94.11s.	£172.4s.11d.	220	414
St. Mary, Quarry Hill	£65	£118.15s.1d.	186	265
,, , Newton	£65.19s.	£102.11s.6d.	194	281
St. Paul	£55.14s.	£95.10s.4d.	140	207
St. George	£133.12s.4d.	£373.16s.11d.	279	479
St. Philip	£107.1s.10d.	£106.12s.11d.	234	219
St. Andrew	£94.5s.3d.	£153.8s.4d.	240	337
St. Luke	£40	£117.9s.5d.	130	210
All Saints	£54.16s.	£73.4s.3d.	130	215
St. Matthew	£35.6s.	£137.2s.3d.	115	236
Buslingthorpe	£80	£102.2s.	205	201

(Leeds City Archives, DB 196/19–55)

4B. SOCIAL DISTINCTIONS IN SCHOOL

The views of a Bristol police inspector expressed in evidence to the Newcastle Commission were characteristic of parents in the highest social class which made habitual use of elementary schools. They go far to explain the general failure of voluntary schools to provide for the lowest classes, since there could be no doubt as to whose children would be more likely to be a credit to the school.

In my opinion there is not classification enough in the national schools; children of respectable but poor parents are thrown in with children of disreputable people. This is felt by parents, and they do not like to send their children to such schools, where they get contaminated. In the — school there are a number of boys and girls go to that school. It is a very good school, but the children are not classified. One woman named D—, who is now convicted for receiving stolen goods, and whose husband now carries on a brothel in Deep Street, St. James', employing his daughter, a girl of twelve years of age, to manage the brothel, sent one or two of his children to — school; this has damaged the character of that school, and I would not send my children to it.

(PP. 1861 XXI Part III, p. 212)

4C. THE SCHOOLS OF ST THOMAS, CHARTERHOUSE

William Rogers, incumbent of St Thomas, Chaterhouse from 1845 to 1863, believed in education as a means of religious and social improvement and was a brilliant fund-raiser (during his incumbency he was able to claim £9343.14s.8d. in government building grants, over £6000 more than any other school promoter). His aim was first to create and then satisfy a demand for good education and his original schools in Goswell Street were so good that they quickly attracted parents of varied social classes from outside the district. Capitalising on these people's demand for more advanced education, he raised fees and established, in effect, a secondary department; then used the resultant profits to finance Golden Lane School for his own parishioners. Three documents follow: (i) Roger's account of Goswell Street and its prospectus for 1856–7 (the year in which Golden Lane School was opened); (ii) Roger's description to the Select Committee on the Education of Destitute Children (1861) of his district, his methods and Golden Lane School; (iii) a list of the occupations of parents in the St Thomas, Charterhouse Schools which reflects the wide social spectrum served by successful elementary schools.

(i) *Goswell Street*

The system pursued in these schools is this: Children are admitted to the infant school at three years of age, in which they remain till they are sufficiently advanced to be transferred to the juvenile school, which is an upper branch of the infant school. Here girls and boys are taught together till they have attained such proficiency as to warrant the managers in drafting them off to the girls' and boys' school, in which the usual national education is given; and when they are of sufficient age to profit by superior teaching, and if their parents are willing, they are admitted to the upper schools, where, in addition to the higher branches of arithmetic, mathematics, book-keeping, &c., instruction is given in Latin, and French, and drawing.

The rate of payments varies from 2d. to 6d. per week . . . In the upper schools . . . all who are transferred from the National Schools are admitted at 10s. per quarter . . . It will thus be seen that the rate of payment depends upon the proficiency of the scholar; and I do not very well see how any other system can be pursued in a community like this, where it is almost impossible to fix the condition of the parent, or to ascertain the rate of his wages; and in the end it comes to much the same thing, for it is only those who are better to do in the world who can dispense with their children's services, and who can afford to leave them a sufficient time in the school to reach the higher classes. At the same time, every encouragement is given to the inhabitants of the district, and any poor person's child, residing in the district, is admitted free, and may go through all the schools and classes without payment, providing the parents are willing to keep them at the school.

ST THOMAS CHARTERHOUSE DAY SCHOOLS

Under the superintendence of the Rev. W. ROGERS, Incumbent of St Thomas Charterhouse, and the inspection of H.M. Privy Council Board on Education.

Boys' School – UPPER SCHOOL. Head Master, Mr W. HAMMOND (Certificated Master). – A superior education is given in this School, including, together with religious instruction, the English, French and Latin languages, Arithmetic, Writing, Book-keeping, together with the elements of Mechanics and Natural Philosophy, affording great facilities to tradesmen and the middle classes, of obtaining a sound practical education for their children. Prospectuses to be had at the Committee Room. *Terms*: Senior Division, £1; Junior Division, 15s. per quarter. *Hours of Attendance*, from half-past 9 A.M. till 3 P.M., daily.

Boys' Second School – Head Master Mr J. SMITH (Certificated Master). – In this School elementary instruction is given, including, together with religious instruction, the usual branches of a national education, reading, writing, spelling, geography, grammar, history, and arithmetic. *Terms* First Class, 5s.6d. per Quarter; or 6d. per Week. Second and Third, 3s.8d. per Quarter; or 4d. per Week. All others, 2s.9d. per quarter; or 3d. per week. *Hours of Attendance* from 9 to 12 A.M., and from 2 to 4 P.M. daily. Exhibitions to the Upper School are given to the most proficient scholars at Christmas and Midsummer.

Girls' School – Head Mistress, Miss C. HOLDWAY (Certificated Mistress) – The instruction given in this School is the same as in the boys' Second School, with the addition of needlework, marking, and the elements of domestic economy. There is also an upper class where the higher branches are taught, together with French, and fancy needlework. *Terms*: Upper Class, 10s. per quarter or 1s. per week. *First Class* 5s.6d. per quarter or 6d. per week. Second and Third, 3s.8d. per quarter or 4d. per week. All others, 2s.9d. per quarter or 3d. per week. *Hours of attendance* 9 till 12 A.M. and from 2 till 4 P.M. daily.

Juvenile School. – This school is for young children, boys and girls, who are taught together till the age of 10, when they are drafted into the Boys' and Girls' School. *Terms*: 3s.8d. per quarter or 4d. per week.

Infant School – Mistress, Miss C. BUCKINGHAM. For Children from 2 to 6 years old. *Terms.* First, Second, and Third Classes, 2s.9d. per quarter or 3d. per week. All others, 1s.10d. per quarter, or 2d. per week. *Hours of attendance,* same as Girls' School daily. – *Saturday is a holiday in all the Schools.*

Instruction in drawing is given to the scholars by a master and mistress appointed by the Privy Council Board of Trade, on Tuesdays and Thursdays, from 3 to 5 o'clock, in the Drawing School. Charge 1d. per week, or 4d. per month, paid in advance. N.B. – Parents are particularly requested to take notice that every child is required to have a copy-book, slate and pencil, and spelling-book, and other class-books, in order that the children may prepare lessons at home. Children are expected to attend on Sunday, unless their parents wish them to attend elsewhere. There are Sunday Schools for young people who have left the Day Schools, conducted in separate rooms, by voluntary teachers. There is a *Clothing Club*, for the benefit of the scholars. Deposits received every Tuesday at 12 o'clock. Interest, 3d. in the shilling. *Provident Club Deposits* are received every Monday morning at the Committee Room, and repaid, with interest, on December 21st every year. – *Baptisms* are performed every Sunday at the Church, at half-past 3 o'clock, *free of expense*. – Attendance is given at the Committee Room every Monday Morning, from 9 to 10, to admit children, and to see parents who may wish to communicate with the Rev. W. ROGERS.

ST THOMAS CHARTERHOUSE EVENING CLASSES

Held in the school rooms, Goswell Street. A Separate room for Adults.

ADVANCED CLASSES FOR YOUNG MEN

Monday – Latin and Scripture, Rev. W. Rogers; French, Mons. F. Quesnel; Mathematics and Bookkeeping, Mr W. Hammond. *Tuesday* – Geography and Use of the Globes, Mr W. Greenstreet; Writing, Mr C. H. Palmer. *Wednesday* – Scripture, Rev. R. Holme; French, Mons. F. Quesnel; Penmanship, Mr C. H. Palmer. *Thursday* – English Grammar, Mr J. Brabham. *Friday* – Reading and English History, Mr J. Smith; French, Mons. F. Quesnel.

Terms 21s. yearly, or 12s. half-yearly, entitles the member to all the above classes (Latin 5s. per quarter and each additional French class 2s.6d. per quarter extra). 5s. per quarter entitles the member to attend one of the above classes (except French) and the elementary instruction; to each additional class, 1s. per quarter. Entrance fee, 1s.

The READING-ROOM is supplied with the daily and weekly newspapers, publications, and a good lending library for the use of members of the above classes only, and is open every evening at 7 o'clock. Terms of admission to the library for non-members – 1s. per quarter.

ELEMENTARY DIVISION FOR ADULTS. In this department instruction is given in writing, elementary arithmetic, English grammar, geography, reading and spelling, and dictation. *Terms*: 2s. per month, or 5s. per quarter. Entrance fee, 1s. Superintendent – Mr W. GREENSTREET.

BOYS' EVENING SCHOOL – The instruction comprises geography, English grammar, slate and mental arithmetic, composition, dictation, writing, reading, and spelling. Terms: First Class, 6d. per week, or 5/- per quarter; Second and Third

Classes, 4d. per week, or 3s.8d. per quarter. All others, 3d. per week, or 2s.6d. per quarter. Schoolmaster, Mr M. THOMPSON. The rooms are open from 8 to 10 every evening.

ADVANCED CLASSES FOR YOUNG WOMEN
A separate room for Adults

Monday – Scripture, Rev. R. Holme; French, Mons. F. Quesnel; Arithmetic, Mr W. Hammond; *Tuesday* – Geography, Miss M.A. Butler. *Wednesday* – English Grammar and History, Miss A. Williams; Writing, Mr C.H. Palmer. *Thursday*, Reading and Dictation, Miss A. Williams; Writing, Mr C.H. Palmer. *Friday*, – French, Mons. F. Quesnel.

Terms 21s. yearly, 12s. half-yearly, 8s. quarterly, or 3s. monthly, entitles the member to all the above classes, (except French), including one French class 10s.6d. quarterly, or 4s monthly; additional French class, 2s.6d. per quarter extra. A single class, 5s., each additional class, 1s. per quarter. A good lending library for the use of members of the above classes. Entrance fee, 1s.

GIRLS' EVENING SCHOOL. – Conducted by female teachers. Course of instruction the same as in the boys' school. Terms: First Class, 6d. per week, or 5s. per quarter, Second Class, 4d. per week, or 3s.8d. per quarter. Third Class, 3d. per week, or 2s.6d. per Quarter. On Monday, Wednesday, and Thursday, from 7 to 9 o'clock. Schoolmistress, Miss A. Williams.

Drawing and singing classes, for which see separate prospectuses. A set of chemical apparatus will shortly be purchased, when a class in chemistry will be formed. The whole of the above classes are under the superintendence of the Rev. WILLIAM ROGERS, M.A., Incumbent of St. Thomas Charterhouse, assisted by Teachers of experience, who are furnished with Certificates of Merit by the Committee of Council on Education. Further information can be obtained of Mr PHILLIPSON, at the Schools, every evening after seven o'clock. Examinations are held at Midsummer and Christmas, when Certificates of the first, second and third degrees, together with prizes, are awarded.

(W. Rogers, *The Educational Prospects of St. Thomas, Charterhouse* (new edition, 1856), pp. 15–16, Appendices I, II)

(ii) *Golden Lane*

. . .I am far from asserting that there are no other poor districts in London. I am sorry to say that there are; perhaps here or there an odd street or two might be found . . . poorer than our own; but I still maintain that there is a singularity in the utter unmixed poverty of this district; that, as a legally constituted district, there is none so utterly destitute in all its parts, none which is such a complete bundle of rags, without any particle whatever of the purple and fine linen which is to be found in other parts of this city. . . The population is 9,500. . .

We have in the Golden-Lane Schools, which are confined to the parish, 868 . . . in addition to these there are many of the children residing in the district who attend the higher schools . . . the lowest rate of payment is 1d. a week . . . any child who cannot pay is admitted free. . . At present we have about 100. . .

We have children without shoes, and if they had shirts they would protrude from their trousers; and in the school there is a most unmistakeable bouquet about them, showing the class from which they come; no child is refused on account of the state of its clothes. . . I should be sorry to call them ragged schools; I have striven hard against that because I disapprove of the term "ragged," and I am sure that the people disapprove of it too. . .

A child would be removed [from the register] after a month's continued absence, unless some excuse were made. If requested he would be re-admitted. We desire only to keep our books straight. . .

. . .[On attendance] I should say, fairly, regular. . . I do not see how anything is to be taught unless the children attend regularly. . .

. . .when we first thought of establishing the Golden-Lane Schools, I thought it would be necessary that the children should be admitted free . . . but through my visitors, I canvassed the district, and we found that the people were very anxious indeed about these schools, and took great interest in them. I asked which they preferred, and they unanimously preferred to pay the penny. . . I think that the first thing to be done is to get up something like public opinion in favour of schools, which I think we have done in our district, and when it becomes to be considered a disgrace not to go to school, the children generally are sent. . .

. . .we do a great deal in the way of assisting them with clothes; we lend them pinafores . . . which do not fetch very much at the pawnbrokers, and yet make the children look decent. We do not enquire what they wear under the pinafore . . . the parents are pleased at the clothes being lent, and seeing their children more decent, they are induced to provide better clothes. . . I have been two or three times into a ragged school, and I have found that they are exactly the same kind of children. . .

. . .My system is, to throw all the receipts and expenses into one balance-sheet, and those who pay larger fees, if there is a surplus, contribute towards the support of the Golden Lane Schools. The entire fees received in the last year, amounted to £1,294.13s.2d. . . .

. . .I think the schools are popular with the children; I think they like to come when they once get attached to the teachers; but that their first impulse is voluntarily to go to school I do not believe; they are sent by their parents in the first instance.

[On denominationalism] . . . we take anyone who comes into the school. Three Catholic priests came about a year ago, and went all through the schools, and they were perfectly satisfied, and said that they should not object to their children coming. . . [On teaching the catechism] . . . if there were any objection, we should make arrangements, but the parents of the children are not in a condition to object to the catechism. . . I do not know the difference between religious and secular. . . I am unable to separate the two; there is always a religious lesson given, and the teachers are all religious people, so far as I know. We are not teaching the catechism all day, if you mean that. . .

[On cleanliness] . . . it is much better to throw the *onus lavandi* upon the parent and not upon the schools . . . I think there are a great many good people that are very dirty; it would be difficult in our school to establish a washing department. . .

[On children admitted free] . . . no one knows whether they are paid for or not; it is an arrangement amongst ourselves. . .

We have one master and two mistresses . . . they are all certificated, and we have 12 pupil teachers altogether; six male and six female. . .

. . .we are easy with some of the children, and do not require very punctual attendance; if their parents say, for instance, that they want them to attend the market in the morning, we allow them to come later; but the parent comes and states this or any other excuse he may have for sending the child late to school . . . ours is, if I may so call it, a "regular irregularity;" we do not allow a child to come in at any time he likes, unless he has some reasonable excuse for his lateness, or unless his parent states that he is occupied and cannot send the child until a certain time in the morning. . .

. . .I have large meetings with [the parents] three times a week . . . the regular weekly meetings are for religious services, and for short addresses to them on religious subjects; and then we have other meetings in the winter; lectures, illustrated with the magic lantern; and entertainments of that sort . . . and the people seeing that the children who go to this school are much improved, and are in a better condition than others, take an interest in the school, and encourage each other to send their children.

(PP. 1861 VII 395, pp. 47–54)

(iii) Returns of the trade, calling or employment of the fathers of all the children in . . . Charterhouse, St. Thomas' School.

	Number of			Number of	
	Fathers	Children		Fathers	Children
Accountant	1	1	Cabman	14	18
Actor	1	3	Cabinetmaker	45	63
Apothecary	2	2	Carman	18	25
Artificial flowermaker	2	3	Carpenter	95	137
Artist	2	4	Chimney-sweeper	6	8
Baker & confectioner	52	82	Cigarmaker	4	5
Basket-maker	6	11	Clerk	22	35
Blacksmith	19	31	Coachmaker	3	3
Blindmaker	8	11	Cook	7	14
Bookbinder	26	38	Cooper	9	13
Bookseller	2	3	Cork-cutter	6	8
Brazier & bellfounder	27	37	Costermonger	72	96
Bracemaker	4	5	Curate	1	2
Bricklayer & mason	37	58	Currier	10	11
Broker	7	8	Cutler	14	21
Brushmaker	5	5	Dairyman	5	6
Butcher	23	30	Dentist	2	4

	Number of Fathers	Number of Children
Distiller	3	5
Drover	4	7
Dyer	4	7
Engineer	7	10
Engraver	11	13
Fireman	8	9
Fishmonger	1	1
Furrier	2	3
Gardener	2	2
Gasfitter, &c	10	13
General dealer	24	37
Glass-blower	15	22
Greengrocer, &c.	18	24
Grocer	8	9
Hairdresser	15	22
Hatter	15	24
Hawker	15	17
Horsehair-worker	3	4
Inspector (G.P.O.)	1	1
Inspector (police)	1	1
Ironfounder	16	23
Ironmonger	7	8
Jeweller & silversmith	42	57
Labourer	112	141
Lawyer	1	1
Newsvendor	5	7
Oilman	8	11
Optician	2	2
Organ-builder	1	1
Paper-stainer	4	5
Pawnbroker	1	1
Pinmaker	2	3
Plumber, painter & glazier	31	56
Policeman	10	15
Postman	6	8
Printer and compositor	38	55
Publican	8	8
Railway-guard	1	1
Sailor	9	12
Sawyer	10	16
Scripture-reader	1	3
Secretary	1	3
Servant	5	6
Sexton	1	1
Shoemaker	90	140
Shopman	7	10
Soapboiler	3	(sic)1
Soldier	4	5
Stationer	11	15
Stoker	3	4
Superintendent (police)	1	2
Tailor	47	69
Tax-collector	1	1
Tea-urn & scale-maker	12	14
Tinman	11	11
Tobacconist	4	4
Traveller	11	15
Turner	27	46
Turnkey	2	3
Typefounder	5	5
Umbrella-maker	10	15
Undertaker	6	8
Upholsterer	7	13
Warehouseman	8	14
Watchmaker	49	83
Waterman	2	2
Wheelwright	4	6
Whipmaker	5	7
Weaver	4	5
Widows & orphans	84	133
Total	1,464	2,110

(PP. 1857–8 XLVI 261)

4D. THE DECLINE OF CHARITY SCHOOL ATTITUDES

The recognition by practical managers that charity-school attitudes were out of date and harmful to a school's prosperity was often criticised by subscribers. The following example from St.

Chad's School, Shrewsbury, brings out the issues clearly. It is unusual only in that ladies' committees were normally less liberal in outlook than were men; but this school's records suggest that it was fortunate in the women who served on its committees.

March 30th 1863: Annual Meeting

. . .Proposed by Dr Watts & seconded by Mr Oldfield that the hair Cutting in the Boys' school be discontinued.

The question of all the Children in ye girls school wearing the same Clothing on Sunday, and of their scouring the school room, having arisen, it was thought desirable that the managing Committee should consult with the Ladies' Committee upon the subject.

The meeting was adjourned. . .

April 4th 1863: Adjourned Annual Meeting

. . .The Secretary reported he had communicated with the Ladies' committee about the meeting the managing Committee on the subject of dress, and of scouring the school room, & that he had a communication from the former to lay before the present meeting.

He then read the following minute made at a Ladies' Committee meeting held for the purpose of considering this matter.

"This Committee having heard from the Hon Sec[y] of St. Chad's national schools yt the annual meeting have thought it advisable yt ye managing Committee s[d] consult with ye Ladies' Committee respecting ye expediency of Compelling all ye girls attending the school to wear like Clothing as also to scour & clean the school-room, submit ye following statements for ye Consideration of ye adjourned annual meeting.

With regard to ye dress – "That since ye removal of ye restriction on ye dress the average attendance at the school has increased nearly threefold.

"That there is a strong feeling on the part of many of the Parents ag[t] their Children wearing such dress."

"That making the wearing it Compulsory would greatly lessen the numbers attending the school, in which case the funds would suffer both as regards pence, and also Capitation grant."

"That out of 138 now on the books only 45 care to accept the dress though it is offered to all."

"That supposing the present number could be maintained the funds of the school w[d] not be sufficient to Clothe every child, the cost for the present year would be more than £40."

With regard to the Cleaning

"That the following are the ages of the Children attending the girls school

Under 10 years of age	102
Above 10 and under 12	24
Above 12 and under 14	12
	138

"That from the size of the present school room and the distance to carry water, both hot and cold, up 30 steps it has been found by experience that the Children are altogether unable to do the work properly, and if it were insisted on their health would materially suffer."

"That they dust and sweep the room twice every day, and light the fires, and scour and clean thoroughly the ground floor of the premises" –

"That as the school is partly self supporting there is not the same Claim upon the children as where the education is entirely" [free]

"This Committee therefore are of opinion that to enforce the wearing a prescribed dress would be most inexpedient and that it would greatly diminish the numbers, as well as lower the tone of the school; and also that the scouring the school room by the Children, is altogether impracticable. This Committee are quite aware of the evils of unbefitting and excessive dress, and ye necessity for industrial training, they have given their especial attention to these two subjects and among many difficulties have aimed at producing practical results in the school, if they have failed in their aim or have not given satisfaction to the subscribers, they are quite willing to resign their office to others who may be considered more efficient."

After some discussion as to whether this communication from the Ladies' committee could be received by the present meeting it was proposed by Mr Haycock & seconded by Mr Lowe "That the communication from the Ladies' Committee be regarded as satisfactory." . . .

(Minute Book, Salop CRO, 1048/4584)

4E. PARENTAL CONTRIBUTIONS TO A BUILDING FUND

It is clear from records, central and local, that by the 1850s Lancashire contained some of the most advanced schools in the country. The half-time system brought a wide cross-section of the population into the schools; and communities which were articulate and relatively prosperous were quick to recognise the value of a good school and to support it. This attitude is reflected in a letter reproduced by W. J. Kennedy, HMI, in his report for 1859–60. Of the teacher who wrote it, Kennedy remarked, 'If he seems to speak favourably of his own work, I can certify that he says no more than the occasion of his letter and the facts of the case warranted.'

. . .I may add further, that during the last twelve years the schools have increased sevenfold in numbers, and that this increase (if the annual reports of Her Majesty's Inspectors may be credited), has been accompanied by a proportionate increase or improvement in general attainments and efficiency. I am happy to inform you that our school-building prospects are of the most cheering character. At the commencement of last month Mr — canvassed the principal people in the town for subscription, and succeeded in obtaining £330, when he handed the subscription book to me, with an intimation that the trustees wished me to make an appeal to the parents of those children who either were, or had been, in connexion with the schools.

I looked up all the admission registers I could find, and made out a list of 678 names of parents who, I had reason to think, were still resident in the town. To every one of these I addressed a circular, and in the next ten days made upwards of 650 calls, and was successful in almost every instance, in obtaining either a subscription or a promise, which in due time will be fulfilled. These subscriptions range between £1 and 3d. and in the aggregate amount to £257.13s.9d., a sum which I could not have believed it possible to raise from such a class of people. The frequent expressions of thankfulness for benefits received at S—'s National schools made to me, in the course of my canvass by many of my old pupils, who are fathers and mothers of families, was gratifying in the extreme, and the substantial tokens which they gave of their sincerity was satisfactory proof to me that I have not laboured in vain, nor spent my strength for nought during the last thirteen years.

(PP. 1860 LIV, pp. 96–7)

4F. THE PURPOSES OF REGISTRATION

The Education Department's attempt to improve standards of registration at source, by including a question on registration in the certificate examination in 1855, produced disastrous results – 'every species of mistake which can be committed seems to present itself'. The colleges were then ordered to set fortnightly exercises on registration; and probationers who had answered badly were threatened with the loss of their first augmentation grant if the state of their registers was unsatisfactory. To show that they were not asking the impossible, the Department printed the two best answers, one of which, from a girl at Warrington College, is reproduced below.

What are the advantages of registration to teachers, managers of schools, and parents?

A careful system of registration enables the teacher, by whom it is pursued, to supply *the Government* with the statistics which they require, without having recourse to guessing, which is not very creditable, and besides often very far from correct. These statistics are very troublesome to make up, unless the register is regularly and carefully kept; while, if attended to, at regular and stated times, the trouble is but slight. The register is also a kind of protection to *the Teacher* from unjust blame, since it enables her at once to point out the cause of an irregular scholar's want of progress. And, if a register of rewards and punishments is kept, a powerful check is established over the children, with whom a reward or punishment will have double weight, when it is known to be registered. *Managers* may ascertain from the registers whether their school improves, and whether a sufficient number receive the benefit of the school, to compensate them for the outlay. *Parents* may learn from it whether their children really attend when they are sent to school, and the teacher may convince them how much is really lost by irregular attendance. Absence, if always taken notice of, and obliged to be accounted for, becomes much less frequent.

(PP. 1856 XLVII, p. 15)

4G. SCHOOL ATTENDANCE

Once registers had become more accurate, the twin problems of irregular attendance and short stay in school were fully revealed. Two examples, one urban, the other rural, are reproduced below. The second, summarised from an attendance register covering the period from March 1855 to December 1856, is distorted by the absence of the second quarter of 1856, so that only 530 possible attendances are recorded. Both sets of figures serve to underline the difficulties with which the schools were faced. The problem was perhaps less acute in villages than in towns, because there were fewer opportunities for changing schools; but the figures from Winston show that it was real.

(i) From the admission and attendance registers of St Stephen's Boys' School, Newton Row, Birmingham

	Admitted	Age	Left	½ days attended
1.	4/2/50	8	16/1/51	189
2.	11/2/50	10	4/2/54	1001
3.	11/2/50	10	24/7/50	102
4.	11/2/50	8	19/7/50	169
5.	11/2/50	8	12/3/50	22
6.	19/2/50	7	21/5/50	26
7.	4/3/50	8	5/8/51	391
8.	4/3/50	9	15/3/50	3
9.	12/3/50	9	29/3/50	16
10.	12/3/50	6	29/3/50	16
11.	19/3/50	8	30/4/51	120
12.	19/3/50	9	24/12/51	160
13.	7/1/51	10	2/4/51	63
14.	7/1/51	7	27/2/51	45
15.	14/1/51	7	16/5/51	68
16.	14/1/51	6	16/5/51	68
17.	14/1/51	10	16/3/51	27
18.	14/1/51	7	21/3/51	62
19.	21/1/51	7	20/6/53	394
20.	21/1/51	13	4/6/51	28
21.	21/1/51	9	6/4/51	31
22.	21/1/51	7	7/3/51	44
23.	27/6/52	9	23/3/54	372

	Admitted	Age	Left	½ days attended
24.	27/6/52	9	30/6/53	302
25.	12/7/52	7	10/3/54	268
26.	12/7/52	6	2/3/53	227
27.	12/7/52	7	11/11/52	115
28.	12/7/52	6	19/10/52	120
29.	12/7/52	6	3/12/52	124
30.	12/7/52	6	6/12/52	90
31.	27/9/52	10	23/10/52	32
32.	27/9/52	7	27/10/52	34
33.	4/10/52	8	3/2/54	677
34.	4/10/52	6	5/8/53	200
35.	25/10/52	8	3/6/53	252
36.	25/10/52	7	6/6/53	100
37.	28/10/52	9	27/10/52(sic)	13
38.	28/10/52	7	27/10/52 ,,	13
39.	28/10/52	7	29/12/52	68
40.	28/10/52	8	14/7/53	75
41.	5/1/53	8	22/9/53	241
42.	5/1/53	9	18/5/53	120
43.	5/1/53	9	16/3/53	63
44.	5/1/53	9	18/6/53	153
45.	5/1/53	8	25/3/53	30
46.	12/1/53	8	18/2/53	29
47.	12/1/53	10	29/3/53	59
48.	24/1/53	9	12/2/53	30
49.	24/1/53	9	26/5/53	142
50.	24/1/53	6	30/11/53	120

(PP. 1854–5 XLII, p. 422)

(ii) From the attendance register, 1855–6, Winston CE School, Co. Durham

	Admitted	Name removed	½ days attended
1 RB		1/8/56	268
2 WP		21/12/55	52
readmitted	4/8/56		82
3 GH		4/9/56	337
4 JH	on roll throughout		398

(ii) From the attendance register, 1855–6, Winston CE School, Co. Durham – *cont.*

		Admitted	Name removed	½ days attended
5	CG	on roll throughout		416
6	TP		21/12/55	50
7	HH	on roll throughout		411
8	RM	,, ,, ,,		433
9	WW	,, ,, ,,		389
10	FT		before 23/6/56	277
11	WHS		28/2/56	291
12	MAS		21/12/55	169
13	JAB	on roll throughout		439
14	SH		before 23/6/56	{ 187
readmitted		27/10/56		{ 53
15	CT		before 23/6/56	221
16	JP		7/3/56	199
17	TA		18/7/56	254
18	SD	on roll throughout		335
19	JD	,, ,, ,,		367
20	JAP	25/6/55		440
21	RP		7/3/56	209
22	JP		4/9/56	370
23	AB	on roll throughout		500
24	IP		before 23/6/56	222
25	MP	25/6/55		448
26	MJB		21/12/55	66
27	EB	on roll throughout		439
28	TS		28/2/56	287
29	JB	on roll throughout		470
30	TW	,, ,, ,,		515
31	RT	,, ,, ,,		416
32	JP	,, ,, ,,		401
33	GS	,, ,, ,,		502
34	MAH	3/7/55	before 23/6/56	223
35	WH	3/7/55	,, 23/6/56	269
36	CT	4/7/55		480
37	GS	16/7/55	28/2/56	240
38	AP	23/7/55	before 23/6/56	274

		Admitted	Name removed	½ days attended
39	TB	30/7/55		292
40	JA	21/8/55	21/12/55	19
readmitted		3/11/56		45
41	SA	21/8/55	21/12/55	19
42	HH	8/10/55	4/7/56	106
43	MAH	8/10/55	21/12/55	52
readmitted before		23/6/56	18/7/56	14
44	JB	8/10/55	21/3/56	199
45	CS	15/10/55	21/12/55	43
readmitted		23/2/56	18/7/56	33
46	TH	15/10/55	21/12/55	16
readmitted before		23/6/56	24/10/56	29
readmitted		2/12/56		7
47	JP	15/10/55	before 23/6/56	114
48	CG	5/11/55	before 23/6/56	158
49	GP	5/11/55	before 23/6/56	312
50	EH	5/11/55	before 23/6/56	83
51	JH	12/11/55	25/6/56	97
readmitted		3/11/56		33
52	AH	12/11/55		280
53	MH	12/11/55	21/12/55	54
readmitted		24/6/56		166
54	MJT	19/11/55	before 23/6/56	83
readmitted		24/11/56		19
55	JH	20/11/55	8/7/56	83
readmitted		1/12/56		9
56	JH	20/11/55		202
57	JP	26/11/55	before 23/6/56	131
58	AA	7/1/56	28/2/56	10
59	BC	14/1/56	before 23/6/56	49
60	WP	before 23/6/56		115
61	ET	4/7/56		188
62	SN	7/7/56	18/7/56	8
readmitted		24/11/56		15
63	JN	7/7/56	16/7/56	8
64	TN	7/7/56	18/7/56	18
65	WK	8/7/56		175
66	BK	8/7/56		176
67	JS	15/7/56		162

(ii) From the attendance register, 1855–6, Winston CE School, Co. Durham – *cont.*

		Admitted	Name removed	½ days attended
68	RC	21/7/56	21/11/56	125
69	MS	23/7/56		130
70	SS	29/9/56		95
71	JS	20/10/56		61
72	HH	27/10/56		52
73	TD	11/11/56	21/11/56	5

(Durham CRO, EP/Wi 87)

4H. STATUTORY HALF-TIME

The half-time system posed many problems for the average school. Some of these are described in H(i), a complaint from the schoolmistress of Finedon, near Wellingborough, who encountered it after the Act of 1867. In textile areas, however, where half-time was an accepted part of the way of life, some half-time schools were very successful, taking advantage of the enforced regularity of attendance and the consequent assured income in fees. One of the most celebrated was Rochdale Parochial School whose master, James Wrigley, was consistently praised by HMIs, the Factory Inspectors and J.S. Winder, whose report to the Newcastle Commission is quoted under (ii).

(i) During the past year, I have had over 30 girls in attendance under the Workshops Regulation Act. Of these I am afraid not more than half have derived much benefit, while their coming has seriously interfered with the *order* of the school and the instruction of the other children. It is most difficult to make many half-timers take the same interest in their lessons that other children do, their one idea seems to be to get through the two hours of school time each day with as little trouble as possible to themselves, consequently they cannot well be taught in the same class with others who are not half-timers, their progress being so much slower. This is particularly the case with those whose mothers work in the same factory, and are anxious to have their needlework done by the girls when at school. Such mothers have contrived that the girls should come almost always at the hours when needlework is done, so that the girls, though great dunces, rarely have a reading or writing lesson, as I *must* keep to my time table, for the sake of the rest, and of course all the class must work together, the numbers being too large to admit of my attending to anything but the needlework at that time. The great difficulty is, that I have never been able to make them all come at one time, say from 9 to 11, 10 to 12, or 2 to 4. The masters will send them only at such times as are convenient to themselves each day, consequently they miss so many lessons that those which they do receive are almost unintelligible to them. Then most of the half-timers are rarely, if ever, present at a scripture or catechism lesson, which they always try to avoid, this I think is most objectionable. When work is scarce, as it has been lately, they have stayed away altogether for three or four weeks at a time, then when they go to work again, they return for the 10 hours a week. I have inquired why they do not come the whole time to school when their masters do not want them, and the parents say they cannot afford to pay when the children have no wages.

Finedon, Wellingborough,
January 22nd, 1870
(PP. 1870 XXII, p. 104)

(ii) *Rochdale Parochial School*

. . .There could hardly be a more striking sight to the understanding eye than the interior of this school, in which I have seen 600 children present at one time, all under the most perfect command, moving with the rapidity and precision of a machine, and learning as though they were learning for their lives. It is difficult indeed to overrate the greatness of the work which Mr James Wrigley, to whose intelligence and unflinching energy the success of the school is entirely due, is effecting in the town. Not only are 700 children receiving in the school the benefits of a most awakening and stimulating instruction, and of an exact and intelligent discipline, but by means of an admirable system of night work not less than 400 or 500 families in the town are made to take an interest in the education of their younger members. I was assured over and over again by parents who had children at the school, that the scholar's slate of night questions frequently concentrated the attention of his whole family, who are thus associated with the work of the school most beneficially both for themselves and for him. Night work is usually a mere sham; in this school it forms one of the most essential features of the system of teaching, and involves no less than an hour and a half every day of additional school time for both master and pupil-teachers. Nearly half the scholars are half-timers, and it is from this school that I was able to form the best idea of what the half-time system can do, under the unfavourable conditions of attendance which always accompany it in considerable towns.

I satisfied myself that a child of ordinary abilities entering this school, even as a half-timer, between 8 and 9, with an average rudimentary instruction, and continuing in it till 13, as a half-timer might do, would almost certainly arrive at the first class. Clever children might reach it, as in fact the analysis of the classes . . . shows that they do, much earlier, and remain in it a long time. What does that imply? Fluent and intelligent reading in any book or newspaper; the power of writing from dictation ordinary sentences, such as would naturally occur in a letter, almost faultlessly as far as spelling is concerned, and in a very tolerable hand; a knowledge of all the practically important rules, and, probably, of the whole range of arithmetic, integral and fractional; a sound general notion of the map of the world, with an accurate knowledge of British geography; a connected, though slight, outline of . . . English History; and an ability to parse, and probably to analyse, any ordinary sentence.

A child, in fact, who has spent some time in the upper division of the first class . . . has received a sound education, abundantly sufficient for awakening his mind, enabling him to go on with self-instruction, and fitting him for any situation in life which he is likely to be called on to fulfil. Even if he never pass beyond the second or third class he will have been taught to read well, write fairly from dictation, and to make a simple calculation. . .

(PP. 1861 XXI Part II, pp. 224–5)

4J. VOLUNTARY HALF-TIME

Voluntary half-time could only be established when a large employer was prepared to experiment and was therefore dependent upon patronage (cf. 5B, 5M(iii)). An interesting aspect of the scheme run by Charles Paget in Nottinghamshire was his success in involving parents engaged in the stocking-knitting industry. Paget described his scheme in a pamphlet published in 1859, *Results of an Experiment on the Half-time System of Education in Rural Districts*; nine years later it aroused the interest of Edward Stanhope, one of the Assistant Commissioners reporting on the employment of women and children in agriculture. He took evidence from Paget, the schoolmaster and some parents and pupils, part of which is reproduced below.

Evidence of Mr William Spencer, master of the Free School at Ruddington

The half-time system described by Mr Paget was introduced here in 1854. Since that time Mr Barker, one of the farmers here, has adopted it, and another farmer sends his two girls on alternate days. Besides this, several of the stockingers send their children almost in the same way, but with less regularity. These children come when they can be spared, and not on any certain days. On the whole their attendance is about the same as in the case of Mr Paget's half-timers, and I am unable to distinguish between the results obtained in the two cases.

Mr Paget's boys come every alternate day, but on Saturday all go to work. They are also all taken away when there is any very great press of work. It will be seen that as a rule this method requires no alteration in the mode of conducting the school, for necessarily the pupil must be present on Monday, Tuesday, Wednesday, Thursday, and Friday during any two weeks. The total attendance in the year of Mr Paget's boys is, on an average, 90 days, and the stockingers' children, mentioned above, attend about the same number of days.

To get on really well in school matters boys ought to come a part of every week, as a rule; and at a meeting of the Schoolmasters' Association, held last month at Nottingham, a resolution was unanimously passed in favour of that principle. . .

I find that the half-timers take as good a position in our school as those who come whole time, and do not have any great difficulty in keeping up with them. In the case of some boys the change is almost necessary, and I sometimes say to one, "Can't you get a few days work somewhere?" They hardly know whether they like school or work the best. . .

The rule which Mr Paget laid down, that every boy admitted to work upon half-time should be able to read fairly, exposed the fact that vast numbers of boys at the age of 9 years were unable to read with any degree of intelligence, although there had been a free school in the parish over 200 years. To remedy this evil a committee was formed in 1857, with the clergyman of the parish as its chairman, and a subscription made which enabled a prize of about 1s.6d. worth of educational materials to be offered to every child in the parish over 9 and under 10 who could read the Gospels nicely, and besides this prize a certificate of merit was also to be given . . . at the present time we find that about 90 per cent of the children do present themselves for this examination, and that, whereas 10 years ago only 55 per cent were able to read and 12 per cent to read well, now nearly 80 per cent do so. Nearly every certificate so obtained is now ornamenting the best room in the cottage of the parent, set in a good frame. The results of this experiment were at once so astonishing, that in 1861 Mr Paget offered a second prize of 5s. worth of educational materials to every boy or girl who, at the age of 13 and under 14, could read, write and account to his satisfaction.

The number of these prizes that have been awarded by Mr Paget has increased year by year, and among the competition the half-timers have held their own. Out of 63 that have passed for them, of whom only 30 were boys, no less than 13 of the boys have been half-timers; 28 have failed in passing, and of these two only were half-timers. Think also of the effect of sending 404 bundles of slates, books, etc. into the cottages of this village during the last ten years, besides 163 large dictionaries, etc.

The result of this system has been to extend "home education", if I may so call it. The half-timers have had to do work at home in order to keep up with their class, and a desire for self-improvement has been developed. There is in this village a "juvenile self-improving" class for boys over 13, who elect their own teachers and manage their own funds. It meets once a week all the year round, and helps to carry on education after the school has been left.

Wm. Sanday, team-man. – My lad, who is now 24, went to Mr Paget's half-time at 9 years old, and stayed till 14. Before that he had been at infant school. He is a gardener, but what will show that his education is good is, the fact that he has been employed in taking stock for the co-operative store.

My other boy (18) went to Mr Spencer's school at 7. He began to work on the farm tenting crows at 8 years old. He worked every other day; then he got to leading horses and so on. He stayed at school till he was 14. The school is a mile from where we live. When it was his morning to work he had to be up at 6; when it was his morning for school he was not called till I had gone to work; but I did not find that he had any difficulty in getting up on work mornings. On the contrary, the rest made him the fresher for it. . .

Mrs Beecroft, milkman's wife. – My boys Will. (19) and George (15) were both at Mr Paget's; they were on the half-time plan. The oldest is apprentice to Danks and Nixon at Nottingham; the other helps his father. We never had any trouble getting them up on work mornings; but boys that go every day to work seem to me to be overtired by it.

They both went to infant school, but we hadn't a good schoolmistress here till the last year or so; the other couldn't write herself hardly. Now we have a very good one. One of my boys is there, but both my elder boys could read before they were 9 years old.. . .

William Beecroft, aged 18, bellhanger, apprentice to Messrs. Danks and Nixon, Nottingham. – I was one of Mr Paget's half-time boys. I went to work on his farm when I was 10. I could read and write pretty well them [sic]. We could all of us read and write before we began, though some of us not very well.

When we went to school, we were not put next each other, nor treated differently from other boys. We took our places in our classes with the other boys as if we had never been away. We were obliged to do work in the evenings to keep up.

The day's rest from work was very good for me. A change of boots was the great thing. There are plenty of boys about who have their feet bent and twisted by the boots they have to wear in the fieldwork, but we were able to change our's every day, and never suffered at all from it.

There's not one of us that has not got on a bit.

(PP. 1867–8 XVII, pp. 318–19)

4K. THE 'TRIPARTITE SYSTEM'

Henry Moseley's 'tripartite system', intended to ensure for every pupil daily contact with an adult teacher, was tried with varying degrees of success in many schools. West Ashton school, Wiltshire, described below by the vicar, F. H. Wilkinson, who introduced the system in 1848, enjoyed a considerable reputation in the early 1850s and was attended by many children from outside the parish; but its success probably resulted less from the 'system' than from the farm and dairy in which the pupils spent the afternoons, the games room in the vicarage which they could use during the evenings and the excursions organised by Wilkinson, which included a marathon twenty-four hour trip to the Great Exhibition (PP. 1852 XXXIX 337, pp. 7–8).

. . .The school buildings consist of three rooms, of which one is devoted to reading, another to writing and arithmetic, and the remaining one to oral instruction. The latter is fitted up with a gallery for sixty children; the writing-room with parallel desks; and in the reading-room the seats are arranged for distinct classes, such as are usual in National schools, only that we place them in parallel rows instead of the more common square form.

The children, 150 in number, are divided into three large sections, consisting of about 50 in each. Of these, the first, containing the more advanced children, is called the *A Division*, the second is named the *B Division*, and the third, which really with us forms an infant-school, is called the *C Division*. The morning school-time consists, as usual, of three hours. We have thus three localities, viz. the reading room, the writing and arithmetic room, and the oral instruction room; three sections of children, the A, B, and C; and three hours of instruction. It is evident that by a system of rotation, the changes being made at the hours of ten and eleven, each section will pass an hour in each room. This is the Tripartite system . . . presuming the acquaintance of your readers with the method as explained by the Rev. H. Moseley . . . I at once note down what appear to me as its most important results. And first, I name a great economy of time, labour, and mental energy. Of time, because the teacher or teachers, assistant or pupil-teachers, and monitors, are all engaged . . . in that employment best suited to their several powers. . . The monitors, superintended by the mistress, in a mixed school, or pupil-teacher, can teach efficiently the mechanical art of reading; and one-third of the school is always thus being instructed by monitors. The pupil-teachers can teach writing and the rules of slate arithmetic; and one-third of the school is under their care. The head-teacher, of course, ought to be fully competent to give the oral instruction, and especially to explain the subject of the lesson read in classes in the reading room; and the remaining third of the school is receiving from him, that religious, moral, and mental training, which is of the highest importance, but which the monitorial system notoriously fails in supplying . . . no time is wasted, because neither teacher nor scholar has a task allotted beyond his power to accomplish, and there is a generous rivalry as to which shall do so most successfully. The economy of labour is a simple matter of fact; 150 children in this school are instructed by one head teacher, three pupil-teachers, and five monitors. This is the largest staff we ever require, though I hope to exchange one of the monitors for another pupil-teacher. . . Contrast this with the staff that would be required in a school of a similar size under the monitorial system . . . and the economy of labour is apparent; the average number of children in a reading-class, with us, is eight or nine only. The economy of mental energy is hardly less apparent. While the connexion of the instruction given in the gallery with that . . . in the reading and arithmetic-rooms enables the head teacher to keep the reins of the whole school in his hands, and while he can at any time interchange duties with his pupil-teachers if necessary, he ordinarily feels at liberty to give the whole energy of his mind to the instruction of each section as . . . it comes before him in the gallery lesson. The mind of every child . . . thus comes into contact with, and receives the impress of his mind, and will probably carry this influence with him throughout life. The mental energies of the pupil-teachers, again, are expended on objects within their grasp; while the monitors are freed from requirements the successful accomplishment of which is quite beyond the reach of the great majority of children of their tender years.

The second great advantage . . . [is] the facility the system affords for the advantageous classification of children. Few things are more perplexing to a teacher than the admission into his school of a child of advanced age, intelligent, and with a perfect knowledge of the art of reading, but almost wholly uninstructed in writing and arithmetic. If tied to the old system of monitorial classes, he is compelled to place the child in a very low one, thus discouraging him at the outset by putting him on a level with children only half his own age, and depriving him of the general instruction of the higher classes, which he is fully competent to receive. On the Tripartite system the difficulty is removed at once; there need not be . . . the slightest connexion between the child's position in the reading-room and in the writing and arithmetic room. Such a child would take his place at once in the first class in the reading-school, and would then feel no injustice done him when he found himself in the place suited to his acquirements in the other school; while in the gallery lesson he would share equally in the general instruction. . .

A third advantage of the Tripartite system consists in its great quietness compared with the ordinary methods. . . In the room for oral instruction not a sound is heard, except the teacher's voice and the replies of those on whom he may call. In the reading-room five voices only are heard, one in each class; while in the writing and arithmetic room, as half the division are engaged in a silent occupation, the study of arithmetic is pursued under the most favourable circumstances. . .

In conclusion, I would describe the chief characteristic of the Tripartite system to be this, – it appropriates the advantages of the systems in common use, while it avoids their defects. . . The one hour's oral instruction, bearing as it does on that given in the other two rooms, brightens and adds an intelligent interest to the hard application and perseverance required during the remaining two hours, without superseding the necessity for the exercise of these valuable qualities. . .

(National Society, *Monthly Paper* (1851), pp. 47–9)

4L. TIMETABLES

Increased collective teaching and the desire to ensure that all pupils had regular contact with adult teachers inevitably led to the introduction of set timetables. Those of large schools were very complex, e.g., Goswell Street (R. H. Hadden, *Reminiscences of William Rogers* (2nd edn, 1888), pp. 68–70) or Stockport British School (PP. 1857–8 XLV, pp. 517–8). There are fewer records of smaller schools; but for several months of 1864 the teachers of the schools of Whitwick, Leicestershire, recorded their daily timetable in their log books. It varied from week to week; the following is the record for one week of April. Whale was a pupil-teacher; the other named persons were monitors. The boys' school was unusual in having a fifth class which relieved the mistress of some of the older infants.

Timetables, Whitwick, 25–29 April, 1864

BOYS' SCHOOL

	Class I	Class II	Class III	Class IV	Class V
Monday					
9.30	Scripture (Self)		Scripture Texts (Self)	Reading (Whale)	
10.0	Mapping (Self)		Reading (Self)	Arithmetic (Whale)	Writing (Self)
10.45			PLAY		
11.0 to 11.45			Writing in Copy Books		Writing on Slates
1.30	Reading (Self)			Reading (Whale)	Writing (Whale)
2.30			PLAY		
2.45 to 3.45	Arithmetic (Whale)		Arithmetic (Benistow)	Arithmetic (Counting) (Self)	
Tuesday					
9.15	Scripture (Self)		Grammar (Self)	Reading (Whale)	
10.0	Mapping (Self)		Reading (Self)	Arithmetic (Whale)	Writing (Whale)
10.45			PLAY		
11.0			Writing		
11.45			Singing		
1.30	Reading (Self)			Geography (Whale)	Writing (Whale)
2.30			PLAY		
2.45 to 3.45	Geography (Self)		Reading (Whale)	Writing (Self)	Reading (Harrison)
Wednesday					
9.15	Scripture (Self)		Writing (Self)	Catechism (Whale)	
10.0	Mapping (Self)		Reading (Whale)	Counting (Self)	
10.45			PLAY		
11.0 to 11.45			Writing in Copy Books		Writing on Slates

1.30	Reading (Self)		Arithmetic (Chester)	Reading (Whale)	
2.30	PLAY				
2.45 to 3.45	Grammar (Self)		Reading (Self)	Arithmetic (Whale)	Writing (Whale)
Thursday					
9.15	Scripture (Self)		Writing (Self)	Reading (Whale)	Writing (Whale)
10.0	Putting down Numbers (Self)		Reading (Whale)	Writing (Whale)	Reading (Benistow)
10.45	PLAY				
11.0 to 11.45	Writing in Copy Books				Writing on Slates
1.30	Reading (Self)		Transcription (Self)	Reading (Whale)	
2.30	PLAY				
3.0 to 3.45	Dictation (Self)	Arithmetic (Self)	Reading (Self)	Counting (Whale)	
Friday					
9.15	Scripture (Self)			Catechism (Whale)	
10.0	Mapping (Self)		Reading (Whale)	Reading (Self)	
10.45	PLAY				
11.0 to 11.45	Writing in Copy Books				Writing on Slates
1.30	Reading Psalms for the Day and for Sunday Next (Self)		Arithmetic (Self)	Reading (Whale)	
2.30	PLAY				
2.45 to 3.30	Music and Singing				

GIRLS' AND INFANTS' SCHOOLS

	Girls Cl. I	Girls Cl. II	Girls Cl. III	Girls Cl. IV	Infants Cl. I	Infants Cl. II	Infants Cl. III	Infants Cl. IV
Monday								
9.10	Read Scripture (Monitors)		Catechism (Monitors)		Repeated Scripture Text (P.T.)			
9.50	Dictation (Self)		Reading (Monitors)		(10.0) Reading (P.T. and Monitors)		Writing (P.T. and Monitors)	
10.20	Arithmetic (Self)		Arithmetic Ballframe (S. Carter)		(10.35) Songs and Exercises			
10.45	PLAY				PLAY			
11.0	Writing (Self and Monitors)				Gallery-Counting			
11.35	Tables (Self)		X Tables (Burgess)	Making Figures (Dent)	Singing			
1.30	Sewing or Transcription (Self and P.T.)				Writing (P.T. and Monitors)		Reading (P.T. and Monitors)	
2.30	PLAY				PLAY			
2.45	Reading (Each class heard by self)				Reading (P.T. and Monitors)		Writing (P.T. and Monitors)	
Tuesday								
9.10	Scripture (Self)				Scripture (P.T.)			
10.0	Arithmetic and Tables (Self)		Arithmetic and Tables (Monitor)			?	?*	
10.45	PLAY				PLAY			
11.0	Dictation (Self)	Spelling (Self)	Copy Book and Slate Writing (Monitors)			?	?*	
11.45	Repeated Catechism (Self)				Learnt Keble's Hymn (P.T.)			
1.30	Sewing or Making Figures (Self and P.T.)				Writing (P.T. and Monitors)		Reading (P.T. and Monitors)	

*Not recorded

Time		
2.30	PLAY	PLAY
2.45	Reading — (Self) (Monitors) (Self) (Monitors)	Reading — Writing (P.T. and Monitors)
Wednesday		
9.10	Collect Article and Catechism (P.T.) — Repeating Catechism (Monitors)	Gallery – Parable of Tares (Self)
10.0	Arithmetic (P.T.) — Arithmetic (Monitors)	Reading in Classes (Self and Monitors)
10.45	PLAY	PLAY
11.0	Writing in Copy Books or on Slates	Gallery – A Fish (Self)
11.45	Tables	(11.30) Exercising and Catechism (Self)
1.30	Sewing or Writing	Writing — Reading (P.T. and Monitors)
2.30	PLAY	PLAY
2.45	Reading — (Monitors) (Self) (Monitors)	Reading — Writing (P.T. and Monitors)
Thursday		
9.10	Read Scripture (Monitors) — Scripture Lesson (Self)	Gallery – Learning a Psalm (P.T.)
10.0	Arithmetic (Monitors) — Numeration (Self) — Number (S. Carter)	Reading (P.T. with Teachers from Class I)
10.45	PLAY	PLAY
11.0 to 11.30	Dictation (Self) — Copying (Self) — Writing (Monitors)	Writing and Figures (P.T.) (Singing and Exercises at Intervals)
1.30	Sewing or Copying on Slates	Writing — Reading (P.T. and Monitors)
2.30	PLAY	PLAY
2.45	Reading — (Self) (Monitors)	Reading — Writing (P.T. and Monitors)

GIRLS' AND INFANTS' SCHOOL

	Girls				Infants			
	Cl. I	Cl. II	Cl. III	Cl. IV	Cl. I	Cl.II	Cl.III	Cl. IV
Friday 9.10	Writing Scripture Texts (Self)		Catechism (Monitors)		Learning and Singing a Hymn (P.T.)			
10.0	Arithmetic (Self)		Number (Monitors)		Reading (P.T. and Monitors)			
10.45	PLAY							
10.0 to 11.45	Writing				Spelling (P.T.)		Writing (Monitors)	
1.30	Sewing							
2.30	PLAY							
2.45	Singing							

(Based on Log Books, Whitwick National Schools, Leics. CRO, E/LB/364)

CHAPTER 5

TEACHERS, PARENTS AND PUPILS

In the late 1860s the master of Leyland Endowed School, a trained teacher, was asked[1] why he chose to work there rather than in the better paid post in an annual-grant school to which his certificate entitled him. He replied that he valued his independence; in a voluntary school he would be under the authority of the clergyman and would have more work to do.* He had a point. Old Macer, badly paid and unqualified, was more his own master than his successors whose function, as Lingen said, was executive only.† Deviants like the political activist, who in 1852 paraded through Blackburn at the head of a rampaging election mob, did not last long;[2] and they were rare. As a group, elementary teachers were conformist, even submissive. Mr Joyner was more typical than Mr Noad.[3]

The old-fashioned parochial schoolmaster who supplemented his income by acting as a parish clerk, surveyor, rate-collector and the like was, whatever his deficiencies as a teacher, part of the community in a way that his successor was not. Clergy like Sanderson Robins saw the teacher's role as semi-sacerdotal and teachers' own writings show an acute awareness of a gulf, moral even more than social, separating them from the people who used their schools. Their position was isolated and was seen to be so. They were passing through 'a self-conscious stage, sensitive and impatient', wrote a friendly observer, J. P. Norris, HMI.[4] The popularity of harvest schools and of reunions at those training colleges which maintained contact with their old students was partly the result of a desire for the company of their fellows. They showed some signs of developing into a caste; they intermarried and their children became pupil-teachers. In towns they sought each others' company and formed associations, many of which developed into pressure groups and coalesced into the National Union of Elementary Teachers in 1870.‡

Although even Lingen acknowledged that elementary-school teaching was hard work,[5] the hours and the holidays were better

* 5A. † 5B. ‡ 5C.

than in most jobs. Salaries rose steadily in the 1840s and 1850s and then reached a plateau. As with many Victorian occupations, the worst disadvantage of teaching was the absence of any career structure. A young certificated teacher could expect a salary which compared favourably with that of a curate and very favourably with that of a nonconformist minister;* but unless he was lucky he would be earning no more at forty than at twenty. Nevertheless, there was no real shortage of teachers. In 1867, for instance, a post in Bayswater with a basic salary of £80 attracted fourteen experienced applicants. For women, elementary teaching was arguably the best possible career – 'an honourable independence and greater advantages than are offered elsewhere' – as the philanthropic Miss Burdett-Coutts said when, with Education Department approval, she circularised middle-class schools for girls, urging them to become elementary schoolmistresses rather than governesses.[6] Some commentators considered that there were other advantages since the schoolmistress's lady-like manners, ability to keep accounts and knowledge of domestic economy gave her an exceptional chance of marrying above her station!

The small but growing class of assistants ranged from girls of fourteen or fifteen earning one or two shillings a week to teachers in large schools receiving as much as many masters. Until 1862 the grant system in practice discouraged their employment. Although it offered £25 p.a. to ex-pupil-teachers or later to probationers serving as assistants,[7] there was general agreement that such people must be paid £35 or £40 a year because they could not live respectably on less; and, in efficiency, there was little to choose between them and senior pupil-teachers who could be had at no cost to the managers. They were therefore relatively uncommon except in very large schools in which adult assistance for the master was essential.† With the Revised Code the position changed. As early as October 1862, indeed, the managers of one London school used the demands of the Code to justify the spending of an additional £120 a year on three extra assistants; and an increasing number of managers appointed assistants in place of some pupil-teachers. They were not universally popular. On the whole only the least able probationers took assistantships, though few were as bad as the assistant who, after

* 5D. † 5E.

seven unhappy months, confessed to the schoolmistress that she could not manage even one girl, still less a class.[8] If they were competent they soon left for schools of their own. Nevertheless, by 1870 most of the larger schools had one or more adult assistants.

The pupil-teacher system was devised both as a method of recruiting and training adult teachers and as an alternative to dependence on child monitors who were largely unwilling or incompetent, or both. The pupil-teacher, even at thirteen appreciably older than most of his pupils, legally bound to five years' service and supervised and instructed by qualified adults, was a different proposition; whilst apprenticeship bridged the gap between school-leaving and adulthood. The solid financial advantages built into the Minutes of 1846 meant, inevitably, that most managers who could meet the prescribed conditions hastened to replace monitors with older apprentices whose continuance was guaranteed and who cost the school nothing. Rogers, for example, had seventeen pupil-teachers in Goswell Street by 1850.

A pupil-teacher had to be physically and psychologically tough. Five years of unremitting toil punctuated by annual examinations gave little scope for adolescent ailments or adolescent rebellion. The proportion who cracked under the strain was surprisingly small and, of these, the larger number were forced to give up for health reasons. Nevertheless, there were always certain tensions between the pupil-teacher and the school authorities.* The former's prime aim was to prepare for his future career, the latter's to improve the immediate efficiency of the school; and a good test of a school's quality was the degree of concern shown for the interests of the pupil-teachers. The bad teacher made them responsible for the most difficult groups and scamped their instruction; the bad manager did nothing to ensure that they received the attention that was their due. Good managers took seriously their duty of supervision, watching their pupil-teachers' progress and sometimes reporting it annually to the subscribers. Thus in 1860 the committee of the Manchester Jews' School wrote that Wolf Levy, who had just completed his apprenticeship, '. . .pursued his tasks steadily and perseveringly, – faithfully seconding the efforts of the master, and attaining a control – mild yet firm – over the pupils, which is scarcely hoped

* 5F.

for in his successor, John Harris, who, however, promises improvement as he advances in the term of his apprenticeship'.[9]

Such paragons needed no discipline; but the evidence of school records shows the extent to which teachers relied on managerial support in dealing with their apprentices. Trouble often resulted from a change of teacher, when a third- or fourth-year pupil-teacher was confronted with new demands and expectations. Not all teachers were capable of educating adolescents. The need for more adequate provision, to some extent masked in schools whose clergy took part in the instruction of the pupil-teachers, was beginning to be recognised by the later 1860s. Canon and Mrs Fry held Saturday morning classes for the Anglican pupil-teachers of Leicester[10] and some teachers' associations experimented with joint programmes of instruction.* But all this was in embryo. The pupil-teachers' centre was a development of the future.

The disappearance of the monitorial system left monitors in a subsidiary role. The provision for stipendiary monitors in the Minutes of 1846 failed, since the conditions laid down were almost as strict as those for pupil-teachers; but many schools retained some monitors aged eleven or twelve, either as substitutes for pupil-teachers or as potential candidates. They helped with the routine subjects – the 3Rs, sewing – and were paid between 6d. and 2s. or even 2s.6d. a week, the latter being the going rate for diocesan monitors.[11] Monitors chosen from the body of the school were normally only used regularly for reading groups. In the panic after the Revised Code some schools tried to revert to a general reliance upon unpaid monitors, but in most cases the resistance of parents and children was too strong for them.

Where did managers fit into this picture? Their primary duty was supervision, to ensure that funds, from whatever source, were used effectively.† The Education Department urged this duty with increasing emphasis; the evidence suggests that, at least in Anglican schools, weekly visits, supplemented by quarterly or annual examinations, were the norm. Managers had the last word on curriculum – the ladies of Kendal British School, for instance, studied a book on kindergarten before agreeing to try it; and some interpreted their duty more widely. Thus on Wednesdays at

* 5G.

† 5H.

St John Baptist, Manchester, Rev. Peter Marshall assembled all the assistants and pupil-teachers in his three schools for a criticism lesson, or a model lesson given by one of the teachers, or occasionally a lecture from Marshall himself, as on 21 October 1863 on the art of investigating a subject.[12] How much actual teaching managers should do was a more disputed question. Teachers, who regarded them as amateurs, were often critical of their efforts – like the schoolmaster who remarked of a lesson from the rector that the children were 'backward in comprehending the Rev[d] Gentleman's mode of reasoning', or the mistress who said of the curate: 'The Rev. T. Ansell visited morning school, but his *familiarity* with the First Class is *absurd*.'[13] Nevertheless some, like Dawes, were exceptionally able teachers; and when they were prepared, as many were, to teach regularly at set times, they could do much to compensate for understaffing and for the teachers' weak points. The vicar's wife who was 'very persevering with the "awkward squad" of Standard I' must have been an asset, as must the curate of whom an unmusical master wrote, 'I feel right pleased to find that my boys have made such progress in Singing since Mr Dodd began his weekly lesson.'[14]

But for pupils, managers were probably most significant as providers of school treats, regular features ranging from tea and buns on the vicarage lawn to ambitious excursions.* Such experiences, it was felt, made school more attractive and encouraged attendance. At a time when they had no means of enforcing attendance, managers and teachers tried varied ways of inducing it. Thus homework was valued primarily as a means of involving the pupil's whole family in his school work. The problem of enlisting the support of parents was much aired and most possible solutions were discussed.† But many teachers were not adept at establishing good relations with parents. The conscious moral superiority, one element of the missionary zeal which fired so many of them, must to many parents have seemed sanctimonious conceit. Discussions often ended in acrimony: 'She said she would send her children to the Baptist School – Told her I should not consider the school any worse if she did so.'[15]

School authorities were resigned to absence caused by inability to pay fees, to seasonal absence in farming communities, to regu-

* 5J.

† 5K

lar absences in areas of cottage industry where children were required to fetch and carry materials. Their most bitter complaints were of restless changes of school, or motiveless absence, which they usually attributed to ignorance, selfishness or failure of discipline in the home. No doubt they were often right; yet it is possible to discern consistent patterns underlying many parental reactions. One group, sharing the views of the Bristol police inspector, removed their children if they thought they were being contaminated by bad company. Conversely, others objected to the schools' struggles to impose standards of cleanliness and tidiness. (It was 'quite enough to pay 4d.', complained one Birmingham mother, 'without having to send him so clean'.)[16] Parents wanted their children to 'get on' and generally believed this to mean progress in the orthodox curriculum. A number of promising schemes for the introduction of practical subjects foundered on the unwillingness of parents to send their children to learn them. They objected, too, if they thought their children were being inadequately taught. Parental complaints of a teacher's failure to make a child learn could often be triumphantly refuted by producing his attendance record. But in the absence of any obvious cause, most managers took a fall in attendance as *prima facie* evidence of the teacher's inefficiency and acted accordingly. In contrast to the position in endowed schools, a teacher who was really disliked by the parents rarely lasted long.

'Punish little Jack or Bill for any fault', wrote Harry Chester, formerly the second-in-command in the Education Department, 'and immediately he will be transferred in state by his affronted mother to the opposition school.'[17] Parental reactions undoubtedly influenced policies in the field of punishment. Corporal punishment was less frequent than in previous generations or in contemporary schools for the upper classes. Many managers attempted to restrict its use especially, since this angered parents most, its use by pupil-teachers. The Wesleyans, following Stow, made great play with 'moral training'. Others, more cynically, relied on lines and detention; but all were very conscious of their duty to provide moral guidance. It is clear from log books that time which, in a later age, would be devoted to patriotism and the empire was, in the middle years of the century, spent on exhortations to moral improvement.* Teachers undoubtedly took their civilising mission seriously.

* 5L.

Pupil's reactions to the experience of school are more obscure.* Victorian children were not encouraged to comment on their education whilst it was taking place; and reminiscences recorded in old age are not necessarily reliable. There is evidence – the framed certificates at Ruddington, for example[18] – of parents' pride in their children's achievement; a pride presumably shared by the children. If the present rate of truancy in an age of compulsion is evidence of a negative attitude towards school, then perhaps attendance in an age of non-compulsion should to some degree be the reverse. By the 1860s an increasing number of schools were recording attendance averages of over 70 per cent. In 1869, 696,540 children over six years of age (about 82 per cent of those qualified by attendance) were examined under the Revised Code and had learnt enough to achieve a pass rate of slightly over 85 per cent.[19] This tells us a little about these children, but not much. Perhaps the best evidence that their education had achieved some success dated from fifteen or twenty years later when they were parents themselves and when parliament had at last made up its mind to impose compulsory education. The relatively high attendance levels achieved by 1890 would not have been possible if a majority of parents had not grown up to regard school attendance as the norm.

Notes

1. By an assistant commissioner of the Taunton Commission: PP. 1867–8 XXVIII Part XIV, p. 306.
2. Blackburn Coucher Book, St Clement's Bottom Gate, 1852 (Lancs. CRO).
3. See IB, IG, 3K.
4. PRO, 30/29, Box 19, Part 2, 14/12/1855.
5. PP. 1852 XXXIX 337, pp. 74–5.
6. Paddington & Bayswater National, correspondence, 3/6/1867 (GLCRO); B.M. Add. MSS. 46404, pp. 19–21 (1857).
7. See Appendix 2.
8. Lambeth Parochial Minute Book, 23/10/1862; St Andrew's Holborn G., Log Book 6/11/1866 (GLCRO).
9. *Annual Report* (1860–61), p. 7.
10. Leicester County Girls, Log Book 22/8/1864 et seq. (Leicester City Museum). For Fry see 2D.
11. See above, p. 58.
12. Kendal British Girls, Minute Book, 18/11/1858 (CRO Kendal); St John Baptist Log Books, Boys, Girls and Infants (Manchester Archives).

* 5M.

13. Teston National, Log Book, 21/10/1864 (Kent Archives, P365/25/1); Stoke Abbott National, Log Book, 1/12/1864 (Dorset CRO, S55).
14. Crowle CE, Log Book, 28/6/1865 (Worcs. CRO); St Margaret's Boys, Durham, Log Book, 26/10/1866 (Durham CRO, E/C18).
15. Hugglescote National, Log Book, 20/11/1865 (Leics CRO, E/LB/150/1).
16. See 4B; St Paul's Boys, Birmingham, Log Book, 8/5/1868 (Birmingham City Library).
17. H. Chester, *Hints on the Building and Management of Schools* (1860), pp. 6–7.
18. See 4J.
19. PP. 1870 XXII, p. 4.

Documents

5A. A CASUALTY OF REFORM

When Gregory took on the district of St Mary, Lambeth (above, p. 56) a new, equally zealous rector was presented to Lambeth Parish Church. He found the parochial school still monitorial; the master had hitherto had a free hand, choosing his own assistants, nominating boys for clothes under the endowment and acting as secretary to the committee. The rector changed all that and persuaded the other managers to invite inspection and apply for a government grant. In consequence the master was told in March 1855, and again in June, that he must pass the certificate examination at the end of the year or leave. At the time he agreed to sit the examination but his resentment grew, especially after the rector appointed a temporary assistant without reference to him; he resigned in August. His letter contained legitimate complaints of staff shortages (pupil-teachers, of course, could not be appointed until he had a certificate); a complaint that worry about his position had affected his wife's health; and a strange assertion that the proposed staffing of a master, one assistant and five pupil-teachers would be insufficient for government requirements. Its core, however, vividly reflects the bitterness which many of the old dispensation must have felt towards the new; these sections are given below.

To the Treasurer and Committee
Sir and Gentlemen
I am obliged to you as the Treasurer for your Kind enquiry

at the School this morning respecting an assistant master. That your enquiries may be directed aright, I deem it my duty to inform you that it will be needful to obtain both an assistant and an head master for the School as for the reasons following, it is my intention to resign my connection with both the School and the Parish at Mich[s.]

More than 7 years ago, Sir, I received from Mr Nixon, one of your predecessors as Treasurer afterwards from the Committee, and the foundation Trustees, my appointment as Master of the School. That the Committee were satisfied for $6\frac{1}{2}$ years that I had done my duty in the School, I have written and printed evidence of. For 7 months last past, so entirely has my position in the School been altered, I may not select boys for clothing; I may not be trusted with the Minutes of the Committee; I may not be consulted about any proposed changes in the School, however much they may concern my teaching duties, my leisure hours, and my Salary, that I am but one remove from a mere automatum [sic]. Until about Christmas last the Committee gave evidence that they placed confidence in me: but of that feeling I have yet to receive the first evidence this year. . .

The second reason for my leaving the parish is the Minute of the Committee dated I think June 21st which after 7 years service expels me from office at the end of the year, but permits, after such expulsion to sit in January 1856 for a government certificate, the result of which sitting would not be known till March even to HM Privy Council. So that for 3 months I should be without an engagement* with a wife & family depending on me for their support a condition both unreasonable and unscriptural (*vide* Matt vii. 12) This is the sympathy and encouragement offered me beforehand to undergo a severe ordeal – an ordeal, the preparation for which has, according to a return produced in the House of Commons moved for by Mr Hadfield "ruined the health" of 180 persons for life (vide page 159 of the enclosed pamphlet). . .

(Lambeth Parochial Boys' School, Minute Book, *esp.* 21/6/55, 17/8/55, GLCRO, A/LPB/15)

* There is no evidence that the committee intended this, though the tone of their minutes suggests that they were sceptical about his intention to sit; and some were certainly anxious that he should leave.

5B. COLLABORATION IN A VILLAGE SCHOOL

The following passage from the second *Report on the Employment of Women and Children in Agriculture* illustrates the triangular and amicable relationship between patron, parson and schoolmaster characteristic of many successful rural schools of the period. The benevolent paternalism of Lord Lyttelton and his brother, the rector, made his estate village, Hagley, resemble a village in a novel by C. M. Yonge (see B. Askwith, *The Lytteltons* (1975)); the school, inevitably, was part of the structure (cf. 6L).

Evidence of Mr W. Stephens, Schoolmaster, Hagley National School

I have been master here for 24 years. This is a mixed school. There are 56 boys on the books and 18 girls. Last week the average in attendance was 47 boys and 17 girls. About a quarter of the boys come from other parishes, but only one of the girls. Nearly half belong to the agricultural labouring class. The poorest class pay 3d. a week; the artizans and small tradesmen pay 4d. each; small farmers, 5s. a quarter, and large farmers 7s.6d. No deduction is made if more than one in a family attends. Many of the poorest are helped by the gentry. The school is inspected by Government, but is not quite self-supporting. Before the introduction of the Revised Code we allowed the scholars over 12 years old to be absent on any alternate days or weeks, or during the busy times of the year, according to their convenience, but such absences were not to exceed half the time the school was open. That plan worked very well. Lord Lyttelton used to give them a capitation prize (worth 3s. to 2s., but not given in money). We have had to give up that plan on account of the introduction of the Revised Code. There are 10 small allotment gardens attached to the school, 100 square yards each. They are given to 10 of the boys as a reward for good conduct. They cultivate them out of school hours. Lord Lyttelton finds manure and lends tools. The land is rent free, and the boys have the produce of the gardens themselves. On an average they make 6s. or 7s. a year profits. There is also a carpenter's shop. A carpenter comes to give instruction on two afternoons in the week. About 16 of the elder boys take that up. They are divided into sets of four each, and each set has one lesson per fortnight. The rector pays the carpenter and provides tools. There are a few (perhaps six) children who don't come to school at all. That is owing to the indifference of the parents. Some come to school three miles; they are quite as regular as those who live nearer. Labourers' sons, as a general rule, stay up to the age of 11 or 12. They go away a little before that, usually to plant potatoes in the spring, but not for long enough time to interfere much with their school work. The old half-time system enabled us to keep the boys longer than we have been able to do since. The school was open last year 464 times, and on an average each boy attended 438. There is an infant school here; they come here from that school at the age of 7. I think that a boy could read, write, and cipher a little with ease by the age of 10 if he attended school regularly. Eight boys passed the fourth standard last year; they were aged from 11 to 13. But we are in the habit of keeping them back in order that they may be sure of passing a standard every year. A good many of the labourers' sons are diverted from farm work in consequence of the good education they receive here; but there is nothing in the system of agricultural labour in the neighbourhood which interferes with the education of boys. . .

(PP. 1868–9 XIII, pp. 286–7)

5C. TEACHERS' ASSOCIATIONS

Teachers' associations were regarded with suspicion by the Education Department which feared them as potential pressure groups; but many observers, amongst them Frederick Watkins, HMI, who published this list of the activities of one association, believed that they should be encouraged as expressions of a zeal for professional improvement. (Cf. P. H. G. H. Gosden, *How They were Taught* (1969), pp. 201–3). Groups of this sort joined to form the Associated Body of Church Schoolmasters which ultimately developed into the NUET (see M. Seaborne and G. Isham, *A Victorian Schoolmaster, J. J. Graves* (1967), pp. 9, 15–16).

Papers Read at the Halifax Church Teachers' Association, 1854–5

The benefit of mathematical studies in a liberal education, and their application to the mathematical course of instruction in our National schools.

Whether Sunday schools are fulfilling the objects for which they were originally designed.

The art of teaching
Teaching geography
Sunday schools
Drawing and design
The form and magnitude of the earth
Discussion on "Home lessons"
Principles of success in a National school
Discussion on the "Games to be allowed in the playground"
The training of pupil-teachers
Discussion on the "Educational measures then before Government"
Separation or non-separation of the sexes for the purposes of instruction
Training the intellectual faculties
The Minutes of Council for 1854–5
Illustration as an auxiliary to the teacher
Rewards and punishments in schools
Works of Macaulay
Electro-magnetism

(PP. 1856 XLVII, p. 281)

5D. TEACHERS' SALARIES

This list of salaries for the posts obtained by students who left Durham Training College at Christmas 1866 includes an estimate for accommodation (£6 for an unfurnished, £10 for a furnished house); but it still lends some substance to the Education Department's claim that even after the Revised Code certificated teachers were not badly paid (for comparison, the living of St Thomas Charterhouse was worth £150, that of St Mary, Lambeth, £90). The true problem was not the initial pay of qualified teachers but the low salaries of the unqualified and the fact that these young men, under the existing system, would probably never earn much more in the future.

Name of School	*County*	*Gross Value*	*Remarks*
Belmont	Durham	£90	Including proceeds of night school
Branxton	Northumberland	£105	Do. do. and sewing mistress

Coanden	Cumberland	£65	—
Coundon	Durham	£125	Including sewing mistress and proceeds of night school
Harton	Durham	£115	Including proceeds of night school
Harwood	Durham	£85	Do. do.
Holme Eden	Cumberland	£70	To increase next year
Langleydale	Durham	£90	Including proceeds of night school
Lamplugh	Cumberland	£112	—
Leadgate	Durham	£115	Including sewing mistress
Stanley	Durham	£115	To commence in June – until then the arrangements are provisional
Startforth	Yorkshire	£90	—
Wantage	Berkshire	£100	—
Whickham	Durham	£75	To increase next year
		Assistant Masterships	
Hetton	Durham	£65	Including proceeds of night school
West Rainton	Durham	£65	Including night school

(PP. 1867 XXII, p. 426)

5E. A SCHOOLMASTER AND HIS ASSISTANT

New Jerusalem, Peter Street, Manchester, was the most important of the twenty Swedenborgian schools in Lancashire. It was founded in 1827 and extended in 1857; even more than the Rochdale Parochial School it represents the type of highly organised school developed to serve the skilled workers of the industrial north. It was in these schools that assistants first became common; but the situation at Peter Street was unusual. It is surprising that Mr Moss, unlike many of his contemporaries, did not sit the certificate examination when it began in the late 1840s.

This account was written in 1914 by R. Race who attended the school in the 1860s. His praise is confirmed by contemporary references. Peter Street retained its reputation when it was taken over by the School Board in 1880 and became the most distinguished of the Manchester Higher Grade Schools (below, p. 238).

. . .the New Church Society sought to educate children in order to prepare minds for their propagandist labours. No "conscience clause" restricted school management, so that Bible reading was taken as frequently as the headmaster chose. . . Each child was taught the New Church doctrines, and studied the Word as expounded in accord with these doctrines. The very writing lessons were utilised in this work by constructing headlines of doctrinal statements. Finally, children of the day school were compelled to attend the Swedenborgian church to which it was attached. . .

The school may be said to have entered upon a new era from. .[1857]. .not merely because of the enlargement of the accommodation, but because Mr James Scotson, who had been both scholar, pupil teacher, and uncertificated teacher under Mr Moss, gained his teacher's certificate in 1857. Now, Mr Moss was an uncertificated teacher; the Education Department was gradually eliminating such teachers . . . and Mr Scotson became in the eyes of the department the only recognised head. Having been brought up from childhood under Mr Moss, having a profound respect and affection for him, and fully recognising his ability and worth, it was impossible for Mr Scotson to oust his old chief from the appearance of headship with any degree of suddenness. We therefore find that for many subsequent years Mr Moss was generally regarded as chief and Mr Scotson as assistant; indeed this was carried so far that in making the annual statement of the school staff in the log book Mr Scotson placed Mr Moss first in the list and himself second every time until the year 1870. Hence the change produced by the new mastership was very gradual, and no pains were spared by Mr Scotson to prevent Mr Moss from feeling any indignity from the reversal of their positions. Scholars working in the school only saw an aging master relinquishing work and responsibility as his years advanced, while the young disciple took them upon his shoulders with ready loyalty; the former lost none of his dignity, and the latter never failed in according full respect to his veteran colleague.

It must never be forgotten, however, that Mr Scotson succeeded to a school already celebrated throughout the length and breadth of the land for its discipline, efficiency, system, and the soundness of the education its scholars received – an establishment whose secondary title, "Moss's School", which it never lost, pointed inevitably to the originator of its fame. . .

Indeed the general impression produced upon the children could not fail in its effect on their future life and the development of their character. They learnt that ambition need have no limits; industry and ability need never cease to climb. They found by experience that idleness and incapacity dragged people down, down, down, eternally; that one could not remain stationary; one must either make sufficient effort to rise, if only occasionally, or one must surely sink. . .

I remember that so far back as 1866 the subjects included reading, writing, arithmetic, geography grammar, object lessons in the lower classes, elementary science in the upper classes, and Scripture lessons, including Swedenborgian doctrines throughout the school. At one time the top class received a special course of lessons in political economy, and for several years boys in the same class could learn book-keeping on payment of an extra weekly fee of one penny. . .

In 1864 Mr Scotson gave a special series of lessons to the pupil-teachers in physical geography, but long before this it was customary for them to study Latin and mechanics. Whenever opportunity arose they were encouraged to attend lectures outside the school, such as those on chemistry at Owen's College by Professor Roscoe in 1866, and through a number of years the political economy lectures at the same place by Professors Jevons, Helm, Brewer and Adamson.

(*City News* (Manchester), 11, 18, 25/4/1914)

5F. PROBLEMS OF PUPIL-TEACHING

The letters reproduced below are two of the comparatively rare surviving expressions of opinion by pupil-teachers. F(i), printed in the journal connected with Cheltenham Training College, illustrates the sort of petty friction between master and pupil-teacher which was probably common enough; (ii) is a much more serious case of victimisation. Pupil-teachers apprenticed in schools other than those in which they were educated could find themselves in a position of great isolation. E.D. at least decided to go to the top, to the Yorkshire HMI, Frederick Watkins, who was much impressed by her letter. 'Who would doubt that the writer . . . is a young person whose heart and mind have both been strongly and beneficially influenced by her education at school. . .'; and he reproduced it to illustrate the ability and right-mindedness of the rising generation.

(i) Sir, – A short time ago I felt much discouraged by the conduct of my master, whilst teaching geography, I had, as I thought, well prepared my lesson, which was upon the motions of the earth. By means of diagrams drawn upon the black board, and the use of a small globe, I was endeavouring to explain, in as simple a manner as I possibly could, the causes of day and night and the seasons. I was just in the middle of my lesson, the children were listening with deep interest, and I felt delighted in imparting to them something which they were almost entirely ignorant of, when my master came up to the class, cleaned out my diagrams, and led the children's minds into quite a different channel. This I thought was really too bad; if he had taken up the same subject, or begun explaining some point which he thought I had omitted, then I should have felt glad; but as it was, I thought he cared little about my teaching, or the methods which I was employing. Masters, encourage, and not discourage, your Pupil-Teachers, and you will find they will work with more energy, interest, and cheerfulness.

By inserting the above in your valuable and useful periodical, you will much oblige

A PUPIL-TEACHER

(*Papers for the Schoolmaster* (1855–56), p. 168)

(ii) REVEREND SIR,

My father wishes me to write to you and ask your advice upon a subject that gives me great uneasiness. I am a pupil-teacher at St. — school, and am now in my third year. The schools became mixed in the early part of the year, and for some time I taught a mixed class, but since midsummer I have taught the first class of girls, and have had them *entirely to myself* in the girls' school.

I have had no system but my own to work by, no judgment but my own to depend upon; in short, I have just taught them as I liked. In the afternoon I have taught needlework to *all* the girls. The reason why I have had to do this is because we have had no mistress.

But this is not the worst. I have not had a lesson this year. I asked once if I might not receive lessons from the master, since there was no mistress, but was told that the Government would not allow girls to be taught by a master.

Now I think, in the first place, that it is very wrong to intrust me so young, and consequently so inexperienced as I am, with so important a charge; and, secondly, I think I shall not pass the examination. The Inspector will say, 'She is not qualified to teach what a girl ought to teach at the end of the third year;' and so I shall lose a whole year's salary besides a whole year's tuition, though I shall have had *double* the work, and *more than double* the care that I ought to have had.

Shall I be sent home at the examination, or might I be transferred to some other school? Please to send me your opinion upon the subject, and you will greatly oblige,

Your obedient servant,

Rev. F. Watkins. E.D.

(PP. 1857–8 XLV, p. 302)

5G. THE EDUCATION OF PUPIL-TEACHERS

Whilst the content of a pupil-teacher's studies was rigidly controlled by the official syllabus, the ability of a single teacher adequately to instruct him was often queried. The Education Department expected managers to remedy the deficiency and the more conscientious tried to do so, e.g., the vicar and curates of Kidderminster who taught Latin, German and mathematics to a pupil-teacher in the 1850s (PP. 1898 XXVI 417, qq. 7108–9). But this, like the Owen's College lectures at Peter Street, was external support. Signs of the recognition by teachers of the need to pool their resources, which ultimately produced pupil-teacher centres, began to appear in the later 1860s after the individual gratuities for instructing pupil-teachers had been abolished by the Revised Code. Two such experiments, by teachers 'who have given much time and trouble and have been put to some expense, with the sole object of improving their pupil-teachers', were described by an undenominational inspector of schools.

Proceedings of the Tyneside Association of Teachers

Twenty-one departments (including two national schools) are represented, and about 70 pupil-teachers with 20 candidates attend the monthly examinations, after which the answers in each subject are carefully marked by the teacher who set the paper, and are returned to the different schools, there to be again read by the candidates and their own teachers who point out and discuss the errors. The marks are carried forward to the final list, which is eagerly looked for at the end of the year. At Christmas 1868, of six pupil-teachers from these schools who competed for admission to training colleges, five obtained good places in the first class, and one was at the top of the second. These examinations have had the following good effects, – (1), they have in no small degree improved the pupil-teachers in actual knowledge, readiness, and style; (2), they have had a beneficial effect in making the pupil-teachers in outlying districts acquainted with their fellows in other schools, and in establishing an *esprit de corps* amongst them; (3), they have diminished the difficulty of obtaining suitable candidates by making the position better known and more popular, in fact this difficulty scarcely exists at all in these schools. It is remarkable that on no single occasion has there been an attempt to shirk an examination.

South Durham Association

A similar association was founded at the beginning of 1868 in Darlington, about 90 pupil-teachers from 43 schools belonging to it. The general plan does not materially differ from the Tyneside scheme, but it is worthy of notice that five Church of England schools are included, and that no objection on either side has hitherto been made to any of the questions on religious knowledge. One difficulty – the expense of travelling from the schools to Darlington – has been greatly lessened by the liberality of the directors of the Stockton and Darlington railway, who allow pupil-teachers and teachers to travel from any station to Darlington and back again, for the purpose of attending the examination, for sixpence only each time.

(PP. 1870 XXII, pp. 341–2)

5H. SUPERVISION BY A MANAGER

Managers were constantly exhorted to the duty of examining and assessing their schools. Reflections occasioned by these activities appear in the parish day-books kept by W. J. Butler, the famous vicar of Wantage. In 1865 his chief concern was with the state of the boys' school which had acquired a new master (Eley) at the beginning of the year (he was replaced at the end of 1866 (above, 5D)).

Tuesday April 4th [misdating: it was the 3rd]

Began the Ex^n of the Boys School, & carried it on to Wednesday, April 4th.

It is certainly inferior both in tone & knowledge to its usual average. The smallest Class are terribly backward & the first Class want style in their composition. They know neither Geography, nor Grammar, both which they knew in former years. I am seriously anxious about them.

Wednesday July 26th [Government inspection]

. . .The boys made more failures than last year – & were more restless & fidgetty than they should have been – Also some *would* 'look over' their neighbours – in spite of all warnings. The Ex^n began too late – 11-45 – & the day was very hot – This accounts for something. But I do not think that Eley is quite up to the mark.

Monday Dec. 4th

. . .Some murmurs about Boys School reach me. It certainly lacks the keen brightness of other years. The boys seem duller and less interested. Possibly the necessities of the revised Code have helped to bring this about.

[From the annual survey in which he recorded his successes and failures in 1865.]. . . The Boys School is not up to its usual mark, either in acquirement or intelligence. There is a want of smartness everywhere. This must be remedied else a long established character will pass from us & we shall feel very materially the deficiency at the Govern^t Ex^n in July. The Revised Code and its requirements has had a good deal to do with this – but I feel that with real care & vigour we might meet all this, & brighten the School as well. . . . The great material need is now an Infant School. We must work on towards this.

(Wantage Parish day-book, 1862–5, pp. 235, 259, 285, 293–4: Berks. CRO, D/P 143 28)

5J. A SCHOOL TREAT

Treats ranged from the simplicity of an afternoon of organised games to the elaborate outings to Hawkstone Park, Rhyl and Llandudno arranged by the LNW Railway for Christ Church Schools, Crewe. A particularly zestful account of a trip to Blackpool appears in the log book of Park Lane British School, Whitefield. Its patron, R.N. Philips, the Manchester Radical whose daughter married George Otto Trevelyan, supported the local brass band, providing a bandmaster and a band shed on the school premises for the benefit of both the adult and the school brass bands which figured largely in the trip.

Friday, July 8th, 1864

To day the School closed for the usual Summer vacation. . . To morrow (Saturday) nearly 400 scholars, parents & friends will have an Excursion Trip to Blackpool. Mr Philips, with his usual liberality, gives a large round of beef cooked which will be cut up and made into sandwiches for the Scholars bread being provided at Blackpool, I engaged a large room in the Waterloo Hotel, South Beach last Saturday for the accommodation of the party.

Saturday July 9th

The school trip to Blackpool was a complete success 386 Scholars, Teachers, parents and friends joined the excursion. We started from Clifton Junction at 6-30, AM, and arrived safely in Blackpool at 8-30. The party marched through the town preceded by the two bands which created quite a sensation, hundreds of people lining the streets and promenade, many cheering as we passed along. We arrived at the Waterloo Hotel at 9-30 and found everything ready for our comfort and convenience. The first thing done was to replenish the inner man, this took about an hour, Each then went out for enjoyment some to bathe, donkey and carriage riding, boating, Trip by the Steamer in the Channel etc. At 12-30 returned to the Hotel, served out the beef and bread to the scholars, each being amply supplied, and there being some left it was given to some old folks who had come with us. At 2 P M, took the bands on the Pier played a few selections; marched back; another rest; Out again at 5 returned at the call of the Bugle at 6-15, formed in procession marched to the Station, Left at 7-15 and arrived at Clifton at 9. Everybody seemed highly satisfied with the out, no accident of any kind occurred; The day will not soon be forgotten by those who went with us.

(Log book, Lancs. CRO SMPi, 2/1)

5K. HOW TO HANDLE PARENTS

In an age without compulsion school attendance depended upon the goodwill of parents; the question of how to enlist their support was therefore much canvassed. The following extracts from a prize essay by Mr Hobley of Brightwell, Berkshire, show that teachers fully understood, at least in theory, how good relations should be built up. But, in spite of the good sense, the characteristic air of conscious moral superiority might easily have produced friction in practice. The subject for the essay was 'How can the master best secure the cooperation of home influence with his work in school?'

. . .Ignorant themselves, and often unthoughtful, the parents look upon life as a period for providing only for their bodily wants, labour being its sole occupation; and so they consider their children in the same light, namely, as a number of beings born to go through certain troubles, to endure similar privations and toils and then to pass away. How grievously do they forget that in these children – their own offspring – talents and energies exist, which, if rightly brought out, would be productive of much happiness, and much usefulness to themselves and to others. And sadly, thoughtlessly, do they forget that they are placed here to be prepared for another and eternal existence. So the school is considered by them as only a convenient place, where their children can be put out of their way till old enough to earn a trifle towards their daily bread. Thus the work of the teacher is not prized or valued by them; the children are kept at home for the least excuse, and they are often late in their attendance; and no sooner does a chance of labour offer itself, than the child is at once and finally removed from the school, with his mind uncultivated, and his faculties not developed; and so the little smattering of knowledge he has picked up, soon vanishes away, and he descends to the level of his parents' ignorance, instead of helping to form part of a wiser and better generation.

Such, then, being the state of affairs . . . it is really of the utmost importance that the parent and teacher should *both* be on *one* side – the teacher's side – the side of good . . . But how? Let us consider that next.

1. *His general bearing towards the parents will either facilitate or hinder the attaining this object*. – Any prohibition to the parents, or dictating as to how they are to dress their children, &c., would appear to them an encroachment on their freedom of action, to which they feel they have an equal right with their superiors in station. He must endeavour to know the nature of the material upon which he has to work, the dispositions and peculiarities of the parents; and not forget that he cannot treat all alike; that he cannot adapt all the parents to the "Procrustean bed". . .

His own character must have a decided moral tone to it; he must be consistent, reasonable, gentle, and obliging; standing in high esteem among the parents of his scholars; behaving as one with whom they can safely entrust the care and instruction of their children; becoming as it were, for the time being, a parent to each child in his school. He must not exercise too much authority, or assume a lofty bearing towards the parents; but uniting firmness with gentleness and humility, gradually lead them on to listen to, and then to act upon, his admonitions and advice. . .

2. *His treatment of the children*. – . . .The teacher must endeavour to secure a place in the affections of his pupils; there must be a deep sympathy between him and them; his presence must be a source of gladness and happiness to them, and not one of reserve and fear; therefore, let him secure a place in their most agreeable associations, let him in some way be connected with that which gives them most pleasure. Then, through these things will he gain the parent; for having won over the child is the easist [sic] and most direct way to the parent's heart. Then . . . urge upon them the necessity of exercising care and pains with their offspring while young, that they may become, when they grow older, real comforts to themselves and all about them. Show them that they are best furthering the interests of their children by endeavouring to carry out, at home, the course of lessons, and the good moral influences, which have been begun, and are still being carried on at school. . .

3. *The Nature of the School-work*: . . .The instruction should be adapted to the resources and employments of the district. In a

mining locality, the nature and use of minerals and also mining operations should take a prominent place in the education of the child; near the sea, navigation, &c., should be attended to; and so on. Such subjects, if skilfully handled, will greatly interest the children; naturally, will they speak of them at home; and, the parents, finding that it is all connected with that employment in which they themselves are constantly engaged, will feel greatly interested also. Here "home lessons" might be made very effectual; they greatly encourage private study; they strengthen the school-work, and check loose and idle habits, by giving employment in the evenings, when, otherwise, the child might be lazily sauntering about the streets. . . The parents often take pleasure in rendering a little assistance to their children in this home-work; they take great notice of it, for they like to know something about what the child is learning; then, seeing how much it bears upon their future work and duties, they value it; they see its advantages; and so are gradually led on to take an interest in the improvement of the school. . .

4. *By Judicious Visiting.* – By occasionally visiting the parents, speaking to them kindly, listening to their complaints, and helping them in their difficulties; he may lead them to look upon him in the light, not of an hireling, but of one really anxious for their children's welfare. But his visits must be well-timed; he must go at the right *time*, in the right *way*, and not stay *too long*; he must avoid going when the father of the family, having returned from his work, is eating his supper; for the feelings of the poor must be respected, and they do not like to be visited at mealtimes. . . His visits should not be merely systematic calls, as if they formed part of his ordinary duty; for then that friendly regard, which is shown by incidental and occasional calls, might be destroyed. Children kept at home through illness, would certainly form opportunities of visiting. . . Again, kind enquiries after scholars passed away from school, and holding situations in distant places, will help to cement these friendly feelings between parent and teacher. Then, there are many little acts of kindness, that the teacher, by visiting, may be enabled to do for the parents themselves, which will greatly help to unite their good influences. Thus, a widow wants a letter written to an absent son: who can so well do this as the teacher? Again, an old man, near death, has a few things to leave, and wishes for a "will" to be drawn up, but cannot afford the

lawyer's fees: who can so well aid him in this as the teacher? Or again, an illiterate mother receives a letter concerning a situation for her son or daughter, but is unable to read it, from her ignorance and the indistinctness of the writing: who can so well decipher it for her as the teacher? These, and others might be mentioned, will all help to bear their weight and influence in leading the parents even to consider it a duty and a privilege to second the efforts of the teacher.

(*Educational Guardian*, 20/11/1860, pp. 174–7)

5L. MORAL INSTRUCTION

Log books abound in instances of zeal in the cause of moral and spiritual improvement. A few entries are given below; most teachers jumped at any opportunity which presented itself – even if, as at Crewe Green, it misfired. Most of the instances are self-explanatory; a note is added if explanation is needed.

(i) [A reaction to the Cotton Famine from R.N. Philips's schoolmaster]

10/10/1862

Closed the week's work by addressing a few words to the whole school on forethought, & industry. Alluded to the present distress of the Neighbourhood, enumerated a few examples of persons who by their habits of carefulness were enabled to hold up against the bad times, without appealing to the benevolent, or applying to the Parish for relief.

(Park Lane, Whitefield: Lancs. CRO, SMPi, 2/1)

(ii) *30/7/1863*

It having been announced that two females were to perform on a high rope at a circus which was to come into the town today, I spoke to the children of the sinfulness of attending such an exhibition.

(Stourbridge, St Thomas' Boys': Worcs. CRO, 250.6 BA1017/31)

(iii) *17/8/1863*

Gave the children some good advice respecting being honest over gleaning.

(Brackenfield C. of E.: Derbys. CRO, D83 C/EFI)

(iv) *25/2/1864*

The Rev. J. H. Thompson visited [with the Chaplain of Worcester Gaol]. . . The latter Gentleman very nicely explained to the children the folly of intemperate habits.

(Cradley N.: Worcs. CRO, 250.6 BA1244)

(v) [A master leaves after fourteen years]

24/3/1864

Gave my last advice to the School in the gallery on some important points, moral and religious – was pleased with their serious and affectionate attention.

(Penryn Wesleyan: Cornwall CRO)

(vi) *24/11/1864*

Spoke to the children about races find their parents went with them; and could not say much to them it was not their own fault.

(Crewe Green N.: Ches. CRO, SL38/2/1)

(vii) [Mary Anne Brett having died of croup, on the day of her funeral lessons ended early]

19/2/1867

. . .in order that I might speak to them of the uncertainty of the life even of little children. I intended also to have read to them the XIV chapter of St. John, a chapter that Mary Anne was very fond of spelling out by herself, but was prevented from so doing, by a strange lady entering and requesting that she might be allowed to speak to the school. After making a suitable address, she referred to the death of Mary Anne. The children seemed much impressed, and I think they will not readily forget their little schoolfellow.

(Stowmarket N. Inf.: Suffolk CRO, Ipswich, A402/1)

(viii) *20/5/1868*

Gave a lesson this afternoon to the whole school on the "hog" – with the object of impressing upon the boys the moral lessons of good behaviour cleanliness &c.

(Macclesfield Old Church (Duke St.) Boys: Ches. CRO SL74/3)

5M. PUPILS

The actual words used by elementary pupils were not often recorded. Matthew Arnold once reproduced a letter from a schoolgirl (F. S. Marvin (ed.), *Reports on Elementary Schools* (1910), pp. 122–3) and W. H. Brookfield, HMI printed the famous composition on the racehorse (PP. 1857–8 XLV, p. 385). The compositions collected in the Manchester Secular School (PP. 1857–8 XLVI 331) are disappointing; they are mostly mere recapitulations of lessons. The most interesting is included below as M(ii). The artlessness of M(i) suggests that it is a genuine confession. M(iii) is a letter written to J. P. Norris, HMI, by a boy who was absent during his inspection of Rostherne School, being one of ten pupils involved in a half-time scheme (cf. 4J) on Lord Egerton's estate. It might be said of this letter, as Arnold said of the one he published, that it bears 'the stamp of plainness and freedom from charlatanism' to be found in public elementary schools.

(i) *A Six-Year-old*

. . .The guilty boy persisted in asserting his innocence, though the most satisfactory proof of his having done it was given. At last he made the following statement which I took down in writing & he signed it

"I did throw a stone at the pump and did not mean to hit Mrs Slaney on the head. I did not mean to hit the window. I threw a piece of tile like what I have got in my hand. I am a bad boy for having told you so many stories. I told you I did not throw the stone because I was afraid you would punish me. I ought to be punished a dozen times on the hand to make me good."

(Whitwick N. Boys' Log Book, 18/6/1863, Leics. CRO, E/LB/364)

(ii) *An Eleven-Year-old*

I have on a velveteen jacket which is made of cotton, a cloth waistcoat, which is made of sheeps wool, and a pair of corded trowsers which are made of cotton, a calico shirt which is made of cotton, a blue and white striped neckerchief which is made of cotton, and a pair of woollen stockings, which are made of sheeps wool, and a pair of clogs, which are made of wood and leather.

(PP. 1857–8 XLVI 331, p. 30)

(iii) *A Twelve-Year-Old*

REVEREND SIR,

Mr HODGKINSON, our schoolmaster, told us that you had been here the afternoon that we were at work, and that you very much desired a letter from each of us, which we are all very glad to write. I'm sure we shall all be very glad to see you again this year if you come, and I hope we shall get a very good account, even better than ever we have got before. I have only been one year at field work last July, so I shall go on till this time next year, unless I am made a pupil-teacher. I don't know whether my parents will allow me, for Mr Gainsford* said it would not be advisable, as things were in such a very unsettled state. But I will now describe the half-time system. There are five boys on each side; two on each side of which are helping two men to feed up the cattle for sale, and another helping a man to cut hay for them, which is done by steam, and to boil turnips for the horses, and myself and another are doing odd jobs, such as cleaning turnips and mangle, and driving horses with the plough, and fearing birds off the new sown ground, and many other odd things. Our governor's name is Mr Henry Newhouse, who is very kind to us all. We are paid by him every Friday at one o'clock, but before we can receive our wages we must give him a certificate from our schoolmaster, and also before we can obtain the service we must have a certificate both from Mr Gainsford and Mr Hodgkinson to show that we are well up in our lessons, and have been good boys. I think I have now told you all about the half-time system, and every thing else that is worth mentioning, so I now conclude by remaining

Your obedient Scholar,

(PP. 1862 XLII, pp. 89–90)

* The clergyman; he meant the proposals for the Revised Code.

CHAPTER SIX

THE CURRICULUM

WHATEVER the scepticism expressed by later generations as to the value of education in voluntary schools, their sponsors had few doubts: 'To what but the spread of a sound and scriptural education can we attribute the improved tastes, the orderly demeanour, the patient endurance, the kindly sympathy, now so prevalent among the poorer portion of our fellow-countrymen and country-women?'[1]

The British and Foreign School Society's form of scriptural education consisted of daily Bible reading and study of the strongly pious contents of the society's *Daily Lesson Books*. Doctrinal statements were memorised in denominational schools with results of which such observers as W. H. Brookfield, HMI, frequently complained.* After the appearance of cheap readers from Dublin and from the societies, the Bible gradually ceased to be used as a reading book but the Department itself emphasised the importance of Bible study, refusing grants to schools in which it was not read daily. Theoretically, at least, religious instruction was as central to elementary education as was compulsory chapel in an Oxbridge college.

An elementary school existed, by definition, for the teaching of the elements; but these might be interpreted as either the basic knowledge appropriate for the poor or, as was the view of a number of educational reformers, the skills and knowledge basic to any education which the children of the wealthy picked up at home but which the poor could only acquire in school. The difference was more than one of emphasis; the second attitude opened possibilities for development which were absent from the first. Certain assumptions were, however, common to both. The 3Rs must be taught; apart from their utility they were the necessary tools of self-education. For girls, irrespective of social class, sewing was as much a necessity as reading. Beyond that point there was less agreement. Some general knowledge was usually considered desirable; so was knowledge relevant to the future careers of the pupils and to their moral development; and, ideally, this

*6A.

knowledge should be presented in a way that would stimulate their powers of thought. Out of these confused and pragmatic assumptions the elementary curriculum evolved.

The National Society's organizing masters, employed to raise schools to a minimum level of efficiency, assumed that as well as the 3Rs, sewing and music, the more advanced children should acquire a modicum of grammar and geography, the one supposedly necessary for the mastery of language, the other for the understanding of public events and for the future emigrant. It is possible to see that standards were gradually raised, by examining the criteria used by the inspectorate in classifying the schools which they visited. In his report for 1855, for example, Brookfield summarized what he expected of the top 20 per cent of children in a school classified as *Fair* – 'a school of average creditable kind, but with nothing to boast of'. They should be able to read a page of natural history and answer some collateral questions on it, to work a sum in compound multiplication and write an account of an object they had seen or read about 'with trifling errors of grammar and spelling'; to describe the distribution of land and water over the globe and name the counties of England and the kingdoms of Europe; and they should possess a knowledge of the leading incidents of Genesis and the Gospels and verbal accuracy in the catechism and a few texts.

By 1860 he demanded more. The children were expected to read intelligibly from a book like *Robinson Crusoe*, to have reached compound multiplication in arithmetic and to show a knowledge of measurement and a correct judgement of height and distance; and to write legibly and in fair spelling a composition about 'an animal or a railroad or a ship'. In addition, they should have a knowledge of the globe and of the topography of England and Europe and some knowledge of the animal, vegetable and mineral kingdoms. They should have learnt some elementary grammar and a little history and, finally, demonstrate that they knew the life of Christ and the ten commandments.[2] A *Fair* inspected school would have been above the general average for all schools; nevertheless, the elementary curriculum in its standard form had clearly evolved by 1860.

Of the 3Rs arithmetic had changed least. It remained what it had always been, computation and ciphering. The cost of arithmetic textbooks meant that most sums were either dictated or worked from the blackboard, though occasional instances of a more sophisticated approach are recorded: 'Drew up Cards for the four compound Rules 40 for each class, each card containing 6 sums where thought is required. This I find the easiest method of testing individual boys, as they cannot copy . . .'[3] Such 'slate arithmetic' (the term was often used in timetables) was clearly distinguished from mental arithmetic, which was much cultivated as a sure means of impressing visitors and parents.

The abandonment of the Bible as the instrument of teaching reading inevitably led to greater changes in this area.* In Kay-Shuttleworth's time official influence strongly favoured the phonic method; after he left the council office, HM Inspectors became noticeably more tepid in their advocacy, complaining that it was too often used without understanding. Simultaneously there were attempts to apply the principles of *Little Charles* to reading material for the poor; so that the classic rivalry of phonics and 'look and say' already existed in the 1850s. Most of the reading material at this time, published by the voluntary societies and the Irish National Board, was dull, stuffed with piety, information and long words, but bought because of its cheapness. Recognition by publishers of a potential market and the need for books simple enough to be read to HM Inspectors by the average child led, after the Revised Code, to an improvement acknowledged even by Matthew Arnold.[4]

The elementary schoolmaster, 'actively and positively teaching . . . from first to last',[5] was no longer able to prepare copies while his pupils 'learnt their book'. Consequently, when children graduated from filling their slates with words copied from the blackboard, they had to proceed to copy-books – luxuries whose expense brought about a decrease in the amount of time spent on copywriting. An official campaign to improve handwriting was, however, begun in 1854, after a complaint from Palmerston that the 'great bulk of the lower and middle orders write hands too small and indistinct, and do not form their letters'.[6] Dictation, as a means of testing spelling and accuracy, was general and composition was frequent in the higher classes.†

Singing had been common enough in monitorial schools as an accompaniment to organised marching round the barn-like

* 6B.

† 6C.

buildings; but the continental reformers who so much influenced Kay-Shuttleworth laid much greater stress on music as the sweetener of labour – their ideal was the merry peasant. Hullah began his classes in the late 1830s and his handbook and his classes for teachers were both subsidised by the Committee of Council in 1839–40; singing was everywhere encouraged in State-aided schools. Simultaneous encouragement came from Anglican efforts to increase congregational participation in church services. School children could be trained to take the lead – a purpose which explains why so many impecunious schools were nevertheless equipped with a harmonium. The Catholics – especially Cardinal Wiseman – laid even greater stress on school music; and all these influences ensured it a permanent place in most timetables.[7] It was chiefly singing, of what one teacher called 'Hearty, Merry, Moral Songs'; though the adjectives may not have been wholly appropriate to such ditties as *Rosalie the Prairie Flower*, in vogue in Cheshire in the mid-1860s.[8] A brass band, as at Park Lane, Whitefield, was a rarity. Drum-and-fife bands were less uncommon and might be associated with physical activities. The gymnastic apparatus placed in many playgrounds in the 1840s was usually left to rust away in peace, but some teachers, caught up in the Volunteer movement, introduced military drill into their schools in the early 1860s.[9]

The general knowledge deemed necessary for nineteenth-century living was provided through object lessons* and, in the higher classes, by geography, grammar and history, in that order of frequency.[10] These were, *par excellence*, the subjects for oral teaching. Geography, much the most common, included some physical geography but was mainly topography and map-drawing. 'Is it not ridiculous', said one indignant lady, after watching a class of girls draw the map of Europe from memory, 'to see girls who will probably be my servants taught to do that which I cannot do myself?' Occasionally a teacher might make the work topical, like the master who seized the opportunity of the Austro-Prussian War for lessons on the geography of Germany and Italy – 'the Seat of the War'. The boys, he added, were much interested.[11]

These subjects, together with sewing for the girls, formed the standard elementary curriculum. But the child who attended

* 6D.

regularly for several years had time for more. The possibility of giving him knowledge useful to society was obvious and attractive and led to the most successful nineteenth-century example of State influence on the curriculum. By the late 1840s the failure of attempts to improve the artistic skill of British workmen by means of evening classes in schools of design had been recognised; the schools had become the preserve of the middle classes. The idea of catching and instructing the future workman in his childhood seems to have occurred to a number of people,[12] but it was Henry Cole who, by firmly associating instruction in drawing with financial advantage, made it a subject as commonly taught as grammar or history. As early as 1855 the Science and Art Department reported that 18,988 children were learning drawing under its regulations.[13] The normal pattern was for lessons once or twice a week in preparation for the annual examination. Some ambitious day schools – St Thomas, Charterhouse and St Mary's Lambeth among them – had schools of art attached to them, with evening classes for adults.

Other forms of useful knowledge were of more general application than drawing. A combination of the Pestalozzian view that education should be based on things rather than words and the claim that a curriculum seen to be relevant to the pupil's future occupation would encourage attendance produced a vogue for 'industrial education'. Through practical work pupils would prepare for their vocations; their parents, seeing its usefulness, would send them to school more regularly; and they would learn, in the words of one committee, 'not only to *know* but to *do* well, morally & physically'.[14] Carpentry was the commonest handicraft, but the most popular areas of study for boys were agriculture and gardening.* A number of schools held classes in gardening; some developed agriculture on an elaborate scale, growing crops, keeping livestock and making and repairing equipment. More schools might have followed suit had it not been so expensive an innovation; most recorded examples depended on such patronage as that of the Lytteltons at Hagley for their survival.[15]

Much the same was true of 'girls' industry'. All girls learnt needlework and the provision of materials was expensive. Something could be gained by organising the sale of their work but, increasingly, the schools relied on supplies from 'the ladies'. Thus

*6E.

the girls of St Stephen's, Westminster learnt the basic stitches by making sets of child-bed linen for Miss Burdett-Coutts's charities in the slums.[16] Patronage was similarly important in a major innovation. Training in household work for girls about to go into service had been provided in many charity schools but the teaching of domestic economy primarly to prepare girls for their vocation as wives and mothers was characteristic of the Victorian desire to use education for the moral regeneration of society.* When the Birley family, for example, founded a free school in the Manchester slums they laid especial emphasis on domestic economy because of its civilising effects.[17] The teaching of theoretical domestic economy became increasingly common and was included in the curriculum of all the women's training colleges. Provision for practical work depended on the generosity of patrons.

Despite the claims of educationists there is clear evidence that, far from appreciating its relevance, most parents regarded practical work as an insult or, at best, a waste of time. The non-elementary subjects which they preferred were more conventional – navigation in coastal areas, surveying, commercial arithmetic and book-keeping and even, for the academically ambitious, a smattering of Latin and mathematics, taught to a few top boys in a number of schools, sometimes by the master, sometimes by the managers.

A conviction that in an age of progress education ought to extend beyond the elements was undoubtedly widespread.† If some parents demanded subjects hitherto only taught in secondary schools, many middle-class theorists preferred a curriculum geared to the realities of nineteenth-century society. Secularists, for example, favoured the teaching of social economy, as did the Irish National Board which included long extracts from Archbishop Whately's manual, *Easy Lessons on Money Matters*, in its reading books. The reason why classical economics was considered so valuable a study becomes clear from an abstract written by a nine-year-old at the Manchester Secular School: 'Generally the results of a strike are, that the people become poor, run into debt, spend all they have saved, and are thrown out of work, because their places are filled up with other people who are

* 6F.

† 6G.

willing to work for the wages they have refused, and by machinery.'[18] The Education Department tried to make the subject part of the certificate course and it was taught in schools of varying types: New Jerusalem, Peter Street, for instance, St Thomas, Charterhouse, Hagley and Lord Ellesmere's day schools in Lancashire.

But contemporary experiments in the teaching of science were more significant and more widespread. Their origins were various. Ever since the beginnings of Mechanics' Institutes science had been regarded as the form of knowledge most useful to the intelligent artisan. Practical subjects benefitted from the application of scientific information. The best agricultural schools taught chemistry; the best domestic economy included some physiology. More fundamentally it was argued that to include science in a religious education would ensure that it would be understood as part of the divine order, not as opposed to it; that, in Samuel Best's words, 'The book of Nature and of Revelation are but two volumes of one and the same Divine Author.'[19]

The work of the three major innovators in this field, Dawes, Henslow and Moseley, has recently been studied in detail.[20] Henslow showed that a combination of field work and uncompromisingly scientific method could lead ten-year-olds to a successful study of systematic botany.* Moseley's Bristol Trade School was a school of applied science, an experiment in technical education.† Dawes's 'teaching of common things' aroused the greatest interest at the time.‡ Essentially a community-based general science, having much in common with the Nuffield approach, it was often misinterpreted as the transmitting of scientific information, as a species of object lesson and, after enjoying a great vogue in the 1850s, went out of fashion. In fact, Dawes worked on the principle that education should stem from the child's urge to understand his immediate environment. Science played a large part simply because it satisfied natural curiosity. The purpose of the school should be to make the child 'observant and reflective'; knowledge was the tool by means of which this end was to be attained.

The range of scientific study in some schools, even after the Revised Code, was far wider than for later generations when 'nature study' was dominant.§ There is not much evidence before

* 6H. † 6J. ‡ 6K. § 6L.

1870 of influence from the Science and Art Department. Huxley's assertion to the Devonshire Commission that current scientific instruction was the result of a battle between two official departments was wide of the mark. Science was prescribed in the curriculum of a number of important schools – St Thomas, Charterhouse, for instance, and Abbott's Ann, St Stephen's, Westminster and the British School at Banbury, under Bernhard Samuelson's patronage.[21] Moreover it is clear that wherever someone was interested, science was taught. Sometimes it was a manager – the rector of Hagley, or Miss Maria Salter, the Baptist minister's daughter, who taught astronomy in Leamington British School. Sometimes it was a teacher – the master at Staveley, whose pupils kept a natural-history diary and borrowed his microscope to study their specimens; the Manchester teacher who regularly took his pupils to the park and the museum to look at the birds and to study their nests and their eggs; the master of a Kentish school who showed 'a few experiments to illustrate the workings of common pump, diving bell etc.'; or the Cheshire teacher whose course on astronomy was enlivened by discussion of phenomena as they occurred: the aurora borealis, shooting stars, the eclipse of 6 March 1867.[22]

Thus children who progressed beyond the lower classes might, if they were lucky in their school, encounter a great variety of non-elementary subjects. Some of the innovators were undoubtedly conscious that they were in fact experimenting with alternative forms of secondary education. When in 1854 Prince Albert sought advice on the structure of Wellington College, then about to open, he consulted four experts in elementary education, all of whose proposals were directly based on their elementary experience.[23] The concept associated with higher-grade schools of a non-classical, scientifically-biased secondary education, unaligned with the universities, has a long ancestry; whilst the criticisms of this concept which Morant and his associates were to voice in the early twentieth century were also anticipated in the 1850s. W. J. Kennedy, HMI, who repeatedly argued the case for separate schools for boys over the age of nine, would have limited their curriculum to language, mathematics, music and drawing: 'One great well chosen study, deeply pursued, both enables a youth to master all other studies, and serves as a nucleus round which other knowledge grows'.

He was bitterly critical of the popular current towards 'materialism . . . sometimes dignified with the name of science . . . Have the promoters of these views asked themselves what end they propose . . . Do they propose to cultivate, to educe, a MAN, or simply an ARTISAN?'[24]

Kennedy's curriculum resembled that of St Mark's School, Windsor, the creation of the Eton mathematics master, Stephen Hawtrey.* Although some science was taught in this school, the curriculum was centred on English literature and music, Latin and mathematics, subjects which, in the words of one pupil, 'turned his brain inside out'. There was none of the mechanical discipline normal in elementary schools. The boys and the staff ate together and went on holidays together; their relationship was intended to approximate to that of Eton boys and their tutors. St Mark's, though not much imitated, was publicised as a proof that the public-school ethos could be made to apply in the elementary system.[25] The demarcation lines of twentieth-century battles over the nature of mass secondary education were already being drawn before 1870.

Notes

1. British and Foreign School Society, *Annual Report* (1864), p. 30.
2. Summarised from PP. 1854–5 XLII, p. 501; 1860, LIV, p. 78; cf. 4H.
3. Crewe, Christ Church Boys, Log Book, 12/8/1863 (Ches. CRO, SL 370/4).
4. PP. 1864 XLV, p. 190.
5. Lingen's words: PP. 1852 XXXIX 337, p. 75.
6. PP. 1854–5 XLII, p. 18(n).
7. I. Taylor, "Music and the Victorian Elementary School", *History of Education Society Bulletin*, 18 (1976), pp. 44–52; O. Chadwick, *The Victorian Church*, Part 1 (1966), p. 519; *The Catholic School* (1849), pp. 51–3.
8. Castle Eden Colliery, Log Book, 25/1/1865 (Durham CRO); Audlem National, Log Book, 8/12/1863; Christleton CE, Log Book, 20/1/1866 (Ches. CRO).
9. See below, 7A.
10. Of a sample of 181 schools between 1863 and 1867, 75 per cent taught geography, 48 per cent grammar, 41 per cent history.
11. Cf. 4L; National Society, *Monthly, Paper*, (1855), p. 177; Grappenhall CE, Log Book, 26/6/1866 (Ches. CRO).
12. E.g., Canon Richson, of the Manchester and Salford Committee, who published manuals of drawing; Principal Rigg of Chester College whose

*6M.

drawing master, Ellis Davidson, produced a Science and Art Department manual; Bishop Short (see 6B), PP. 1852–3 LIV, p. 10; 1854 XXVIII 269, pp. xiv–xv.

13. PP. 1856 XXIV, p. xxviii.
14. National Society files, Finchley, 15/7/1847; for a fuller discussion see N. Ball, "Practical Subjects in Mid-Victorian Elementary Schools", *History of Education*, vol. 8, no. 2 (1979), pp. 109–20.
15. See 5B.
16. Society of Arts, catalogue of the Educational Exhibition (1854), no. 227.
17. PP. 1860 LIV, pp. 98–9 (St Philip's, Hulme).
18. PP. 1857–8 XLVI 331, p. 32.
19. S. Best, op. cit., p. 5.
20. D. Layton, *Science for the People* (1973), cc. 2–5.
21. Charterhouse, Abbott's Ann, *v.s.*; Society of Arts, *Report of the Committee . . . to Inquire into Industrial Education* (1853), p. 190; British and Foreign School Society, *Annual Report* (1856), p. 50.
22. Leamington British Girls, Log Book; Staveley, extracts, 18/3/1863, 19/3/63; St John's, Cheetham Boys, Log Book, esp. 6/8/1865 (Manchester Archives); Teston, Log Book, 30/3/1868; Grappenhall, Log Book.
23. See N. Ball, 'Education for life' in *Journal of Educational Administration and History*, vol. XII, no. 1 (1980), pp. 18–24.
24. PP. 1856 XLVII, pp. 359–62.
25. *The Times*, 2/12, 4/12/1858; PP. 1861 XXI Part III, p. 375. There is a recent study of Hawtrey by E. E. Cowie in *History of Education*, vol. II, no. 2 (1982), pp. 71–86.

Documents

6A. RELIGIOUS INSTRUCTION

Excessive zeal and fear of irreverence undoubtedly produced some very bad doctrinal teaching. Brookfield reproduced A(i) in 1856, lamenting that an eleven-year-old 'who wrote something pretty legible, intelligible, and sensible about an omnibus and about a steamboat, should, after the irksome . . . , the weary, the reiterated drilling of four or five years' produce such a version of his Duty towards his Neighbour'. A(ii), a report of a conversation in a Thames-side school shows that some teaching was more successful. If over-persistent questioning eventually drove the boy to a platitude, that was Brookfield's fault rather than his.

(i) My dooty tords my Nabers to love him as thyself, and to do to all men as I wed thou shall do and to me – to love onner and suke my farther and Mother, – to onner and to bay the queen and all that are pet in a forty under her, – to smit myself to all my gooness, teaches, sportial pastures and marsters, – to oughten myself lordly and every to all my betters, – to hut no body by would nor deed, – to be trew in jest in all my deelins, – to beer no malis nor ated in your arts, – to kep my ands from pecken and steel, – my turn from evil speak and lawing and slanders, – not to civet nor desar othermans good, but to lern laber trewly to git my own leaving, – and to do my dooty in that state if life, and to each it his please God to call men.

(PP. 1856 XLVII, pp. 346–7)

(ii) 'Tell me of any state of life to which it may, perhaps, please God to call you.'
'A waterman.'
'Well, how would you do your duty in that state?'
'Take no more passengers than the licence says.'
'Well, anything besides?'
'Behave civil to the passengers.'
'Anything else?'
'Land 'em dry on the other side.'
'Anything else?'
'Ask no more than the regular fare.'
'Anything else?'
'Keep some of the money for my father and mother.'
'Anything more?'
'Try to lead a good life.'

(PP. 1860 LIV, p. 89)

6B. APPROACHES TO THE TEACHING OF READING

The abandonment of the Bible as the primary reading book meant that methods of teaching reading could be examined more objectively than when the text was sacred; and most techniques used subsequently came under discussion in these years. B(i) is an account by Henry Moseley, HMI, of an experiment with backward readers at Greenwich Hospital School. B(ii) is an extract from an SPCK manual by Thomas Short, Bishop of St Asaph, an advocate of 'look and say'. B(iii) is an example of this approach, used by J. D. Glennie, inspector for the London Diocesan Board and subsequently HMI, for developing expressive reading. But B(iv), from a popular series of phonic readers of the 1860s, though showing a certain macabre realism, illustrates the gulf between Victorian and modern ideas of material appropriate for young children.

(i) . . . A new master was . . . appointed . . . called a reading master, and a room set apart for it, called the reading-room. Into this room all the bad readers were sent, to be exclusively occupied in reading all day long, until at length they should be able to read well; and, to ensure the requisite amount of individual labour for this object, they were broken up into small sub-divisions, each in charge of a paid monitor.

The experiment was, in an educational point of view, an instructive one. It resulted in an entire failure. Although the whole effort of the master and his monitors, and the whole labour of the boys, were concentrated on this one object of learning to read, – and with many of the boys it was continued from morning until night, for weeks and months together, – yet they made but little progress; matters remained very much as they were – they could not be taught to read.

It was plain that, in the attempt, some great educational principle had been violated, on which success depended. Shortly after the appointment of the present intelligent master of this class, Mr Connon, the exclusive instruction in reading was given up; other things were combined with it, calculated to interest the boys, to awaken them to the perception of a power to understand, and of a pleasure in understanding, and to relieve the monotony of the constant mechanical action of the faculties, whatever they may be, which find an exercise in reading. This plan, conceived with much judgment and sagacity, and carried out with great zeal by Mr Connon, has been successful. They spend now only a portion of their time in reading, but they learn to read far better than when they gave up their whole time to it; meanwhile their education in a higher sense, instead of being in abeyance, is proceeding . . . All the conditions of such an experiment appear to have been satisfactorily fulfilled. It was made on upwards of 100 boys, and continued upwards of two years. The conclusion is that boys are not to be treated as machines.

(PP. 1851 XLIV, p. 15)

(ii) We set the child to read a story, and do not exercise him in learning unmeaning symbols of sounds which convey no idea; and by reading the story it learns to read. The lessons are progressive;

but they are all stories, they are all sentences, having each some meaning; and through the meaning, which the child easily catches, we give him the habit of reading the words. We take it for granted that he does know English, and we endeavour to select such words as he does really know, and which he is in the habit of using; and by exercising him in these, we try to make him able to read any words.

(T. Short, 'Hints for Teaching Little Children to Read' quoted in J. Armitstead, *Parochial Papers*, V (1851), p. 310)

(iii) Look, children, there is a balloon going over the school.
Why, there is a man in the balloon.
Now don't you see the man putting out a flag?
Hark, I think he is calling. There, he is waving his flag.
I wonder whether he is calling and waving to us.
Do you think that man in the balloon knows us?

(J. D. Glennie, *Hints from an Inspector of Schools. School Needlework Made Useful and School Reading Made Easy* (1858), p. 30)

(iv) Tread gent-ly, for Fred says deaf Nell is very ill.
Nell can-not sip pleas-ant jellies or eat bread and
honey any more. Her head is as heavy as lead and
her breath is very hot.
Nell tosses in her feather bed and cannot rest.
The doctor said, that the hand of death is on Nell.
The clock has just struck six, and Nell is still very sick.
At last Nell is dead and gone to heaven.

(J. S. Laurie, *First Steps to Reading* (1862), pp. 42–3).

6C. COMPOSITION

The purpose of composition in Victorian schools was not to develop the imagination but to encourage the systematic arrangement of material and the accurate use of words. Subjects were, therefore, strictly realistic, as in C(i), composition at King's Somborne as described by Henry Moseley. C(ii), a letter from 'T', was published in a teachers' journal.

(i) All the children in the school, except five, write on slates; and all, except those of the lowest class, are accustomed to write, not only from copies and from dictation, but in some degree from their own thoughts.

Thus a child in the lowest class but one . . . is told to write the names of its brothers and sisters, of all the things in the house where it lives, of all the birds, or trees, or plants that it knows, and the like. Another stage in its instruction associates qualities with things. It is told, perhaps, to write down the names of all the white or black things it knows, of all the ugly or handsome things, or the tall or short ones, or iron or wooden ones. And then, when the child can write sentences, on the uses of things familiar to its observation – it writes of things used for the food of man or animals, used in building a cottage, or as implements of agriculture. Lastly, it is made to exhaust its knowledge of such things by being told to write down all it knows about them; all it knows, for instance, about sheep, or cows, or horses, wheat, iron, or copper, of the village of King's Somborne, or the neighbouring downs and hills, of the farms and holdings in the parish, or the parish roads, of the river Teste which runs through it, of the neighbouring town of Stockbridge, of Hampshire, of the island of Great Britain, of the earth, or of the sun, moon and stars.

To summon together the scattered elements of its knowledge of these familiar things, to combine them in a certain order, and to express them in written language, is an exercise which may be adapted to each stage in a child's intellectual growth, and which seems well calculated at once to accustom it to think, and to give it the power of expressing its thoughts in appropriate words.

(PP. 1847–8 L, p. 7)

(ii) *An Experiment in Teaching Composition*

. . . Soon after I took to this school, about a year ago, I got the bigger boys to bring me, sometimes, a short account of some simple operation in which they were in the habit of assisting their parents, such as reaping, hay-making, planting potatoes, &c. This home-work was written in the form of a letter addressed sometimes to me, and sometimes to one of their parents. In the writing of their task the boys were generally assisted by their parents, who seemed to take a good deal of pleasure in the business. But such letters it is almost impossible to imagine! Sometimes, too, I got them to write an account of what they had been doing in school that day, or of what they had seen in going home;

but none of their productions were worth anything. Frequently they began at the middle of the story and left off at the beginning, or else left out some very important part. I was very much puzzled in trying to alter this state of things, but at last I hit upon the following plan, which I have since found very useful.

One day I told the boys of the first class that I was going to try a new plan of writing dictation. At this piece of information they all seemed highly pleased, and each roused himself up, as though preparing to make a grand charge at the old enemy – Ignorance. I told them to watch me very carefully, and, after I had finished, to write down on their slates all they saw me do, in the exact order in which I did each thing. My performance was something like the following. I reached the easel, which I carefully placed before the class; then I got the black-board, which I fixed on the easel; after that I went to the box and took out a duster, returning with it to the black-board; I then took out of my pocket a piece of chalk, with which I made three straight lines on the board, then rubbed out the lines, shook the duster again, and returned each article to its place. "Now boys," said I, "you may begin, and, when you have finished, please to let me know, and I will look at your slates." To work they went as eagerly as possible, and by and by I was informed that they had finished. But, to tell you the truth, though I was not very sanguine about the matter, the work fell far short of my least sanguine expectations! Scarcely one deserved to be called moderate. One left out something, another gave me credit for doing more than I really had done, and *all* forgot to describe things in their proper order. I suspected the cause of this, and giving them more credit than I thought they really deserved, I told them that we would try again, and that next time they must observe my operations more narrowly.* This time we were more successful, and after a few more attempts, the performance varying every time, and done by one of the boys, they were able to show a very tolerable piece of composition. All this was done in the form of letters, properly headed and subscribed. This plan I carried out among the other classes that could write at all, in a simpler form, and have been successful. This exercise is done by the big boys only occasionally, for I find that

* Before they began writing I got a boy to stand up and go over orally what I had been doing, under the correction of the class. Thus they were better prepared. (Contemporary footnote).

they are now a great deal more accurate in their descriptions of things which they are required to give . . .

(*Educational Expositor* (1853), pp. 382–3)

6D. OBJECT LESSONS

Object lessons, deriving from a debased form of the Pestalozzian doctrine of *sense-impression*, were a normal part of the infant-school curriculum until the early twentieth century. Theoretically a discussion of a concrete object, they were frequently, in practice, a commentary on a picture or a blackboard drawing and were taught to the whole school, or a large section of it, seated in the gallery, standard provision in infant schools. D(i), a list of 'gallery lessons' taught at an infant school in one half-year, illustrates the bizarre lack of sequence to be found in many schools. D(ii) is a plan of an object lesson on a piece of calico from a certificate examination script which Muirhead Mitchell, HMI, thought creditable. The hiatus in the argument towards the end and the abandonment of the 'interrogative method' presumably reflect examination pressure.

(i) *Gallery Lessons, Winchester Central Infant School, January–July 1866*

The cow; the uses of the cow; the squirrel; the dog; the uses of various animals; the cat; sugar; tea; the rabbit; the sheep; the reindeer; the hedgehog; the elephant; the eagle; the kangaroo; tea; the canary; the leopard; the eagle; a quill; the pig; the camel; chalk; the monkey; the bear; butter; the hen; the caterpillar; the whale; the hen; the eagle; the reindeer; the horse; the kangaroo; the hedgehog; the rat; the badger; the whale; the toad.

(Log Book, Winchester City Archives: Hants. CRO, Education Box II, B XVIII, B/8/3)

(ii) What do you call this? yes, a piece of calico; what is the difference between this piece of linen and the piece of calico; the threads of the linen shine more than the threads of the calico; yes, this how we can tell linen from calico. Which is the strongest? yes, the linen is the strongest, but the calico is by far the warmest, and is very useful. To which kingdom in nature does the linen belong do you think? yes, it is a vegetable because it grows out of the ground, then I suppose calico is a mineral; no, calico is made of cotton taken off the apple tree; no, because every tree bears its own particular fruit; we do not grow grapes from thorns, or figs from thistles, so we can only get cotton from the cotton tree. Have you any cotton trees in your gardens? Why have you not? no, cotton does not grow in this country. Teachers, tell them where cotton grows; yes, it grows in India; in which quarter of the globe is India? yes, where Adam and Eve lived; how should you think it grows on the tree? yes it grows in large pods as large as the cocoa-nut; there is great pains taken to make it into nice calico; when it is taken out of the pods it looks very much like rough wool, and is combed or carded in India very much the same as wool is in England; it has then to be drawn out into threads, which is a deal of trouble; then these have to be divided into three or more, and then wound upon bobbins by machines which little girls manage, poor little things; they seldom get any learning; they are called factory children; and then it is woven into calico like this, and some is coloured and printed, which makes nice frocks and pinafores. Let us see whose frocks and pinafores are made of cotton; yes, how very nice to have such comfortable clothing; how thankful we ought to be to God for giving us the useful cotton tree.

(PP. 1851 XLIV 401, pp. 279–80)

6E. GARDENING

The Finchley National and Industrial Schools were typical of the attempts in the late 1840s and 1850s to develop an elementary curriculum with a practical bias. The following notes, drawn up in their first year, refer to the boys' school which aimed at a linkage of theory with practice. There were classes in botany, horticulture and some aspects of agricultural chemistry and the school grounds included a garden for medicinal plants and plants used in manufactures. The resolution quoted was carried out and the schools acquired a considerable reputation. In 1852 the committee published the four *Finchley Manuals of Industry*, text-books which quickly became popular. Thus in C. M. Yonge's novel, *The Daisy Chain* (1856), an heiress about to marry a missionary declares that she will 'go through a course of Finchley manuals' (Part II, chapter 23).

Scheme of Industrial Instruction in the National School of the Holy Trinity District in Finchley

Every boy aged 11 years or more has a garden of two poles, rent free, to cultivate for his own use; and keeps a debtor and creditor account of the value of the produce and of the expenses of his garden.

Every boy is employed one hour and a half in the afternoon, daily, except on Saturday, in cultivating his own garden, or in cultivating a plot of ground for the benefit of the school establishment, or in some other industrial occupation.

The boys are encouraged in working in their own gardens in play-hours and before and after school-hours.

The boys are employed in classes of four, alternately, every Friday, from 8 till 9 o'clock a.m., in cleaning knives, pumping water, and chopping wood, for the girls' industrial school.

Pecuniary and other rewards are given to those boys who cultivate most successfully their own gardens, who keep the best account of the cost and produce of their gardens, and who are most punctual in attendance.

On some occasions, when the boys work in the garden at extra hours, they are paid for their labour . . .

	Hours
Boys' school – hours per week, exclusive of Saturday	30
Industrial occupations	10½
Leaving for intellectual occupations	19½
Industrial on Saturdays	3

Resolved, – "That poultry, rabbits, and swine shall be kept by the school, and tended by the boys; that sheds, hutches, and styes shall be constructed by the boys, with such help as may be provided; that a mill be provided, with which the boys shall grind corn; and that the boys shall be employed in mending shoes and clothes, and in knitting; provided always that the boys shall follow these occupations in the fixed industrial hours, and that they shall be pursued under the direction of the master, with such help, and subject to such orders, not opposed to the principle of this resolution, as the treasurer may at any time direct."

(PP. 1850 XLIII 241, pp. 70–72)

6F. DOMESTIC ECONOMY

The most celebrated of the fairly numerous girls' schools which taught domestic economy was at Sandbach, where the vicar, John Armitstead, and his son and successor made the teaching contribute to the work of the parish and the parish, in turn, solve the knotty problem of financing an expensive subject. The system described by Armitstead in 1857 was still operating in the 1870s; some other experiments, e.g., that described in S. Austin, *Two Letters on Girls' Schools* (1857), were less secure financially and less long-lived.

To the Editor of The Times

. . . I . . . crave the aid of your universal circulation as a medium of reply to many inquiries concerning the system adopted in this parish and the results which have attended it . . . [girls'] avocations . . . admit of instruction at school of a better kind than can be had at home. The most important and of every-day necessity are dressmaking, to the extent of cutting-out and making their own clothes, washing and getting up fine linen, household work and cooking. The method we have adopted has been as follows:-

1. Dressmaking.– Having laid in a stock of materials at wholesale prices, of suitable texture and patterns, we invite the children, nothing loth, to make their own selection. The pupil-teachers and elder children, under the direction of the mistress, cut out the dresses, and each child, as far as it is able, makes its own. When completed they are fitted and tried on before the class, and upon payment by instalments, or otherwise, given to the children to take to their parents. The charge is carefully calculated upon the prime cost of the material, and an account sent home with each article . . .

2. Washing. – . . . the schools are in the centre of the town, and consequently confined in space. The area of the washhouse is only 25 feet by 15 feet . . . in which we contrive to get in one compartment a washhouse; beneath it a tank for rainwater from the roof of the schools; a well with pump for spring water in one corner; along two sides 12 washing-boxes, convertible by letting down a cover into ironing-tables; three boilers. . . A cistern . . . to receive spring water from the pump, at a sufficient elevation to

convey it also by means of pipes to the washing boxes. . . The other compartment embraces a drying closet, space for mangle, and staircase, with room over it, for heating the irons, and airing the clothes. . . The children bring their own clothes in baskets the beginning of each week, which are returned as soon as they are completed. A laundress was employed at first to teach them, but of late the pupil-teachers have been found fully equal to the duty.

3. Household Work. – This is taught to the pupil-teachers and elder children by admitting them in rotation for a week at a time into the master's house, which, as six or eight young people are boarded with him and form part of his family, affords an excellent opportunity for initiating them in the ordinary matters of domestic economy.

4. Cooking. The culinary department will require greater details, which I enter into more willingly . . . from the experience I have gained how much in connexion with a school it may be made to supply a want most painfully felt in almost every parish in the kingdom. If there is one thing of which our poor stand in need more than another it is suitable nourishment in the time of and upon recovering from sickness. . . How often are relapses experienced from the use of improper food, or, what is pretty nearly the same thing, food roughly and improperly prepared! . . . To supply what is wanting the following plan has been adopted. . . For a kitchen a shoring has been raised, 10 feet long by 4 feet wide, in connexion with the master's house. In it a small gas stove has been placed . . . which, with the addition of a few saucepans, completes the apparatus; for with the aid of the stove, small as it is, a dinner may be cooked for 20 people. . . At first, for a few weeks, an experienced person was required to instruct the pupil-teachers in the art of cooking. Now they are able in their turn, a week at a time, to do everything. It is an occupation they like very much. . . They have four books to keep, – an order, waste, cash, and delivery book, and thus acquire a knowledge of bookkeeping as well as of domestic economy, in the purchase of meat and other necessaries, and the best method of preparing them; and above all, they learn to sympathize with the poor, to whose wants it is their privilege to minister. . . The order book is always open for the clergyman, the medical men, and district visitors to enter in it the names of

such as stand in need of help . . . their title to help, of whatever creed, necessity. All that they are called upon to do is to acknowledge the receipt daily in the delivery-book provided for the purpose. The offertory, alms'-box, and private subscriptions supply the necessary funds.

The principle which has guided us throughout has been to make employment acceptable to both parents and children, by making it in every instance beneficial. The children make and wash their own clothes, and have their dinners given when employed in the cooking department in reward for their trouble. . .

Food Supplied to the Sick During 15 Months, Ending Christmas, 1856

Dinners of	roast mutton	610	Puddings. – Rice, sago and tapioca	134
–	Boiled	48	Gruel. – Arrowroot & meal, quarts	38
–	Hashed & sippets	131	Beef tea, ditto	4
–	Minced ditto	24	Soup, ditto	1380
–	Mutton-chops	102		
–	Roast beef	100		
–	Minced ditto	22		
–	Boiled ditto	9		
–	Irish stew	9		
–	Cold meat and mashed potatoes	150		
–	Fish and rabbit	4		

(*The Times*, 5/6/1857)

6G. PROGRESS AND THE CURRICULUM

The naïve faith in progress which led many managers to extend the curriculum beyond the elements is well reflected in this passage from the *Annual Report* for 1856 of a small Wesleyan school.

. . . The world has rolled onward – Truth and Religion, Virtue and Morality, Art and Science, have cried onward. The rich territory of intellect is laid open, and the golden mines of thought are accessible to all. Our Scholars are now invited to soar high, and walk the paths of science, talking with freedom of yonder stars, telling of worlds of which their forefathers never dreamed, to ascertain at their own fireside by the lightning flash passing events in distant lands, to descend into the earth, and there explore the mysteries of ages past, to master the Surveyor's Chain and Euclid's Elements, to sketch nature with the utmost ease and facility. To become proficient in these and other subjects of a useful and practical nature is the privilege of the rising generation of the present day. . .

(Salisbury Wesleyan School, *Annual Report* (1856))

6H. INNOVATIONS IN ELEMENTARY-SCHOOL SCIENCE: BOTANY

Professor Henslow, Darwin's teacher, taught botany in his parish school at Hitcham in Suffolk by the methods which he used with Cambridge undergraduates: field work followed by systematic investigation in the classroom (for his work-plan, see Layton, op. cit., p. 66). His pupils, mainly girls, because the boys left early for farm work, became sufficiently good field botanists to collect seeds for Darwin's use. The success of such an uncompromisingly scientific approach attracted attention in the Education Department which asked him to prepare a set of 'Illustrations to be Employed in Practical Lessons on Botany'. In spite of this official interest it is usually said that Henslow was only imitated in some public schools, e.g., Marlborough and Rugby under Temple; but see 6L, below. The following passage is from a series of articles written by Henslow in 1856.

Practical Lessons in Botany for Beginners of all Classes. III

HERBORIZING EXCURSIONS – Occasional walks for an hour or two with the children of the first class afford important opportunities for awakening curiosity and imparting information. Sunday walks after divine service admit of the party being joined by some who have left school, but retain a desire for improvement. As a general stimulus to exertion, a pic-nic excursion or two during the summer should include all who have shown an interest in the pursuit, by regular attendance at the lessons and by obtaining a sufficient number of good marks for their botanical exercises. . . I do not envy the feelings of any opponent of popular instruction who could regard with indifference, much less with aversion or scorn, a party of village children actively engaged in examining the results of a half-holiday's research, appeasing good appetities with (to them) a little extra fare, and winding up a happy afternoon with a cheerful song, a thanksgiving hymn, and the national anthem. Such children are not likely to be worse prepared for the more staid proceedings of the morrow's school-room . . . the knowledge which some children have obtained of our native plants is certainly remarkable. They soon learn to recollect what species may have been exhibited, and by whom, on the plant-stands.* They generally know when they have found one new to the plant list. Walking one day through the village, I heard some one running after me, calling out "Mr H., Sir, Mr H.". Turning round, I found a zealous little botanist (M. S., 12 or 13 years old) holding out a bunch of flowers, her features all animation – "A new plant for Hitcham, Sir." "So it is! to what order does it belong?" "Composites." "What genus of our Hitcham Composites does it most resemble?" After a slight examination, the reply was, "Coltsfoot." "You are quite right. But, as you have never been shown the actual genus to which it does belong, I must tell you it is called 'Fleabane'. I don't know the English name for this species of Fleabane, but I will find it out, and tell you more about it when I next visit the school." The plant was 'Erigeron acris". . .

HARD WORD EXERCISES – With young children (perhaps with most beginners) it is advisable to devote a lesson occasionally to the express purpose of showing them how to master the orthography, as well as to obtain facility in the use and application of a botanical terminology. . . One of the first lessons of this description (and there need not be many) should show how the "floral whorls" may be expressed *botanically* in regard to the number (whether actual or apparent) of their subordinate parts. As soon as the first lessons on the floral whorls have sufficiently impressed the fact, that a flower *may* consist of Calyx, Corolla, Stamens, and Pistils, the corresponding adjective terminations "sepalous", "petalous", "androus", "gynous", may be pointed out. If the young botanical volunteers are told they must not expect to accompany the next pic-nic expedition, unless they shall have learnt to spell correctly these four terminations, their slates, in a day or two, will present an amount of orthography which would

*Part of the schoolroom equipment.

surprise persons unaccustomed to witness the facility with which children master difficulties of this character. . .

(*Gardeners' Chronicle* (1856), p. 500)

6J. INNOVATIONS IN ELEMENTARY-SCHOOL SCIENCE: APPLIED SCIENCE

In 1853–4 Henry Moseley planned the Bristol Trade School for the local diocesan board as a deliberate experiment in technical education. After his retirement from the inspectorate in 1855 he supervised it from his nearby parish of Olveston for the rest of his life. There were initial problems and the first master left in 1856; but it prospered under his successor, Thomas Coomber, who had studied science for his certificate at Cheltenham Training College and then gone with an exhibition to the Royal School of Mines. The lower school gave a general education, with some science; the upper, in which most of the time was spent on science, consisted in 1867 of fifty-six boys. The Taunton and Devonshire Commissions both took evidence on the school, as did the Select Committee on Scientific Instruction of 1867, the source of these extracts. They refer only to the day school. There was a flourishing evening school of science (140 pupils) and the school also provided classes for engineers and managers in the South Wales mines.

(HENRY MOSELEY) The declared objects of the school were to teach the boys what is called industrial science; science as applied to industrial pursuits. . . I ascertained from the directory what trades or manufactures were carried on in Bristol . . . which admitted of the application of science with advantage . . . and told the supporters of the school that boys intended for such pursuits would derive very great benefit from knowing the sciences connected with them. Those sciences came under certain general classes; each class . . . would be applicable perhaps to many trades. The idea was to make the school a school in which those industrial sciences were carefully, laboriously and thoroughly taught, as far as they could be carried. . . Boys were accustomed to learn Latin in the old grammar schools, and we wanted to bring science into the place formerly occupied by Latin. . . It was a substitution of one thing for another, with the belief that as much as was achieved in the one case might be achieved in the other . . . the social condition of the boys has risen from the ordinary class of artificers to the first class of artificers, taking in the little tradesmen class, and warehousemen, and overseers, and clerks. . . These may be described as the natural leaders of the working classes . . . the boys generally remain till 14 or 15 years of age . . . we require them to be well instructed in reading, writing, and arithmetic [on entry] . . . but still . . . if they received no more instruction in those subjects than they possess when they come to us, it is probable that when their scientific instruction was completed they would leave school imperfectly educated; we therefore keep up that kind of instruction.

(THOMAS COOMBER) We teach chemistry, organic and inorganic; theoretical and applied mechanics, and experimental physics, including electricity, magnetism and heat; we do not teach acoustics and light, inasmuch as our pupils have no use for them; we also teach descriptive geometry, by which I mean the descriptions of planes and solids, and apply it to the construction of machinery and building, and mathematics. . .

We have four masters: I teach chemistry, electricity, magnetism, and theoretical mechanics; the second master teaches the drawing subjects and the applied mechanics; the third master teaches English, and devotes his attention to mathematics; the fourth master gives instruction of an elementary character in the lower school. . .

The fee for the school is £3 per annum; every subscriber of £3 has the power of nominating a boy to the school without the payment of fees; that is to say, we call on every boy to bring into the school, either by himself or by his friends, £3 per annum. The nomination of a subscriber of £1 would relieve a boy of the payment of one-third of the school fees; of two such subscribers, of two-thirds; and three such nominations would enter him free. . .

. . . the laboratory is used, firstly, for the purpose of the experiments which illustrate my lectures; secondly, for my private work; thirdly, for the education of the pupils in practical chemistry at night. . .

. . . I intend to recommend the Committee to set up a carpenter's bench, with a tinman's bench, with lathe, tools, and so on . . . for almost all my boys are now at work in making experiments which illustrate the science they are studying. I am so strongly convinced of the value of that, that I am disposed to foster it all I can; namely, to teach the boys to handle tools, so that they can make their own experiments. I had to learn it myself; and I look upon it as one of the faults of my original training as a teacher of science that I was not prepared in that respect. . .

The school is growing, and I think we shall grow with the demand. . .

(PP. 1867–8 XV 1, pp. 192–9 (Moseley), 199–206 (Coomber))

6K. INNOVATION IN ELEMENTARY-SCHOOL SCIENCE: COMMON THINGS

The popularity of 'Common Things' in advanced educational circles in the 1850s is shown by its appearance at St Mark's, Windsor, in spite of Hawtrey's bias against natural science. This examination paper illustrates the topical approach advocated by Richard Dawes. It survives because Hawtrey reproduced it in one edition of his account of St Mark's as an example of the work of the school's lithographic press.

Christmas Examination 1857

ON COMMON THINGS

"The Air we breathe"

1. What is Atmosphere? How high is it at least? Why does the Air become more rarified as we ascend mountains? Why cannot water be raised by a pump more than 30 feet above the surface of a well? Describe the construction of the *Barometer*.
2. What is the pressure of the Atmosphere on a square inch of surface? Assuming the surface of the skin to be 2000 square inches, what is the pressure on the human body? Why are we not crushed by it? Why does a sucker hold up a stone, and a cupping glass draw in the flesh?
3. What are the two gases of which common air is composed? Are they mixed or combined? What are the apparent purposes of each?
4. Explain the action of *Respiration*: What change does the Air undergo when taken into the lungs? Why is it unwholesome to remain in crowded and unventilated rooms?

5. What gas is given off by heating Chlorate of Potash and Oxide of Manganese? How can the presence of this gas be ascertained?
6. If a piece of Phosphorus be burnt in an inverted vessel the mouth of which is dipped in water, how high will the water rise in the vessel by the time the Phosphorus ceases to burn? What is taken out of the Air? What remains? What does the above experiment teach us? If a lighted taper be now placed in the vessel what will be the effect? and why?
7. What is Carbonic Acid? From what source is the Air constantly impregnated by it? How is its superabundance got rid of? Why does the number of leaves on trees amount to millions?
8. What is *choke-damp*? Where is it formed? Mention how to proceed in cases of accidents arising from "choke-damp". Give an account of the "Grotto del Cane" or the "Poison Valley" in the Island of Java.

(S. Hawtrey, *A Letter Containing an Account of St. Mark's School, Windsor* (2nd edn, 1859))

6L. ELEMENTARY-SCHOOL SCIENCE: THE SPREAD OF IDEAS

The impact of curricular innovation upon ordinary schools is often hard to trace; but the two passages which follow provide an example. The Lyttelton family (see 5A) were unusual in the extent to which they saw progress in elementary schools in the context of general educational progress; in L(i) the influence upon the rector of Hagley of his elder brother's experience as a member of the Clarendon Commission is obvious. The meeting which occasioned his letter (originally printed in *Berrow's Worcester Journal*) had some success. At least one of those present, Thompson, decided to follow Henslow's pattern (see 6H). L(ii) is a summary of entries in the log book of the school in his parish in the Black Country, which shows his persistence in an obscure area of botanical study.

(i) Sir; – You have asked me for some account of the meeting which met here by my request on November 30th. It consisted of the following members of the Worcestershire Field Club, besides myself: – Mr Edwin Lees, one of its Vice-Presidents, Mr Wm. Mathews, of Edgbaston, its Secretary; Mr Richard Smith, of Droitwich; the Revds. F. J. Eld, of Queen Elizabeth's School, Worcester; W. Lea of Droitwich; and J. H. Thompson of Cradley. Besides these, the Rev. H. Sandford, her Majesty's Inspector of Schools in this district; and Mr John Jones, of the South Staffordshire Adult Education Society were also present. The object of the meeting was to consider what means might be adopted for promoting the teaching of the elements of Natural Science in schools for the working classes. . .

If we are to reach much real success in moulding our pupils, it must be by first carefully studying their peculiar natures and tendencies, and accommodating ourselves to them.

Now experience has, by this time, abundantly demonstrated that in human beings in all classes of society there will always be found several distinct *types* of mind, whose inherent tendencies, imposed upon them by their Creator, cannot, by any interference from without, be interchanged. . . This . . . was illustrated in some rather novel ways in the valuable evidence given by some of the greatest authorities in physical science, before the Public School Commission (which well deserves the careful consideration of all promoters of education). These great authorities drew attention to the important truth that, besides the minds which are drawn by nature towards the study of language, and of what are called the classics, and besides those whose nature impels them rather to pure mathematics and abstract science (the only two for which, till quite lately, much provision has been made in our Universities), there is another considerable class who are attracted by the *applied sciences*, or, as they denominate them, the "*sciences of observation*", and would not be so by any other. . .

Now this evidently applies quite equally to our brethren of the working classes. The counsel which. . . Sir C. Lyell, Professors Airy, Owen, Faraday, Hooker, Carpenter – no light names – so strongly urge upon the public mind, namely, that if we wish to see gentlemen pursue the study of science at the Universities, and in after life, it would be wise . . . to teach at least the elements of science . . . at our public schools – this counsel evidently applies equally to our management of schools, institutes, people's colleges, &c., &c., for the working classes. . . Let it be observed that it is not at all necessary for this purpose that the knowledge of these subjects which we give during childhood should be complete, or even very accurate; the point to be aimed at is to give our pupils *a taste for the subjects*, to open their minds to their interest. Thus Professor Airy . . . says: – ". . . It is astonishing how much the education of the mind comes, not by precise book-studies, but by little things which boys are able to observe, and upon which the mind feeds unconsciously afterwards."

All this applies even more to the case of children of the labouring classes, because their work in after life is to be, not literary, but practical, and among the great objects of nature to which physical science relates, and to which it gives so deep an interest. Our object ought to be to teach these children that there are things to be thought about, not only in books (as I fear they often suppose), but also, and still more, in all nature around them. . .

Now, as to the practicability of giving such instruction in our National Schools, I am able to appeal to experience, not to mere *a priori* theory. I have long made it my object to do so in my own village school. I have given the elder boys and girls some little instruction in the first elements of a few sciences. For instance, one year it has been human physiology and the elements of sanitary sciences; another, elementary and local geology; and always they have learnt a little drawing (taught by my curates, who have, happily for us, happened latterly to be no mean artists), a little carpentering and turning, a little gardening; and we have succeeded without the least difficulty in rousing many of them to a lively interest in these subjects. They stood a very good examination last year in the elements of sanitary science, and this year (as well as a few years ago) they were examined by Mr. W. Mathews, of Edgbaston . . . in elementary geology, and passed, in his opinion, very creditably . . . I know that many will be ready to object that the time . . . would be better applied to simpler matters – as, for instance, the study of the redoubtable "three R's"; and that inasmuch as a knowledge of those "three R's", and a fourth of infinitely greater importance – religion, is indispensible for obtaining Government money, we cannot expect schoolmasters to prefer the former to the latter. But this objection is grounded upon some great fallacies. It assumes that the hour a week which is devoted to such studies (and that is all we have ever devoted . . . to the teaching of physical science in

Hagley School, as it is also all which Professor Owen thinks need be given in public schools) is wasted so far as the "three R's" are concerned. But the truth is (as my own experience at Hagley, and that of Professor Henslow at Hitcham, and, I doubt not many other instances might be added, abundantly demonstrate) that the diversion of the time and energy that would have been given to the mere drudgery of the "three R's" to these other subjects is much more than compensated by the increased power of mind for reading and writing, as well as for every other work, which is the consequence of the greater breadth of intelligence, the greater liveliness of mind, the keener pleasure in the use of the mind – in short, the powerful *gymnasticising* of all mental powers, which is the fruit of the hour a week devoted to such studies – I remain, Sir,

yours faithfully W. H. Lyttelton

Hagley Rectory.

(National Society, *Monthly Paper* (1865), pp. 165–8)

(ii) *29/9/1865*

Thirty of the scholars were taken by the Rev. J. H. Thompson to Abberley valley for a pleasure Trip, and it passed off very successfully.

1866

12/2 The Rev. J. H. Thompson said that the scholars might begin to pay to the Schoolmaster their pence to the amount of one shilling for an excursion to Hartlebury Common in March or April next.

6/3 The Rev. J. H. Thompson took five girls of the First Class from 9-35 to 12 a.m. and eight boys of the same class from 2-30 p.m. to 4-30 p.m. to the Night School Class Room and gave them Lessons on Mosses.

[Thompson's subsequent lessons on mosses starred and summarised]

**12/3*	2-15 to 4 p.m.	First Class
**2/5*	11 to 11-55 a.m.	4 scholars

4/5 The Rev. J. H. Thompson took thirty of the Scholars who had previously subscribed a shilling each, an excursion to Hartlebury Common, accompanied by myself & other teachers. The children partook of tea at the Infant School on their return & went home at 9-30, after enjoying a pleasant day's recreation. I left the rest of the scholars in charge of the Pupil Teacher. The excursionists were chiefly engaged in gathering mosses.

**7/5*	– –	4 scholars
**11/5*	2 to 5 p.m.	7 ,,

5/6 The Rev. J. H. Thompson visited the School at 2 p.m. & planned an Excursion for those who wished partly to pay for it.

26/6 [from HMI's report] The elder scholars frequently employ themselves in collecting botanical specimens for a museum which has had a good effect in drawing out their intelligence.

21/8 The Malvern excursion for the Day Scholars has proved a failure through apathy on the part of the children and their deposits were returned this morning.

1867		
**27/2*	All morning	12 scholars.
**28/2*	10-15 to 12 noon	12 ,,
**13/3*	3 to 4-30 p.m.	4 ,,

1/4 54 of the elder scholars were taken an excursion to Pedmore Common accompanied by five Teachers. The subscription was 2d. The children were taken from Cradley to Stourbridge by Railway, 2nd class fare 4d. The scholars were each given an orange at Stourbridge.

**11/4*	9-30 to 12 noon, 2 to 4-30 p.m.	5 scholars.
**15/4*	,, ,, ,, ,, ,, ,,	6 ,,
**16/4*	10 to 11-45 a.m., ,, ,, ,,	7 ,,
**3/5*	11-30 to 12 noon	2 ,,
**10/5*	9-30 to 11-30 a.m.	2 ,,
	2-15 to 4 p.m.	3 ,,
**14/5*	11-15 to 12 noon	8 ,,

15/5 [from HMI's report] I am glad to find many of the Scholars take still an intelligent interest in collecting botanical specimens.

24/5 Five of the First Class Girls were taken by the Reverends J. H. Thompson and T. H. Gregge to Rowley Regis for an excursion.

**31/5*	9-45 to 12 noon	5 scholars
**10/10*	'during the morning'	2 ,,
**17/10*	– –	3 ,,
1868		
**16/1*	9-30 to 11-30	2 scholars
**21/2*	9-30 to 12	6 ,,
**3/3*	,, ,, ,,	6 ,,
**10/3*	10 to 12 noon	4 ,,
**19/3*	9-45 to 12	6 ,,
**30/3*	9-30 to 12, 2-3 p.m.	13 ,,
**21/4*	All day	All First Class Girls.

8/5 [from HMI's report] The botanical collection made by the children shows great neatness; it would be well if English equivalents for the Latin names could be given.

[After this, records are only occasional. Perhaps Thompson tired of teaching or the master of recording. More probably it resulted from a decline in the attendance of older children commented on by HMI in 1870.]

(Log Book, Cradley National School, Worcs. CRO, 250.6, BA, 1244)

6M. LIBERAL EDUCATION IN AN ELEMENTARY SCHOOL

Stephen Hawtrey founded St Mark's School, Windsor, in 1846 in a cottage converted by the first pupils. Whilst teaching the 3Rs (using, as reading books, cheap editions of Scott and similar authors) his primary aim was to introduce his pupils to humane studies in an atmosphere of confidence between teachers and taught. He prided himself on the physical conditions – he provided 400 cubic feet per child when the Education Department demanded eighty – but St Mark's fitted easily enough into the government system, being much praised by HMIs and producing an exceptional number of pupil-teachers. Most pupils were working class, only seventeen of 228 admissions being described as of a 'superior grade'; and Hawtrey was at pains to show, by publishing letters from parents and employers, that their education did not make them discontented with jobs as artisans or tradesmen. The following extracts are from an account originally written in 1857; see also Hawtrey's *St Mark's by the Sea* (1861) and *A Narrative-Essay on a Liberal Education* (1868).

. . . We retain the children at school quite as long as can be expected; and we keep up a connexion with them after they have left school.

And how is this accomplished?

I have no hesitation in saying, that the way to do this is to make the school children feel *they are loved and cared for*. If this is secured, almost every thing is secured; and without the consciousness on the part of the scholars that an interest is felt in them, I cannot conceive that any teaching will produce satisfactory fruit. . .

With regard to the intellectual part of Education, I believe it to be an essential element of right teaching, that boys should be set, as soon as they are prepared for it, something hard to work at; something that they will not be able to master without painstaking and intellectual effort. I think this is too much lost sight of in our National Schools. . .

Hence it is, that while there is a good deal that is striking and showy on the day of examination, there is less permanent fruit from the teaching, than might be expected. . .

To guard against this disheartening result, as soon as boys are fit for it, it has been the custom, in our school, to give them something hard for their minds to work on. The subjects that present themselves for this purpose are obvious, – *Language and Geometrical Reasoning*. And in order the better to make the study of the structure of language a means of mental cultivation, they learn Latin.

It is not much that we are able to accomplish, Cassell's Latin Grammar, price 8d, being pretty nearly the limit of our classical literature. However, though little, what is done, is of the highest value in an intellectual point of view. Its value perhaps consists in this, that there are so many things to think of at the same time, in constructing a simple Latin sentence, – gender, number, person, case, mood, and tense. . . About the fact that there can be no doubt; we find that the boy's intellects are manifestly and marvellously quickened by their Latin lessons. Of course, there must be zeal and heartiness on the part of the scholars; this is secured by sympathy with them. . .

With regard to Euclid, though the knowledge of it may have no practical bearing on their after life, the effort to understand a geometrical demonstration is of incalculable service in the cultivation of the intellect. . .

We should never forget that our business at school is to teach our scholars how to learn. That school will not be the best from which the scholars go forth with the largest stock of information. . . The best school will be the one where the training has been such as to fit them for carrying on self-education after they leave school. . .

Nor does it at all follow that it is necessary to forego the knowledge of common things. On the contrary, the acquisition of useful knowledge we find facilitated by the course of study we pursue. Education, based on the analysis of language and the study of geometrical reasoning, gives a boy a power over any book that may be placed in his hands. . .

Before dismissing the question of mental culture, I must refer to another branch of learning, my advocacy of which will, perhaps, be more readily received . . . I mean the learning music from notes. . . I know nothing that is more valuable for fixing the attention of children. . . It can be brought to bear on the culture of their minds at a very early age, long before they have made such progress in elementary knowledge as to take in hand the studies before spoken of; and it is the best preparation for them. . . And think only what you are doing for them: opening, as it were, a new sense – teaching them a new language; a language in which are written works of the highest genius and inspiration. . .

Where it is possible I strongly advise a Bath in connexion with the school. . .

In our case we found in the school-yard a little duck-pond. We raised the sides and lined it with concrete, and put a shed over it. This, an adjoining pump, and a large copper, have answered our purpose hitherto. The elder boys go one by one to the bath, and are allowed ten minutes for a plunge and dressing. A widow women comes twice a week to bathe the little boys. Thus every boy bathes twice a week; or is obliged to bring a certificate from home to say that he has been washed all over at least twice in the week. . .

Further, if possible, let them by all means take a meal together daily, with order and regularity. . . It may be breakfast or tea. . . Possibly it may be more convenient that they should take tea together after the afternoon school. . . This is a very favourite plan among our boys. In the summer-time they might adjourn to the common or playground for a game of cricket.

The value of the tea taken together is, that it gives an opportunity for teaching the boys to take their meals in an orderly manner. It also engenders an affectionate, family feeling among them. The social relaxation of the tea-table affords constant opportunities for bringing matters of interest before the notice of the boys, either by talking or reading to them . . . two points . . . deserve further mention.

First, the attendance at Church. The boys of St Mark's School have attended church every day since the school was opened. And this custom has not engendered on the part of the boys a distaste for going to church. . .

The other matter alluded to is the game of cricket. To attach the boys to their school and to one another, by all means have a cricket club for summer, and perhaps a foot-ball club for winter. . . Let the management of the cricket club be placed as much as possible in the boys' own hands. This will make them staid and manly. . .

As a part of their physical education, if the locality admits of it, let them go from time to time to bathe. Teach them to swim and show honour to those who learn. . .

For industrial employments; the work of the bath-room, pumping, &c. and the preparation of the tea furnishes employment, besides the usual operation of sweeping. . . In addition, I would recommend the frequent use of the paste-pot to fasten in the leaves of books . . . &c. Also a box of nails and screws, and a few tools to keep the school-premises in repair, by replacing a hat peg, or putting a new hinge on a locker, are very useful. . .

. . . In addition to the foregoing, I would urge, where the funds will allow it, the introduction of a Lithographic Press. . . It encourages good penmanship. It requires neatness, skill, and judgment for success. And it is a healthy developer of the muscular frame.

(S. Hawtrey, op. cit. (1859), pp. 25–45)

CHAPTER SEVEN

PROBLEMS: THE VOLUNTARY SYSTEM IN 1870

THE most debated sections of the Education Act of 1870 were those concerned with denominationalism and the conscience clause. These were the key issues for politicians and publicists, for the clergy and the Education League. The National Society had been at war with the Education Department ever since the early 1860s when the latter had begun to make acceptance of a conscience clause a precondition of building grants; whilst the abolition of denominationalism was a principal plank of the League's platform. Yet there is little evidence that the issue was important in the schools. There was some friction over attendance at Sunday service, theoretically compulsory in Anglican, Catholic and some nonconformist schools. In many country areas where it was still normal for dissenters to attend the parish church in the morning and the meeting-house in the afternoon, there was no problem;[1] but in towns attendance was frequently not enforced[2] and it was generally recognized that a clergyman who tried to introduce it where it was not customary was asking for trouble. Even so high a churchman as Gregory never attempted it. In day schools the denominational issue hardly arose. There were a few tender consciences, like that of Mrs Foley, who removed her daughter from an Anglican school in Runcorn 'on account of the prayers, which "will do her no good" ';[3] but they were rare. To many parents the whole issue was no more than a tiresome foible of their betters which, at worst, had to be humoured: 23 November 1865: 'Mrs Gallacher called to say she must take her 3 children away for a time for the priest had given her such a "hearing" they will return after Christmas.'[4]

Such evidence as exists tends to confirm the almost unanimous opinion of HM Inspectorate that in England, as distinct from Wales, the controversy was largely a 'platform question'. When clergy like John Armitstead and Dr Molesworth, the vicar of Rochdale, decided to allow withdrawal from catechism lessons, they found, like their successors after 1870, that few parents bothered to claim exemption. In general parents seem to have felt that some religious instruction ought to be given in school and they acquiesced, then as later, in whatever the school offered; though James Fraser, the future Bishop of Manchester, perhaps exaggerated when he remarked that nobody minded the 'catechiz'.[5] Certainly, even one offended conscience was too many, but the question of denominational teaching in day schools became politically crucial by 1870 primarily because, to Radical nonconformists, it symbolised those privileges of the established Church which they were determined to abolish. In this context the Education Act falls into place beside the abolition of Church rates, the Universities' Tests Act and Irish disestablishment as part of Gladstone's policy of protecting the citadel of the Church of England against his own followers by surrendering the outworks.

The real educational problems were those of attendance and 'educational destitution'. The question of how to induce all children to attend school regularly was bedevilled by two factors. The first was a feeling that compulsion in so private a matter as education was 'opposed to the genius and temper of our people',[6] unacceptable in a free society. Hence the Hereford Diocesan Board deleted even the modest proposal in its memorial[7] and the Newcastle Commission rejected the idea out of hand. Secondly, reformers were too strongly convinced of the obvious value of education to believe that the poor could be so irrational as to refuse it for their children once it was available. In 1867 the committee of the Manchester Education Aid Society, after three years' experience of paying children's fees in schools of the parents' choice, confessed that they had been 'wholly unprepared' to find that 'in so many instances it is impossible to persuade the parent to accept. . .'.[8] Without such a background of experience, discussion of attendance tended to be based on the assumption that in properly conducted schools compulsion would be unnecessary. Despite the propaganda of the Education League and the views of school promoters like Francis Close of Cheltenham who, as early as 1856, declared that forty years' experience had made him an 'absolute convert' to the policy of compulsion,[9] both these convictions were still powerful among politicians in 1870 and consequently the Education Act failed to deal with the problem of attendance. It was left to school boards as, in the past, it had been left to managers and patrons. Only gradually, as it became increasingly difficult to lay the blame for non-attendance upon the failings of the voluntary system, was the machinery of compulsion established nationally.

The problem which the Victorians called 'educational destitution' overlapped with that of attendance, since poor schools, poor districts and poor attendance went together; but the basic use of the term was to describe those communities, the third and fourth classes of the Hereford memorial, too poor to finance adequate schools. The typical Victorian voluntary school, unlike early National and British schools which often served wide areas, was parochial, whether it was attached to church or chapel. In one sense this was fortunate since the zeal of religious revival was harnessed to a particular school; but it hindered the collection of money for national and regional agencies and it made almost impossible the task of establishing efficient schools in districts where there were no rich to subscribe, unless it was undertaken by someone like Rogers. An appeal by the London Diocesan Board, for instance, for funds to support a planned expansion of provision in the capital was a total failure.[10]

The grant system intensified the problem since public money was only available to schools which already had resources of their own. The Department's contention that any school which took the trouble could reach the standard required for government grants was disingenuous: the education bills of the 1850s were proof enough that the problem was real. Yet it was not solved until 1870. There was widespread agreement as to how schools should be supported. Local rates, already raised voluntarily in a few areas, would be a reliable substitute for subscriptions: a far more secure basis for any institution and one which could be adjusted to its changing needs. But by whom should they be authorised and to whom should the grants from the rates be paid? The State, until 1870, was committed to the support of a religious education; and mid-Victorian churchmen of all persuasions shared John Scott's view that a religious education must inevitably be denominational.[11] The rating authorities were the vestries, the scene of annual battles over Church rates. Rates for the support of varying forms of denominational schooling, each, in the eyes of zealots of other persuasions, propagating error, would produce battles far more complex than those provoked by the simple issue of maintaining the parish church. The Newcastle Commission attempted to evade controversy by proposing that grants from the rates should be payable on the results of examinations of individual pupils and administered by county boards; but it is scarcely surprising, a quarter of a century before local-government reform, that the boards were never created and the proposals for examination annexed by central government.

Since, however, Parliament and the administrators never doubted that the provision of mass schooling was a matter for the localities, the Revised Code merely blocked the solution which the Newcastle Commission had regarded as the most feasible. By the time the bill of 1870 became law it had cut the Gordian knot by excluding voluntary schools from rate aid; but it was at least workable in the contemporary context. It extended elementary education throughout the country with the minimum of upheaval; at the same time the school boards gained powers which ensured that they could succeed where voluntary schools had failed. Rates gave them an assured income. They possessed legal rights which voluntary-school promoters lacked: they could pay for their building by long-term borrowing and they could acquire sites by compulsory purchase. Such powers were especially necessary in large towns where the voluntary system was weakest; whilst the creation of the urban boards meant that for the first time school provision in big conurbations could be rationally planned.

The success of the school boards underlines the administrative inadequacy of the voluntary system. It could never have succeeded in providing education for the whole community. Too anarchic to cope with urban problems, its financial resources were insufficient to support its own superstructure and too dependent upon individuals to be secure. Although board schools might suffer after a change in board membership they never faced catastrophe, as happened when a voluntary school's patron went bankrupt or changed his religion and withdrew his support.[12] But administration and finance are not the only significant factors in educational development. In school organisation, teaching methods, attitudes to parents, the introduction of advanced work and of new subjects the thirty years between 1840 and 1870 were arguably a period of more rapid development than any comparable stage of elementary-school history. Since any manager with money in his pocket was free to introduce or support any scheme he chose, the very amateurishness of the voluntary system encouraged experiment. In a climate so favourable, change was rapid. The typical elementary school of 1840 was a monitorial school, teaching the elements mechanically. By the 1860s the classic elementary school was, in essentials, already functioning.*

Notes

1. See Baker, op. cit., *passim*; cf. the rector of Sevington, Somerset, 'I cannot say that none of my people attend any Nonconformist place of worship, but they all come to church.' (PP. 1865 VI, q. 5402).
2. Cf. 4C(i).
3. Weston C. E., Runcorn, Log Book 22/11/1864 (Ches. CRO, SL, 120/1).
4. Marshall St. British Girls, Log Book (Manchester Archives, M66/43/1/1).
5. J. Armitstead, *Popular Education* (1856), p. 47; PP. 1852 XI, q. 576; 1861, XXI, Part II, pp. 60–61.
6. W. J. Kennedy in A. Hill (ed.), *Essays upon Educational Subjects* (1857), p. 234.
7. See above, 2E.
8. Manchester Education Aid Society, *Annual Report* (1867), p. 18.
9. F. Close, *A Few More Words on the Education Bills* (1856), p. 22.
10. R. Burgess, *Metropolis Schools for the Poor* (1846); London Diocesan Board, *Annual Report* (1850), pp. 10–11.
11. See above, p. 55.
12. E.g., Swingfield Minnis (Radnor Papers); Kirtling (CRO Cambridge).

Documents

7A. A SMALL-TOWN SCHOOL IN THE 1860s

The following extracts from a log book are included partly to contrast with 3K and partly to illustrate the extent to which, in some schools, the standards and attitudes of the classic elementary era were already present in the early 1860s.

Dukinfield, a cotton town, was at this time affected by the cotton famine. St Mark's was a good school but in no way excep-

* 7A

tional. The clergyman, William Heffill, like many in the industrial north, was not a university man; the master, Thomas Woode, held an undistinguished certificate (Class III, Division 3). The extracts cover two-and-a-half years, from the beginning of the log book to Woode's departure at the end of 1865.

Note (i) Scholar's Certificates, introduced in 1855 in an attempt to encourage attendance, were issued by the Education Department, countersigned by HMI and presented to pupils over twelve years old who had attended regularly for three years and reached satisfactory standards of attainment and conduct. They recorded attainment in each subject and had been designed at South Kensington with a border of roses and oak twigs entwined and, as a heading, the motto 'Well begun is half done'.

(ii) One of the functions of relief committees was to pay the school fees of children whose parents were thrown out of work by the famine.

1863

1/7. Today, I have been busily engaged in the examination of the first class to mark the progress during the past quarter and thus to fill up the certificates I grant to the successful boys. The Arithmetic pleased me most. Several of the boys read nicely, but as an average I was hardly satisfied. The writing fairly satisfactory. Dictation very good.

2/7. This day has been devoted to the examination of the 2nd class. The work of the class has been good. The Reading best part. The Writing, Arithmetic & Dictation satisfactory.

3/7. Examination of the 3rd class. Not as well pleased with this class as with the first two classes. The lower section not as well up as the upper.

6/7. 4th class examined. Much pleased with the work of the little boys especially with the Numeration & Notation. All of them wrote their names & addresses very nicely.

9/7. The first two classes received Grammar & Geography lessons, the latter being on the physical features of England.

10/7. The Quarterly prizes & certificates granted. 5 of the former & 90 of the latter. 1st class Prize "Clever Boys of our time & how they became famous men". 2nd c. "Take care of Number one.

how to do so". 3rd Class "The life of King Alfred". 4th "The way to do good". Extra class "The Adventures of the donkey".

15/7. . . . Taught the boys a new song entitled "Before all lands in East or West etc."

17/7. Special lesson taught. Drawing to the first two classes. Two lower classes Object lesson on the "Lion".

27/7. Today I have been specially engaged in drilling the 3rd class in Reading, that subject being rather defective in that class. The 1st class has been taught by the 2nd master – Subject the 3 Rs.

28/7. James Booth Hadfield, a clever and intelligent boy has left school to go to work in an office. The School-Certificate obtained him the situation. He is 13 years old & has been to school since he was 3 years old. Very quick indeed at Arithmetic: that subject being the one he delighted in.

5/8. School visited by the Managers who made enquiries respecting the work of the school.

6/8. Gave a lesson on Grammar. Subject "Etymology". Many of the boys gave good sentences.

14/8. This morning at 10 o'clock the children assembled in the School-yard where nuts were scattered amongst them. At the end of this amusement the children were gathered together for a few words of counsel respecting their behaviour at home during the holidays; and after this they were dismissed for a fortnight's holiday.

3/9. The Rev. Wm Heffill visited the school – conversation respecting the work of the New Code.

9/9. Monthly examination of the 4th & 5th classes. The reading of these two classes must receive more attention this next month.

11/9. General Rehearsal of School Songs. The two first classes received a Geography lesson. School visited by the Managers.

17/9. This morning I specially devoted myself to the Reading of the 2nd 3rd & 4th classes. Many children absent this afternoon – Cause The Laying of the Foundation Stone of the Prince

Consort Memorial at Hartshead Pike a place some 4 miles distance.

18/9. The pupil Teacher has given a lesson on the parable of the "Good Samaritan" to the whole School. Considering it is his first attempt it was fairly done. Managers visited the school.

21/9. The Arithmetic of the School has received my Special attention this day. The 3rd class to have 10 minutes each day after School hours, that class being rather deficient in that subject.

2/10. . . . School visited by the School managers who noticed particularly the regularity of the school-children during the past Quarter; observing the fact that out of an average of 152 a number of 120 had not been absent *one* week during the whole of the Quarter ending Sept. 27th 1863. Considering the many difficulties & trials with which the parents have to contend with [sic], this fact speaks well.

19/10. Drilled the first two classes in their military exercises – also in the afternoon took the lower classes to the same exercise.

5/11. Gunpowder plot Day. Special lesson given – Subject Text "If the Lord had not been on our side etc" with Special reference to Historical occasion of the Day. Children dismissed after the lesson for the remaining part of the day.

6/11. Beautifully fine day. Allowed the children a little extra play – air being keen & frosty they enjoyed themselves with one of their usual favourite games. "Shepherds".

11/11. Received from Rev. S. J. G. Fraser H.M. Inspector of Schools "Scholar's Certificate" for John Harrop, a sharp intelligent & a thinking boy – Made the Certificate a Subject for a lesson – Character – Formation of, being my chief aim. The boy is now engaged in a large iron firm near Manchester.

27/11. Composition & drawing in the afternoon first three classes.

10/12. . . . 1st & 2nd classes drilled in Bill making. The penmanship of the School received attention particularly by the master in the morning.

1864

6/1. Read to the children the account of *Six Boys* who have been drowned on the ponds through skating, made this the Subject for a Bible Lesson, the event having occurred on Sunday last. . .

25/1. The relief Committe having issued the notice "That no child be paid for by them unless he received a "Ticket" from District Visitor" a great confusion has been the consequence. Upwards of 50 boys were sent home to get one of these Tickets. The whole of the Day has been spent on the examination of these Tickets.

1/2. Good attendance. More school fees received from the children.

9/2. Shrove Tuesday. Lesson on the *Day*. At 11 o clock each boy received a penny. The money was given by the Rev. Wm Heffill and his Lady. Owing to the serious illness of the pastor Rev. Wm Heffill, the Churchwardens presented the pennies to the children. A Note expressing gratitude was written by G. Farrond 1st class boy, signed by a good number of boys and forwarded to the beloved minister.

19/2. . . . Several children refused admittance this week owing to the School being full.

23/2. Punished a boy for playing with and striking a lucifer match. Punishment "Match" 1000 times.

2/3. A boy in the first class punished very severely for swearing in the play-ground. *Swear* 1000 times to be written neatly. . .

11/3. . . . Punishments. 3rd & 4th classes to be kept in each day next week for 15 minutes spelling.

16/3. Several children absent owing to the cheap trip to Sheffield to view the spot of the late awful catastrophe: the bursting of the Bradfield Reservoir, where upwards of 250 people have been drowned.

24/3. . . . The attendance this week is much lower than usual owing (1) Regulation of Relief Committee (2) Good Friday occurring this week. A few narrow-minded parents keep their children at home.

8/4. The renewal of the Prize Scheme has made a decided change for good in the regularity of the school-boys.

15/4. Several boys in the first class punished for not obtaining 20 marks for Home-Lessons during the week. Punishment Home-lesson 300 times.

28/4. Received a letter from J. R. Lees a late 1st class boy, from America, doing well. Sent an American coin to master as a token of esteem. Prizes the bible I gave him previous to his going.

12/5. The Monitors received a special lesson on the art of Teaching reading to their classes. . .

15/7. . . . Allowed the children to go home this afternoon at 3 o clock so that they might have an opportunity of seeing the Grand Cricket match at Ashton between the All England Eleven and 22 of Ashton.

26/7. . . . Advanced the first class 1st Section a step in Arithmetic. Square root taught.

[From HMI's Report of Inspection, 12/9]

The Boys are cheerful intelligent and orderly. They have passed a very good examination in the elementary subjects and their thinking powers have been well called out – the little Boys are especially quick and accurate in their work. The Master may safely venture on as wide a course of instruction as time will permit. Presented 107

Passed in Reading	107
,, ,, Writing	104
,, ,, Arithmetic	105

20/9. Advanced the Commercial Section a step in Arithmetic.

21/9. . . . Algebra taught to Commercial Section.

23/9. Latin to the Commercial Section – First declension of nouns given.

29/9. . . . Algebra to Class I Sec. 1. Drawing to the first class.

13/10. Football ordered.

11/11. During the whole of this week the master has been unwell and unable to attend School – Been under medical advice. One of the managers kept school.

20/12. Tonight a public Examination of the Boys in the presence of parents and friends. Commenced at 7 o'clock finished at 10 o'clock. Arithmetic of Class I Section A. Decimal Fractions. Compound Proportion. Interest. Stocks. Profit and Loss. Square Root. Section B. Vulgar Fractions. Sec. C. Compound Rules.

23/12. The Rev. Wm Heffill visited School and presented the boys with suitable prizes.

1865

28/3. Quarterly Examination commences.
1 Class. Papers: From 10 to 12 Religious Knowledge.
2 to 4 Dictation & Arithmetic.
The Second Class examined in the 3rd [sic] R's.

29/3. Papers. 10 to 12 Euclid, Algebra, Latin 1st Section.
The 3rd class the 3Rs.
2 to 4 Geography Composition Grammar History

30/3. The General examination of Standards II III & IV in Religious Knowledge.

31/3. Standard I or class 4 examined. The result of the Examination on the whole is good. The Reading of Standards II & III require more care that improvement may be made. Standard V presented very good papers especially in the higher branches.

8/6. The only lesson this morning
The *How* to spend their holidays.
Whit-sun-tide Vacation commences.
Races for nuts i.e. nuts squandered.
Special cricket match – master, P.T. & 2 1st class boys versus 9 of the cricket club.

13/7. At 4 o'clock boys assembled together for the express purpose of presenting Geo. Farron & his two brothers former a bible (3/-) & his brothers a testament each 9d each.
Boys feel the departure of these their schoolfellows very much – they are going to United States of America – George was the cleverest boy in School.

14/7. Granted permission to Classes I & II to go to the station to see their schoolfellows off.

4/9. The annual examination of the 3Rs etc.
No failures. The inspector highly pleased with the Latin & Algebra.

20/12. The last day of Thomas Woode as master of Dukinfield St. Mark's Boys' School.
The testimonial of the boys to the master is a handsome timepiece in value £3.3.0. Inscription:

"Presented to Mr Thomas Woode on the occasion of his resigning the Dukinfield St Mark's Boys' School, Xmas 1865, as a token of esteem and respect by the Pupil Teachers and Boys with their prayers and best Christian wishes.

(Log Book, Ches. CRO, SL, 45/3/1)

CONCLUSION

VOLUNTARY SCHOOLING IN A NEW CONTEXT

LEGISLATION frequently produces unintended and unwanted effects; but there can be few major acts of Parliament whose implications were so misunderstood by both supporters and opponents as the Education Act of 1870. There was no ambiguity about its main purpose: in Forster's words, 'to cover the country with good schools'; nor about the establishment, where necessary, of an *ad hoc* authority, the school board, to implement it. Beyond this point, however, even the framers of the measure seem to have had little idea of how it would work. Whilst many confusions arose from changes hastily made during the bill's passage through Parliament, notably the exclusion of voluntary schools from rate aid and the substitution of direct election to school boards for nomination by vestries and town councils, others were present in Forster's original proposals. The boards were empowered to compel school attendance in their districts but no machinery for compulsion was created elsewhere. The difficulty of finding sites for urban schools had been known to officials for twenty years, yet the proposal that the boards should have powers of compulsory purchase came from Lord Sandon, not from the government.[1] Better drafting might have averted many disputes as to the absolute right of boards to determine whether voluntary schools should be allowed to provide additional accommodation;[2] whilst the failure to define what was meant by 'elementary education', natural enough, perhaps, at the time, became a crucial factor in the events which ended the school-board era.

The National Education League had demanded free, compulsory and unsectarian education. Its leading figures, angry at achieving only a half-measure, scarcely recognised the long-term possibilities opened up by the Act. At the same time they underestimated the resilience of voluntary schools, believing that one more Parliamentary effort would finish them off. Like Forster they showed curious blind spots. John Morley airily dismissed the key question of the size and rateable value of school-board districts as unimportant. 'The question whether there should be a Board for every parish, or a Board for every union, or a Board for united districts . . . is one of detail';[3] although the strongest educational argument against the school-board system was the inadequacy of small rural boards. More sensational in the short term was the loss of the first school-board election in Birmingham by the most efficient political caucus in Britain because, unlike their opponents, they failed to grasp the significance of the cumulative vote.[4]

If Radicals regarded the Education Act in an unduly pessimistic light, the voluntary groups, except for a few prophets of doom like Gregory (treasurer of the National Society since 1869), were mildly optimistic. The British and Foreign Society, seeing their own principle enshrined in the Cowper-Temple clause,[5] announced that in future their resources would be devoted to teacher-training rather than to schools.[6] Anglicans in general felt that they had escaped fairly lightly and believed assurances from Gladstone and Forster that, in future, 50 per cent of expenditure would be met by grant and that school rates would never exceed 3d. in the pound. Wesleyans like Dr Rigg, Scott's successor at Westminster College, anticipated a prosperous future in which board schools would cope with the poorest children whilst discriminating parents would pay high fees for advanced education in voluntary schools.[7] Catholics reacted much as did Anglicans. They immediately realised the possibilities of the cumulative vote and used it consistently to secure permanent Catholic representation on most of the larger boards.

In the autumn of 1870 voluntary-school managers had to decide upon their response to the new situation. A few prosperous British schools were threatened with closure by their committees in order to bring about the establishment of boards in districts with sufficient school places. For schools in financial difficulties the possibility of transfer to a school board was salvation: for Tewkesbury British School, for instance, which had been in dire straits ever since the treasurer absconded to America in 1856.[8] But not all British managers shared the central committee's euphoria; most continued to run their schools as before. There were still more than a thousand British schools in 1900.

Other groups started a programme of hasty expansion. Applications for State building grants (abolished by the Act) were still accepted up to the end of 1870. If new schools were to be established there was an urgent need to collect the local contributions necessary to support such applications. The Anglicans raised £850,000 which, with aid from the National Society's Special Appeal, provided nearly 200,000 additional places. By 1875 the Wesleyans had increased the number of their schools to 900 and of their scholars to 180,000. It was claimed in the same year that, since 1870, voluntary schools had increased by 38 per cent and accommodation by 40 per cent.[9] Catholic expansion was even greater; by 1882 their schools had increased by 117 per cent and their accommodation by 112 per cent.[10] Political excitement in the 1870s, as in the years around 1840, acted as a stimulus to school promotion. In the case of the Catholics the motive power was that of religious duty incumbent upon the faithful; the attitudes of others were more complex. The Anglicans in particular relied upon fears of school rates and of the annoyance and expense of triennial school-board elections to galvanise hitherto uninterested parishes into educational activity; over the years the maintenance of efficient schools in such places became a terrible burden.

In the last four years of Gladstone's ministry, whilst the Education Department was surveying the country for deficiencies, the denominationalists building and the first school boards determining policy, the Radicals of the Education League, expecting that they would soon be in a position to force the repeal of the Act, did their best to keep the issue alive.[11] They concentrated on section 25, whereby school boards were empowered to pay the fees of necessitous children in schools chosen by the parents. This, they argued, was covert subsidising of voluntary schools from the rates. The sum involved was not large and was mostly spent by the boards of Manchester and Salford, whose members simply continued the policy of the unsectarian Education Aid Society[12] to which many of them had belonged. However, the clause obviously presented opportunities for martyrdom to both sides and in 1876 the duty of paying such fees was transferred to the boards of guardians. This provision became a barometer of the relations of urban school boards with local voluntary schools. Where they were friendly the board acted as agent for the guardians, determining eligibility and paying fees through its own officials. Where they were hostile the board remitted fees in its own schools, leaving parents who wished to use the voluntary schools to the embarrassment of associating with paupers in the offices of the guardians.

The election of 1874 showed that the Radicals had overestimated their own importance. Their hostility to right-wing Liberals and to Forster merely helped to put the Conservatives into power. From then onwards there was little likelihood that the settlement of 1870 would be overturned; subsequent legislation was intended to remedy its inadequacies. Experience was rapidly disproving the assumption that, if efficient schools were available, all children would attend them. In the Education Act of 1876 Sandon, Forster's successor, filled a gap left in 1870 by creating school attendance committees in areas without school boards. He thereby forestalled demands for universal school boards to enforce attendance. Mundella's Act of 1880, which imposed upon boards and committees the duty of framing bylaws on compulsion, settled the question of compulsory attendance so far as legislation was concerned; how far it was a reality before 1900 is more open to dispute.[13] In 1870 there had been little support in political circles for free education, but the practical difficulties of collecting fees from reluctant attenders made it a live issue. School boards could easily remit fees, recouping themselves from the rates; for voluntary schools the prospect was more threatening. Eventually the Education Act of 1891 gave parents the right to demand free education and introduced a grant of 10s. per head, the average yield of school pence, to schools which abolished fees, thereby safeguarding voluntary schools except for those in which charges were high.

Voluntary schools had been on the defensive ever since the later 1870s. The zeal of urban boards had demonstrated that income from rates could always outbid income from subscribers who were also ratepayers. Boards could pay larger salaries and buy better equipment. Because most of their buildings were new they could also, even without special expenditure, offer better facilities than the many voluntary schools which were thirty or forty years old. The loss of building grants was a particular grievance. School managers could neither expect to receive 50 per cent of building costs from the State, nor borrow like the school boards, and leave payment to the future. The moment at which managers most commonly gave up the struggle to keep their schools open was not when maintenance became difficult but when rebuilding or extension could no longer be postponed.

In other ways the grant system seemed, to denominationalists, to work to their disadvantage.[14] Gladstone's promise that grants would cover 50 per cent of expenditure had not been fulfilled whilst the grants for subjects other than the 3Rs, initiated in 1867, eventually provided another grievance. Frequently modified and extended by the Education Department in response to pressure groups (amongst them the school-board lobby, anxious to show ratepayers that new subjects brought financial as well as educational advantages), they chiefly benefitted well-equipped schools with a large attendance of older children. Mundella's merit grant, intended as a remedy, had constantly to be defended against accusations that the criterion of merit was a school's ability to earn large grants on attendance and examination.

The entire system, however, was open to a more justified criticism. It still operated on the principle of encouraging local effort by penalising schools in which effort was insufficient. The grant was still reduced by its excess over local contributions which, in voluntary schools, were fees and subscriptions and, in board schools, fees and rates. In rural areas where the yield from rates was often pathetically low, voluntary schools and board schools suffered together; but in towns the preposterous equation of the effort involved in collecting subscriptions with the effort involved in sending a precept to the rating authority gave school committees a legitimate grievance. A clause of the Act of 1876 provided that reductions should not be made unless the grant exceeded 17s.6d. a head. So greatly did the cost of schooling rise in the following decade, however, that this concession became an unfair restriction against which the Cross Commission heard protests from one witness after another.

It is therefore not surprising that, in the 1880s, many school-board enthusiasts hoped and many denominationalists feared that sooner rather than later the voluntary schools would wither away. The Wesleyans, though restrained by Rigg, were moving towards an official abandonment of the denominational principle. Anglican opinion was angry and divided, ranging from the belief of Bishop Fraser of Manchester that the future was with board schools to that of Gregory who was still conducting a tooth-and-nail fight against the whole school-board system. In these circumstances the leadership of the voluntary cause fell to the one man with a coherent and practicable policy: Cardinal-Archbishop Manning, who thus for the second time in his life undertook the defence of Anglican schools – this time because he recognised the strength that would come from a united front of Anglicans and Catholics. His aims were clear: rate-aid, with the maintenance of denominational teaching and, in return, the acceptance of some degree of public control. He took the lead among the denominationalists on the Cross Commission of 1886–8 and, though he did not live to see it, his principles became official Anglican policy in 1896 when Temple succeeded Benson as Archbishop of Canterbury.

In the following year Salisbury's government carried a bill to provide increased aid for voluntary schools and to abolish the 17s.6d. limit. It was recognised, however, as merely a holding measure until the system was changed for, in the mid-1890s, school boards, like voluntary-school promoters thirty years before, suddenly found themselves in a very exposed position. The creation in 1888 of multi-purpose local authorities which immediately found an educational role through the Technical Instruction Act, and the demand for a coherent system of secondary education, altered the context of educational questions. Educationist-politicians like A. H. D. Acland now wanted an end to voluntary schools primarily because, as long as school boards educated only a minority even of elementary pupils, they could not hope, given the existence of county councils, for recognition as all-purpose education authorities. In such circumstances the militant nonconformity which had powered the Education League and which still dominated some school boards was a political embarrassment. Legislation to dispose of voluntary schools could only be carried with the support of the Irish vote whose price would be the conceding of a special status to Catholic schools; and these, for a nonconformist, were the most offensive of all. At the same time the desire to rationalise both local government and the educational structure by removing an out-dated *ad hoc* authority brought strange allies to the voluntary cause; not only Balfour and Morant, but Sidney Webb and, at the last, even Joseph Chamberlain, united with Cardinal Vaughan in support of rate-aid for voluntary schools. In the end the school-board system, like the voluntary system in 1870, succumbed to external pressures beyond its control.

The picture of voluntary schools which emerges from a study of educational politics between 1870 and 1900 is thus one of almost unrelieved gloom, culminating in the Bishop of Rochester's anguished complaint in December 1901 that affairs had reached '*breaking point*'.[15] Voluntary resources could never compete with those of urban school boards; and even the most successful schools often functioned in old and over-crowded buildings. Part of the great increase in voluntary-school numbers in the 1870s resulted from the absorption into the State system of hitherto uninspected schools; and although there are hints that some were much better than the Education Department had formerly been willing to admit,[16] many of them were impoverished. They increased the proportion of schools liable to financial difficulties; and such difficulties were cumulative. In spite of continued Catholic expansion, voluntary-school numbers began to fall in the 1890s as more committees gave up the struggle and closed their schools or surrendered them to a school board.

Nevertheless, the structure as a whole survived. Evidence from other schools presents an alternative picture of peaceful development along lines already laid down before 1870. The later history of two schools already described illustrates both the dangers and the resilience of the voluntary system. St Thomas, Charterhouse, was at a low ebb in the late 1860s. The parish had been subdivided, the schools falling into the new district. In 1863 Rogers became rector of St Botolph, Bishopsgate, where, discovering the dearth of provision for City clerks, he took up the cause of middle-class education. The loss of his dynamism was a blow to the Charterhouse schools and numbers fell. The special character of Golden Lane was lost but Goswell Street revived after 1868 under a new head who developed a science course involving experimental and practical work. The upper department became, in effect, a higher-grade school, charging, with the permission of the Education Department, fees of up to 1s.8d. per week. In 1894 five of the London Technical Instruction Committee's thirty scholarships to higher elementary schools were held there.

The advanced evening classes, renamed the Charterhouse Institute, prospered by providing for ex-pupil-teacher assistants in board schools who were studying for their certificates.[17]

Henry Moseley's death in 1872 produced a similar crisis in the affairs of the Bristol Trade School. Its salvation, curiously enough, resulted from his insistence that the curriculum should include Anglican religious instruction, since the Anglican connection enabled the Endowed School Commissioners to bring it within the purview of the great Colston charity. Endowed and rebuilt, it emerged, still under Coomber, as the Merchant Venturers' School, with a bilateral curriculum (mathematics with applied science and commercial subjects) and a scholarship ladder from elementary schools to higher education.[18]

These two schools survived the loss of their founders partly because the prestige of Rogers and Moseley had given them a national reputation. Individual patronage was still significant; indeed, whether a school board existed or not,[19] it remained a key factor in rural areas. 'The National School at Moreton', declared Lord Redesdale in 1880, 'belongs to the rector and myself';[20] and this situation was common. Many schools accepted as efficient for attendance purposes remained wholly in the patron's hands; for example, those maintained by the Duke of Buccleuch in the Kettering area, or Sir John Maple's school at Childwickbury which, when eventually inspected in 1904, was in good order, well equipped and well kept.[21] The patron's control even of inspected schools might still be absolute. 'I support my school myself. I go under Government because my husband desires it, so that I may be on the same platform as the teachers,' declared the formidable Mrs Fielden of Todmorden,[22] who berated the Cross Commissioners for their ignorance of education. Where the patron was also the employer his influence was far more effective than that of the attendance officer.[23] Perhaps the most interesting example of patronage spans the gap between board and voluntary systems. Sir Titus Salt, a former Voluntaryist, subscribed to the Education League and in 1870 logically demanded the immediate formation of a local school board. Inevitably he was elected chairman of the Shipley Board, built a set of schools just outside the Saltaire boundary and managed, on the board's behalf, both these and the schools in Saltaire. On his death he was replaced, on the board as at the mill, by one of his sons:

. . . Titus took us [Lord and Lady Frederick Cavendish] and Ld. Carnarvon over the magnificent Saltaire schools. I never dreamt of anything on such a scale. He is especially proud of the Board Schools,* which consist of Kindergarten and a great Mixed School; both departments ruled by women, without pupil-teachers, the plan being the class-room one throughout. The big central hall is only used for the religious lesson and for drilling, marching, and games. Of course there is an Admirable Crichton of a Head Mistress of each school, on whom the whole thing depends, and who has the fullest possible freedom of action and control. . .[24]

As long as the Salt family retained control of Saltaire Mill they were, in effect, sole managers of the Shipley Board schools.

Wealthy clergy continued to double the roles of manager and patron. In Sandbach, for example, the boys paraded with their drum-and-fife band and took regular swimming lessons whilst the girls continued the practical study of domestic economy under the genial management of John Armitstead the second, a fox-hunting parson, highly respected by local nonconformists, who later became a member of the first Cheshire Education Committee. Indeed, Sneyd-Kinnersley's reminiscences of his inspections of Cheshire schools show how little they changed from the pattern existent before 1870.[25] Many clergy still played an active part in teaching. The headmaster of St Thomas, Charterhouse told the Cross Commission that:

'We have always two curates about the school, and whatever is going on they are willing to help. One of the curates this morning is helping some boys on with mechanics; another was particularly fond of literature, and whenever he got an opportunity he was doing work in that line. I find that I get most useful help from the managers. . .'[26]

Voluntary involvement in the higher-grade movement will be considered below but, as attendance improved and numbers in Standards V, VI, and VII increased, there were many schools offering curricula to which a well-educated curate might usefully contribute. Some of these were visited by the Samuelson Commission, amongst them St Mary's, Hulme, more than half of whose pupils were in Standard IV and above, learning mathematics, a foreign language, animal physiology and drawing.[27] As, with the reform of endowed grammar schools, the scholarship ladder

* I.e., the post-1870 schools in Albert Road, Shipley.

began to take shape, others set out to act as feeders to the secondary schools: Christ Church, Salford, for example, which by 1895 had gained thirty-seven of the ninety-six scholarships won by Salford boys to Manchester Grammar School. In London the total of 160 scholarships to various secondary schools awarded between 1881 and 1901 to boys from Kennington National School would have been regarded as creditable in a school of similar size in the inter-war years of the twentieth century.[28]

If, as has been argued above, the curriculum and structure of elementary schools evolved very rapidly between 1840 and 1870, the later years of the century would probably have been, in any case, a period of consolidation and extension rather than innovation. Other influences, however, led in the same direction. When compulsion began to force the poorest children into school, sensitive observers soon realised that their needs were social and physical rather than strictly educational. Reformers were more likely to involve themselves in the Penny Dinner movement than in curriculum change. Conversely, if schools tried to attract ambitious parents by means of advanced curricula and high fees, they had to meet consumer demand; and parents preferred conventional subjects to innovations. Moreover the Education Department's well-meant efforts to extend the curriculum by paying for performance in individual subjects led not only to the natural reaction that the subjects most worth teaching must be those which earned money; HM Inspector, who had to approve the timetable, was liable to look askance at subjects on which the Department had refused grant. A National school in Sussex had introduced telegraphy for the older boys. The GPO was interested, lent equipment and provided an examiner and prizes. For three years the school received a specific subject grant; but then the Department changed its mind, the grant was withheld and the experiment abandoned.[29]

This school was unusually enterprising. In 1887 it was planning the introduction of allotment gardening and had tried to teach cookery, all within a budget of £115 a year. In general, however, innovation was confined to a few wealthy patrons like Mrs Fielden, whose school in Todmorden had a national reputation for the teaching of reading and who toured with groups of children to demonstrate her technique.[30] The one major exception was in the age group upon which the elaborations of the Code pressed least heavily. Kindergarten work had appeared sporadically in infant schools ever since Froebel's 'gifts and occupations' had been shown at the educational exhibition of 1854, but had never become common. By 1870, however, interest in kindergarten had revived amongst middle-class educationists and several women's training colleges had begun to teach it systematically. The relaxation of the Code for infants aided its spread, as did the exclusion of very young children.[31] The range of techniques to be found in infant schools thus became very wide. In the 1890s, when some schools were just introducing, under Department pressure, the object lessons which had been common practice for fifty years,[32] others had developed into recognisable predecessors of the modern infant school, the Derby College Practising School, for instance:

Small dual desks were gradually substituted for the old, ugly, long ones. The Babies' Room was given a rocking horse and the main room had a large dolls' house built and furnished for it . . . [there were] some highly prized skin-models of animals capable of emitting appropriate sounds. . . A canary gave interest and gaiety to the room and a pair of pigeons, in a large wicker cage, obligingly brought up a family of two. . . One aquarium was kept for goldfish and another, in due season, for tadpoles. As many bulbs and other plants were grown as space could be found for them. . .

Education in the Infants' School was determined by two different forces. There was the official demand that, before they left, the pupils should be able to read simple books, write legibly, at least with a pencil, and work easy sums. There was again the kindergarten principle that children should be educated by their playful self-activity.

Following the two-fold urge mentioned, the morning timetable was largely filled, after instruction in Religious Knowledge, by short lessons in the "Three R's", relief from too long desk work being secured by play-time, singing and drill. Further, the teaching utilised, as far as possible, the help given by Froebel's "Gift and Occupations". . .

The afternoon timetable was given to "object lessons", recitation, storytelling and, above all, to "Kindergarten Occupations". . .

An experimental "extra" for the top class was a weekly exercise in Oral French. . . The children showed much pleasure in learning the French names for common things, in counting in French, in reciting in French, the days of the week and the months of the year and in singing little French songs. . .[33]

After 1870 voluntary-school managers showed for the first

time a willingness to collaborate with each other. In part this was a simple response to the threat from board schools, but there was also some recognition that cooperation could lead to better education. An early example occurred in the field of domestic economy. Determined experiments continued, as at Sandbach. An instance of cottage cookery over the schoolhouse fire which had caught the attention of an inspector in 1867 had become, by 1879, the Stokesay Cooking School, functioning for three hours on three afternoons a week.[34] In another report there is an idyllic picture of the girls of Chelsea Parochial School sitting on the rectory lawn to eat the dinners they had cooked.[35] But there were problems. The 'good plain cook' could not explain theory whilst, at the other extreme, the grant for domestic economy as a specific subject could be obtained simply by reproducing information from a textbook.[36] Associations of ladies to improve the teaching of needlework by awarding prizes had long existed, but cookery demanded a different approach. Its products could not be collected and assessed at leisure. Associations undertaking to provide central cookery classes began, therefore, to appear in the 1870s.[37] More importantly, the foundation of schools of cookery which trained teachers and made them available to give courses of lessons in groups of rural schools both met the need for teachers and, because they insisted upon practical work in small classes (from ten to fifteen girls), raised standards. The schools of cookery disapproved of much of the work organised by school boards on the grounds that the classes were too large.[38] The cooperation demanded of managers who organised these groups of schools was something which would scarcely have been possible before 1870.

Early attempts by teachers' associations to improve the education of pupil-teachers have already been considered. Common teaching for some Catholic girls developed naturally when nuns and their apprentices returned in the evening from their schools to the convent in which they lived. There seems no reason to doubt the traditional account of the immediate origins of pupil-teacher centres; the concentration of girls from the convent of Mount Pleasant, Liverpool, at the top of the Queen's Scholarship list was sensational enough to make any conscientious school board feel that their pupil-teachers should be given comparable help. Once pupil-teacher centres had come into existence, voluntary school associations to support central classes for their apprentices may fairly be seen simply as a counter-measure. In rural areas, however, the response was to need rather than to threat. The National Society ran correspondence courses and attempts were made to help apprentices in remote schools. In the Staffordshire moorlands, for instance, an annual meeting of managers and teachers, arranged by the diocesan organizing master, agreed on textbooks and a common plan for covering the syllabus; while the organizing master met the pupil-teachers initially to advise them on how to study and then examined them every twelve weeks on one-third of the syllabus.[39]

Anglican diocesan boards continued to function; Manning established a comparable system in the Catholic dioceses as soon as he became Archbishop of Westminster.[40] The end of State inspection of religious instruction gave a new purpose to diocesan inspection and there was a revival of interest in the office of organizing master, whose function was now seen as parallel with that of the school-board inspector. But managers increasingly moved towards more representative associations in which they could play a larger part.[41] One of the earliest was the Manchester and Salford Church Day Schools Association, founded in 1875, which made grants to schools in return for representation on the management committees and the right to inspect. More were founded in the 1880s, some for defence against hostile boards, some, Dover for example, to collaborate with attendance committees. It was soon realised that such associations could give useful advice on dealings with the Education Department; by 1890 some of them had taken the further step of establishing common banking, thus aiding schools without reserves in the lean months which, as the government years varied from school to school, occurred in different schools at different times. By 1897, when the Voluntary Schools Act laid down that the aid grant should preferably be distributed through such associations, they had become a power. In the following year, under Education Department pressure, a complete national network was established for each of the voluntary groups. Some admitted parental representation, a few that of teachers. Had the Act of 1902 not been passed, they might have developed into an interesting experiment in cooperative school management. As it was, they provided voluntary-school promoters with an experience of external control which must have helped them to accept the local education authorities in 1903.

This conclusion has so far been written as if board schools and voluntary schools where wholly unconnected. This was how they appeared to political controversialists and to Radical-dominated school boards like that of Birmingham after 1873, or Walsall, or Norwich.[42] The view was shared by many enthusiasts on the fringes of the educational world. The voluntary schools would have to be done away with, the Cross Commission was told by Lady Stevenson (a conscientious manager under the London School Board whose previous experience of schools had been in Honduras and Mauritius), since HM Inspectors applied lower standards in the 3Rs to voluntary-school children and voluntary-school teachers were a different breed from those in board schools.[43] But any scrutiny of teachers and teacher-training reveals the inaccuracy of this interpretation. All the training colleges: National, diocesan, British, Wesleyan, Congregationalist, even Catholic, had good reason to be delighted with the settlement of 1870 which gave them unprecedented opportunities.

With the Revised Code they had entered a period of extreme difficulty. The new training regulations were draconian[44] and, by the syllabus which followed, the Education Department finally succeeded in excluding the advanced subjects which, to its incessant irritation, had opened for some students the path to the universities and ordination. There were closures and student numbers declined; but the coming of school boards and compulsion meant that, between 1870 and 1885, there were continuously expanding prospects of increased pay and increased job opportunities for teachers. The colleges prospered accordingly. There were some new foundations, notably a revival of Miss Burdett-Coutts's proposal that 'ladies' should be trained as elementary teachers.[45] The market contracted slightly after 1885 but the trained teacher continued to have scarcity value. Even in 1903, ten years after the appearance of day training, the teacher who was trained as well as certificated was more of a rarity than in 1870.[46]

Catholic students were expected to find posts in Catholic schools but otherwise the colleges were in no doubt that it was their duty to supply school boards with teachers. This was to be expected in British colleges and, because of the limited number of Wesleyan schools, the majority of Wesleyan probationers were inevitably appointed to board schools. Except for students from the provincial women's colleges, however, this was almost equally true of Anglicans. In every college except for Saltley and Durham, the majority of men who qualified between 1883 and 1885 went, with college approval, straight into board schools. Nor was this merely a question of condoning the unavoidable. Chester students, for instance, were allowed to include in their magazine a contribution not only assuming, but guying, the migrations of teachers between voluntary and board schools. So far as the Protestant colleges were concerned elementary schools formed a single system within which their students, once qualified, would move freely.[47]

By 1870 the stereotype of the elementary schoolmaster, conformist but self-respecting, strong on religion and morality, unremitting in his efforts to improve the pupils entrusted to him, was fully formed. Its origins were various, but the preoccupation of Kay-Shuttleworth and the Education Department that teachers should not form 'a false estimate of their position in relation to the class to which they belonged' had in the long run less effect on the men themselves than the attitude of the high-church colleges that 'the occupation of the schoolmaster of the poor . . . is as truly liberal as any in the commonwealth'.[48] Their convictions made it, in practice, unlikely that board schools would be secularised, a point emphasised in 1870 by the first president of the National Union of Elementary Teachers in his inaugural address.[49] Many, indeed, welcomed the opportunity to give religious instruction without the interposition of a parson; though if the dubious amalgam of broad-church theology, civics and jingoistic patriotism reported from one London board school is typical,[50] it is not surprising that some boards attempted supervision through panels of clergy.

In general the creation of school boards helped to raise the status of the teacher. This was not in the main a direct result of board policy. If some managers were arrogant, so were some school boards.[51] If in one mood the teacher-turned-journalist, James Runciman, denounced autocratic clergymen who regarded teachers as inferior beings, in another he idealised the old church schoolmaster, the 'affectionate friend' of the vicar, treated with deference by the gentry. Much contemporary opinion held that teachers were less restricted in voluntary than in board schools. Certainly they found it easier to resist the criticisms of organizing masters than those of school-board inspectors, later denounced by Edmond Holmes (admittedly a prejudiced witness) as super-slave-drivers.[52]

Changing circumstances rather than changing systems benefitted the profession. The creation of a unified pressure group (the NUET) and the degree to which it was able to influence official thinking has rightly been stressed as an important factor, but it was as much a consequence as a cause. In the large and highly organised schools of the northern towns, heavily dependent upon fees and therefore upon parental approval, efficient teachers had become increasingly independent of managerial control long before 1870.[53] The policy of the urban school boards was to create many more such units. Whilst some boards sought to maintain a high level of control, others deliberately conceded a measure of autonomy to their headteachers[54] and, in practice, both boards and managers hesitated to interfere with a teacher whose reputation for efficiency was established in the neighbourhood.

The board-school system did something to establish a career structure for elementary teachers. Although salaries continued to vary widely and illogically, there now existed in urban areas a regular progression from assistantships to relatively well-paid headships of large schools doing advanced work. Furthermore, this progression produced a change in the role of experienced teachers. A head, whose only adult contacts in a school of the 1850s were with the managers, became, in a large school, primarily an administrator. His teaching load was reduced and he controlled the work of adult assistants, many of whom, being uncertificated and, in the case of supplementary teachers wholly unqualified, were permanently his inferiors and subordinates. There were sharp divisions in the profession, not between teachers in voluntary and board schools, for qualified teachers passed freely to and fro taking their ideas and techniques with them, but between the trained and certificated, the merely certificated, the ex-pupil-teacher and the permanently unqualified. The existence of such a pecking order inevitably raised the status of those at the head of it.

Records like those of St Mark's, Dukinfield, show that a good school of the 1860s might be well-organised and regularly attended, with a curriculum as wide as that of efficient schools of the 1880s and 1890s. Indeed, with the exception of Swedish drill, examples of all the 'innovations' of the London School Board have already appeared in this book.[55] Even Dr Crosskey, chairman of the Birmingham School Board, admitted to the Cross Commission, under pressure from Heller of the NUET, that the kind of teaching he desired had existed before 1862 'under the guidance of Canon Moseley'.[56] The function of the school boards was not so much experiment as extension; so to organise the schools as to bring this curriculum within reach of the majority of children; and if, by and large, they failed in rural areas, in towns their success was remarkable. Compulsion and efficient teaching kept an increasing number of pupils in school far beyond Standard IV. Standard VII, a term already entering into unofficial usage before 1870, was a flourishing reality long before its entry into the Code in 1882. It was not the fault of the boards that the grant system set a premium on mechanical and unimaginative teaching and on large classes even for practical work.

Elementary-school science provides a notable example. Its appearance as a major element in higher-standard work has, in recent years, been praised as a response to the real needs of mass education. Earlier this century, when the schools were a living memory, it was often condemned as too one-sided to be educational and taught by a deadly alternation of note-taking and tests. It was, however, the Education Department who pointed the way to this excessive bias by accepting secondary work in elementary schools provided it was supported by Science and Art grants. The Science and Art Department itself, by ignoring experimental work in its examinations and by emphasising those sciences which cannot be taught practically without expensive equipment, established the parameters of elementary-school science. Within these the boards did the best they could. Most people would prefer to have been taught science by Dawes or Henslow or even William Lyttelton rather than by the demonstrators of Liverpool, Birmingham or Nottingham, who trundled their handcarts of apparatus from school to school for fortnightly lessons;[57] but the latter at least demonstrated the existence of experimental science to sizeable numbers of children. In the progressive reaction of the twentieth century nature study became the dominant 'science' for the primary age group. It is perhaps unfortunate that no heed was paid to educationists like Cromwell of St Mark's College or Chief Inspector Sharpe who, in the later 1880s, began to call for the return of 'Common Things'.[58]

The establishment of higher-grade schools is recognised as one of the great achievements of the school-board era; and surprise has sometimes been expressed that they were pioneered, not by the pacemakers in London and Birmingham, but by northern boards, several of which had denominational leanings. The early history of higher-grade schools has not been comprehensively studied but the evidence suggests that they resulted from evolution rather than creation. If this is true it explains why they developed under boards which had no desire to make a clean break with the past.

In a memorandum written in 1897 Morant identified three different types of higher-grade schools.[59] The first was an elementary school charging higher fees and providing better facilities than was normal. It was consequently more socially select and kept its pupils to a more advanced age than usual. In a highly stratified society such schools were inevitable. The upper department of Gregory's school complex in Lambeth was one. So, in practice, were those Voluntaryist schools which had survived by charging fees of 9d. or 1s. St James's, Bootle, was a Catholic example, founded to serve prosperous shopkeepers who did not want their children to associate with those of Irish labourers. The higher schools established in 1875 by the School Board of Bradford (a Voluntaryist stronghold) were of this type. They were not admitted to the Association of Higher Grade Schools which denied that they were higher-grade schools at all.[60]

Morant's second type was that in which children were taken through the standards with highly paid teachers and a wide curriculum. The numbers in the upper standards would be disproportionately large and there would be ex-standard pupils working under the Science and Art Department. His third category, to which the Birmingham seventh Standard schools belonged, was the continuation school. Dr Forsyth, of the Leeds Higher Grade School, gave the Bryce Commission a different definition. He dismissed the first type altogether; he disapproved of the third type on the grounds that it gave insufficient time for a coherent course; he regarded the lower standards in the second type as a separate, though preparatory, department (which, in practice, they usually were) and applied the term 'Higher Grade' to a school which admitted children of ten from Standards IV or V and kept them until fourteen, fifteen or, ideally, sixteen. This was the type of school advocated since the 1850s by W. J. Kennedy HMI and by other school inspectors.[61] The Bristol Trade School was such a school; so were the Birkbeck Schools and the upper school at St Thomas, Charterhouse. Other examples existed before 1870 but all owed their foundation to special circumstances;[62] for the evolution of the higher-grade school we must look elsewhere.

Examinations under the Revised Code revealed that in a small minority of schools there was a preponderance of advanced pupils. Of 275 boys in the Jarrow Chemical Works British School who were presented for examination in 1869, for example, 151 were in Standards IV to VI and another twenty-nine in the ex-standard VI established by Corry's Minute of 1867. Thirty took a paper in algebra and eighty a paper in arithmetic which had previously been used in examining the modern side of a public school (Cheltenham College). The managers specifically asked that the top two classes (120 boys) be examined in geography, history, grammar and composition.[63] Clearly this school was already an approximation to Morant's second type.

By 1860 some voluntary schools in the heart of old-established industrial areas were confronted with a form of urban decay. The respectable population moved out; the schools were left surrounded by offices, factories or slums. Most church schools in this position simply went socially downhill with the parish; but some British and nonconformist schools maintained or even raised their fees (of anything from 6d. to 1s.6d.) and looked to the attractions of an advanced curriculum and efficient teaching to persuade parents to send their children into the town centre from the suburbs in which they now lived.[64] The most successful could, by the early 1870s, point to passes in the higher standards and in the new specific subjects and to successes in Science and Art examinations as proof of the high quality of their work; a few of them spontaneously evolved into schools of a 'higher grade'. Parents ambitious enough to pay high fees and make their children travel long distances were parents who kept them at school beyond the normal age of leaving. The consequent overcrowding led some schools to exclude the lower standards altogether. This position, said Scotson of Peter Street, Manchester, 'led to their being regarded more and more as a kind of higher elementary school'. Grimshaw Street British School, Preston, remarked an inspector, 'drifted, in a sort of way, into the position of a secondary school'.[65] Other examples were Lower Moseley Street British School, Manchester, High Pavement British and the People's College in Nottingham, Stockport Wesleyan, Albion Congregational in Ashton-under-Lyne and, interestingly, Plymouth Public School and Stoke Public School in Devonport.[66] In these naval towns the competitive examinations for royal dockyard apprenticeships had always produced a demand for high standards in the schools.

In general these schools prospered in the 1870s. Parental demand for advanced work was increasing. High fees, increased government grants and the possibility after 1872 of turning some classes into organized science schools under Science and Art Department regulations meant that there were few maintenance problems, except in the People's College which received no State grants.[67] Scotson told the Samuelson Commission that he earned as much in the 1870s as later under the school board and that in some years the managers presented him with an extra £50. Difficulties arose only when rebuilding or extension became necessary and school committees showed themselves unwilling or unable, in the absence of building grants, to face the expense. Manchester was fortunate in that the Swedenborgians of Peter Street and the Unitarians who ran its nearest rival (geographically and educationally) in Lower Moseley Street were both faced with this problem in the later 1870s. Both schools were offered to the Board which closed Lower Moseley Street and rehoused and expanded Peter Street, thereby creating the great Central Higher Grade School. The directors of the People's College gave up their independence at the same time and handed their school over to the Nottingham Board as a higher-grade school. High Pavement fell to the Board when rebuilding became necessary in 1891.[68] In all these cases the boards simply continued and developed an already established tradition. The indestructable Mr Scotson continued as head of the Central Higher Grade School throughout its existence, only retiring when it became the Central High School in 1904. The continuity with 'Moss's School' was even clearer in the girls' department, of which Miss Melicent Moss, Mr Moss's niece, was headmistress until 1898, having succeeded her sister Eliza in 1873. Similarly William Hugh, head of High Pavement School since 1861, did not retire until 1905.

The other schools mentioned continued as 'higher grade' voluntary schools, either alongside school-board provision or as a substitute for it, charging fees, but with scholarships from the elementary schools. In Plymouth and Devonport they more than held their own. In 1895 Plymouth Public School had 450 pupils in its upper Department compared with thirty in the board's free higher-grade school; Devonport had 200 pupils in its organised science school as against fifty-four under the Board. Albion School in Ashton had a three-year ex-standard course, a biennial scholarship to Owen's College and a pupil-teacher centre financed by the Technical Instruction Committee.[69] The Boards of Manchester and Nottingham, like others, founded new higher-grade schools and some were established privately: the school at Blyth, for example, run by a limited-liability company of parents, or the higher-grade schools in Cambridge, the work of the great theologian J. B. Lightfoot.[70] Whether the verdict on the higher-grade movement is favourable, or is that of Chief Inspector Sharpe in 1895: 'What they have done has been very little, and it has been very unevenly done, and not very well done in many cases,'[71] it must apply to voluntary as well as to school-board action.

The common ground between voluntary and board schooling has been obscured by the picture of incessant conflict between groups variously labelled as 'board' and 'church', 'unsectarian' and 'denominationalist', 'progressive' and 'moderate' and, at the end of the century, 'Liberal' and 'Conservative'. Part of the obscurity derives from the assumption that the bitter hostilities of London and Birmingham were the norm; in part it stems from the full-blooded abandon with which Victorian election campaigns were fought. Dr Wardle has noted the ease with which, after an election, the members of the Nottingham Board settled down to three years of amicable cooperation.[72] Furthermore, the textbook equation of the two sides with pro- and anti-education lobbies is inadequate and misleading. Lord Salisbury once classified the protagonists as religionists, economists and educationists,[73] a division which cuts right across the traditional dichotomy and makes much better sense. The boards which simply left the vicar to run an outdated church school were economists masquerading as denominationalists; a 'moderate' might be an economist or a religionist bent on undermining the whole basis of the 1870 settlement; some boards used unsectarianism as a cloak for religious intolerance, as in the Dan-y-craig case; and many denominationalists were primarily educationists. Father Burke, a Catholic member of the Manchester School Board, complained indignantly in 1880 that the supposed denominational majority on the board did not exist. There was nothing to choose between the unsectarians and the Church party (led by Herbert Birley). They were equally anxious to spend money on board-school expansion; they had agreed on a 'truncated, dried, sapless' form of religious instruction and the Catholics were left in a permanent minority.[74]

Many school-board members had a simple aim: to carry out the intentions of the Act of 1870 through both board and voluntary schools. They shared the innocent goodwill expressed by the Barnsley School Board: 'We must maintain our friendly feelings with the Voluntary Schools then we shall be able to assist one another in getting the children into school and educating them.'[75] In such communities voluntary-school managers became board members with the intention not of thwarting but of assisting; Herbert Birley, for instance, the working manager of about twenty voluntary departments, sometime chairman of both the Manchester and the Salford School Boards, a believer in small classes and a leaving age of fifteen,[76] perhaps the best example in his generation of Dawes's 'practical and working men'. Or there was William Lea, vicar of St Peter's, Droitwich, a diocesan inspector and a noted midland educationist who, after the 1870 Act, demanded the establishment of a school board to introduce compulsion and, as its chairman, personally checked the attendance sheets every week to see which families should be visited.[77] In Liverpool, a city in which denominationalism was strong, the Council of Education, a body representing the board, voluntary school managers, teachers' associations and other local educational interests, coordinated attendance policy, school hours and holiday dates. It aided school libraries, organised classes for pupil-teachers, gave prizes on the results of the Queen's Scholarship, provided free education for regular attenders and awarded scholarships from the elementary schools to Liverpool College and Liverpool Institute.[78]

Such evidence illustrates the contributions of voluntary-school promoters to development during the school-board era. It is also easy to recognise, in a generalised way, that board-school teachers and, consequently, board-school teaching were to a high degree the product of the voluntary system. A more specific question remains – what, if any, relation existed between experience in a good voluntary school before 1870 and a successful teaching career after that date? There are indications that a thorough investigation of the careers of pupil-teachers from innovatory schools of the 1850s and 1860s might have interesting results. James Scotson never left Peter Street from his entry as a pupil in the 1840s to his retirement in 1904, but his education under Mr Moss was sufficient to enable him to create a school recognised as the equal of the Leeds Higher Grade School under the much more highly educated Dr Forsyth. We know that Mr Wath, under whom the Hereford Bluecoat School had so high a reputation for science work, came from King's Somborne; that Charles Eastburn, also from King's Somborne, went to St John's College, Cambridge as a sizar, was 5th Wrangler, held a fellowship and became mathematics lecturer and vice-principal of St Mark's College; that the master of the Hull Navigation School, celebrated in the 1870s for its teaching of applied science, had been one of the first pupil-teacher candidates to be approved by Moseley at Greenwich Hospital School; and that William Ripper went from a Plymouth elementary school to be apprenticed in a shipyard, left it and trained for teaching at Exeter College and by 1874 had become an assistant in a Sheffield board school. Five years later he was appointed science teacher in the Central School. He ended his career as Professor of Engineering and Vice-Chancellor of Sheffield University.[79] All these men were the products of good voluntary schooling. It seems reasonable to assume that there were other success stories.

School boards disappeared at the beginning of the twentieth century in a blaze of controversy as fierce as that of 1870. If the earlier settlement had demonstrated the declining position of the established Church, that of 1902 demonstrated the decline of Radical nonconformity. The voluntary schools became one element in a national system on terms which were essentially those proposed by Manning in the 1880s. But the schools which benefitted most from the settlement were not voluntary schools *per se* but rural schools, whether voluntary or board. The achievements of school boards were essentially urban. Most rural boards had resources inadequate for their task;[80] whilst by 1900 social and economic forces were eroding the dominance of squire and parson upon which depended the prosperity of rural voluntary schools. If country children were to be treated justly, a new system was necessary.

Fortunately for the new local education authorities they took over schools which shared not only common problems but a common tradition of schooling. This had developed before 1870 partly under Education Department pressure, but principally from the efforts of school promoters to Christianise and civilise their pupils and from their experience of the reactions of children and parents. It was inherited by late-nineteenth-century elementary schools, whether board or voluntary. Through the school boards it was both extended and applied consistently to the schools of a whole district, instead of at the whim of individual managers and teachers. If it thereby became rigid and formalised and hence open to the criticisms of twentieth-century progressives, this is only the fate to which all innovations seem liable as soon as they become normal practice.

The intense individualism of voluntary-school promoters was a major obstacle to the establishment of a national structure but it generated variety and experiment. Schools had reason to be grateful that the self-confidence which stemmed partly from religious conviction and partly from an assured position in society was strong enough to resist official pressures for conformity to a predetermined pattern. In personal terms it was fortunate that mid-nineteenth-century advances in educational practice came from men like Dawes or Rogers or Hawtrey rather than from Kay-Shuttleworth, whose zeal for reform was coloured by his obsessive personality. The inspectors hinted as much in 1858 when, in opposition to a proposal that their views should be combined into one general report, they argued that independent comment on individual experience had helped to save the schools from 'a discouragement of all systems excepting that which happened to be enjoying a transient popularity; . . . attempts to introduce ingenious, but often impracticable novelties which might casually float into favour [producing] . . . a mechanical and pedantic system of elementary instruction'.[81] The common assumption of English educationists that variety of provision is good in itself was already evident; and although some school boards had authoritarian tendencies which were transmitted to some of their LEA successors, the autonomy of voluntary schools was always there, to act sometimes as a drag, sometimes as a stimulus.

At the beginning of the present century the managers of Sompting Mixed National School (average attendance 120) provided a staff adequate in number but of a quality which no conscientious member of an urban school board would have approved. The headmistress was certificated but had been neither trained nor apprenticed nor even, except for one year, educated in an elementary school. She taught all the children above Standard II; her uncertificated sister and two supplementary teachers took the rest. She was Harriet Finlay Johnson, 'Egeria' of Edmond Holmes's *What is and What might be*, the exponent of correlation, activity methods, learning through play and drama. If in one sense she was the herald in the elementary world of the progressive New Era, in another she had affinities with the gifted amateurs of the mid-nineteenth century. Miss Johnson, it seems, did not always satisfy the diocesan inspector. Holmes was probably right in thinking that she would not have survived a school-board inspection. Parallel cases must have been in Sidney Webb's mind when he argued that voluntary schools must be preserved because they gave 'variety and the opportunity of experiment'.[82]

Voluntary schooling, however, had wider significance. By 1870 a pattern of elementary education was established which, at its best, involved purposeful management of committed teachers and a curriculum designed for the moral and intellectual improvement of the masses, without wholly neglecting parental wishes. Few contemporary educationists would have quarrelled with these aims; but the fact that in most cases religion underlay the purpose and the commitment explains why secularists like John Morley, with a single-mindedness equal to that of the most extreme denominationalists, denied any educational merit to schools based upon principles which they condemned. As

Thomas Dyke Acland remarked after an encounter with Huxley, 'These Radical anti-theological people are very intolerant.'[83] After the passage of a century, however, it should be possible to judge voluntary schooling objectively and to recognise the process of continuous evolution from the beginnings of the voluntary system to the classic elementary structure of the early twentieth century. Voluntary schooling belongs to the mainstream of educational development. The Act of 1870 removed obstructions to the flow, but in most respects did not change its course.

Notes

(S. = Section)

1. E.g., PP. 1852–3 LXXX, p. 33; 1859, Sess. 1 XXI Part I, pp. 18–19: 'I have several cases before me in which the friends of education have collected large funds and waited for years in the vain hope of effecting a purchase'; National Education Union, *The Debate in Parliament. . .* (1870), p. 25.
2. Ss. 18, 98.
3. Morley, op.cit, p. 130. In 1897 almost half the 2157 school-board districts had populations of under 1000, 550 of them under 500. *Special Reports on Educational Subjects* (1897), p. 16.
4. S. 29, whereby ratepayers had as many votes as there were board members and could distribute them as they chose.
5. S. 14, excluding catechisms and other distinctive religious formularies from board-school religious instruction.
6. British and Foreign School Society, *Annual Report* (1871), p. 43.
7. J. H. Rigg, *The Natural Development of National Education in England* (1875), p. 7.
8. Minute Book, Accounts (Glos. CRO).
9. Burgess, op.cit., p. 214; Rigg, op.cit., p. 23; B. F. Smith, *Why Hand Over the Church School to a School Board* (1875), p. 15.
10. Figures in D. Selby, *Towards a Common System of National Education* (1977), p. 1.
11. For general developments see M. Cruickshank, *Church and State in English Education* (1963) and J. Murphy, *Church, State and Schools in Britain* (1971).
12. See above, p. 208.
13. E.g., D. Rubinstein, *School Attendance in London* (1969); R. R. Sellman, *Devon Village Schools in the 19th Century* (1967), c. VIII.
14. See Appendix 2. On government policy, H. Roper, *Administering the Education Acts* (1976); G. Sutherland, *Policy-Making in Elementary Education* (1973).
15. Murphy, op.cit., p. 87.
16. E.g., C. F. Routledge, HMI's remark that, in many villages which he had classed as 'black or dark spots', school work had gone on 'unknown . . . to me, and yet in a highly satisfactory manner' (PP. 1875 XXIV, p. 142).
17. PP. 1887 XXIX, qq. 16530 ff.; 1895 XLIV, p. 562.

18. PP. 1884 XXXI, qq. 3760–64.
19. See J. S. Hurt, 'Board School or Voluntary School', p. 13, in History of Education Society, *New Approaches to the Study of Popular Education* (1979); Sellman, op.cit., p. 65.
20. National Society School files, Moreton-in-Marsh.
21. PP. 1876 XXIII, p. 287; Hurt, op.cit., p. 11.
22. PP. 1887 XXIX, q.25957.
23. E.g., Darley Abbey: M. Johnson, *Derbyshire Village Schools in the 19th Century* (1971), p. 199.
24. Oct. 1878: J. Bailey (ed.), *The Diary of Lady Frederick Cavendish* (1927), vol. 2, pp. 223–4.
25. Log Books, Sandbach National, Boys, Girls (Ches. CRO); *Chester Courant*, 18/9/1918; E. M. Sneyd-Kinnersley, HMI (1908).
26. Loc. cit., q. 16708. An excess of zeal was shown by a curate at Christ Church, Northam in 1872, who was scarcely ever out of the schools (Gadd, op. cit.).
27. PP. 1884 XXXI(1), App. p. 155. Other examples: St Margaret's, Whalley Range (ibid.); St Peter's Wolverhampton; Holly Hall, Dudley (1874, XVIII, p. 116); St Paul's Stepney (1878, XXVIII, pp. 493–4); St Matthias, Eccleshall (J. Bingham, *The Period of the Sheffield School Board* (1949), p. 47).
28. PP. 1895 XLVIII, p. 132; P. & H. Silver, *The Education of the Poor* (1974), p. 116.
29. PP. 1887 XXIX, q. 25254 (Selmeston).
30. PP. 1880 XXII, p. 275.
31. See Appendix 2.
32. Johnson, op. cit., pp. 178–82.
33. Description by Amy Fildes, headmistress 1895–8 (Derby Lonsdale College Archives).
34. PP. 1867–8 XXV, p. 127; 1880, XXII, p. 244.
35. PP. 1881 XXXII, p. 274; other examples are recorded.
36. E.g., a boy who inadvertently learnt up a domestic-economy textbook, was examined and refused grant only on account of his sex (Seaborne & Isham, op. cit., pp. 18–19).
37. E.g., PP. 1876 XXIII, p. 382; 1880 XXII, pp. 277–8 (Wakefield); 1882 XXIII, p. 277 (Leamington); 1887 XXIX, q. 33839 (Liverpool).
38. Apart from the South Kensington School of Cookery, the Northern Union had schools in Liverpool, Leeds and Glasgow (evidence of Miss F. Calder, PP. 1887 XXIX, qq. 29054 ff.).
39. PP. 1898 XXVI 417, qq. 5892, 12995–8.
40. Catholic Poor School Committee, *Annual Report* (1866), pp. xlviii–xlix.
41. See P. Gordon, *The Victorian School Manager* (1974), c. 6.
42. PP. 1884 XXIV, p. 459; Gordon op. cit., pp. 109, 120.
43. PP. 1887 XXIX, qq. 26259 ff.
44. No grant could be claimed on any student until he had successfully completed his probation: PP. 1863 XLVII, pp. xliv–xlvii.
45. Bishop Otter College: LMH [ubbard]., *Work for Ladies in Elementary Schools* (1872); PP. 1886 XXV, qq. 13408 ff. (evidence of Miss F. Trevor).

46. See Sellman's figures for Devon, op. cit., p. 86.
47. Figures in PP. 1888 XXXVI 489; Bradley, op. cit., p. 162.
48. F. Smith, *Sir James Kay-Shuttleworth* (1923), p. 107; PP. 1843 XL 217, p. 285 (Derwent Coleridge on the aims of St Mark's College).
49. Reprinted in Seaborne & Isham, op. cit., pp. 26–35.
50. C. Morley, *Studies in Board Schools* (1897), pp. 290–310.
51. E.g., the antics of 'Mr Smith' (Gosden, op. cit., pp. 73–4), or the South Normanton Board's declaration of omnipotence (Johnson, op. cit., p. 150).
52. J. Runciman, *Schools and Scholars* (1887), pp. 95, 200; PP. 1886 XXV, q. 10021; Gordon, op. cit., p. 231; E. Holmes, *In quest of an ideal* (1920), p. 119.
53. See above, 4H(ii), 5E.
54. E.g., Hull, PP. 1887 XXIX, q. 35921.
55. Cf. D. Rubinstein, 'The London School Board', pp. 251–3, in McCann, op. cit.
56. PP. 1887 XXIX, qq. 32746–7. Heller trained at Cheltenham when it was producing teachers like Coomber of the Bristol Trade School.
57. Liverpool, 1876 (PP. 1887 XXIX, q. 32157); Birmingham, 1880 (loc. cit., qq. 30801–22); Nottingham, 1884 (D. Wardle, *Education and Society in 19th. Century Nottingham* (1971), pp. 92–3.
58. PP. 1886 XXV, qq. 12749–54; 1892 XXVIII, pp. 423–4.
59. Reprinted in E. Eaglesham, *From School Board to Local Authority* (1956), pp. 184–90.
60. PP. 1867–8 XXVIII Part IV, qq. 14834–43; W. E. Marsden, 'Social Environment, School Attendance and Educational Achievement in a Merseyside Town', p. 208, in McCann, op. cit.; PP. 1895 XLV, q. 8619. This evidence of Dr Forsyth is a useful source (qq. 8232 ff.).
61. See above, p. 179; PP. 1873 XXIV, p. 104; H. Sandford, *The Gradation of Schools* (1869), p. 7.
62. E.g., PP. 1867–8 XXVIII Part IX 323, p. 55 (Faversham Commercial), Part XVI App. (The Duke's School, Alnwick); 1872 XXV, q. 6388 (Keighley Trade School).
63. PP. 1870 XXII, p. 339.
64. Interview with Mr Smith, former HM of Lower Moseley Street School, *Manchester Evening Chronicle*, 13/3/1914.
65. See above, 5E; PP. 1884, XXXI(1) App., p. 157; 1881 XXXII, p. 384
66. References to these schools are scattered in HMI's reports, before and after 1870; see also PP. 1895 XLVIII.
67. Like other Chartist People's Colleges it had become primarily a day school for older children. The directors gave the foundation of University College as their reason for handing it over to the school board (Wardle, op. cit., p. 130) but an HMI referred to its 'precarious existence' before the take-over (PP. 1882 XXIII, pp. 419–20).
68. Wardle, op. cit., pp. 123–4. The origins of the Sheffield Central Higher School, which apparently took five years from conception to opening, are not clear (Bingham, op cit., pp. 28, 174–85).
69. PP. 1895 XLVIII, pp. 46–7, 165; 1898 XXVI 417, q. 14831.

70. Blyth, PP. 1895 XLV, q. 8389; Cambridge, PP. 1884–5 XXIII, p. 308. Others: PP. 1880 XXII, p. 333 (St Mary Redcliffe, J. P. Norris); 1887 XXIX, q. 22803 (Blackburn, Church); 1895 XLVIII, p. 336 (Bury, Catholic); Gordon, op. cit., p. 111 (Salisbury, the Bishop).
71. PP. 1895 XLIV, q. 1432.
72. Wardle, op. cit., p. 84; cf. P. Nelson, "Leicester Suburban School Boards', p. 57, in *History of Education*, vol. 6, no. 1 (1977).
73. Quoted in Gordon, op. cit., p. 239.
74. J. Burke, *The Manchester School Board: its Personnel, its Work, and its Future* (1880); for Dan-y-Craig, see Cruickshank, op. cit., p. 53.
75. *Barnsley Chronicle*, 1873: quoted in A. M. Davies, *The Barnsley School Board* (1965), p. 196.
76. PP. 1860 LIV, pp. 98–9; 1861 XXI Part V, p. 107; 1887 XXIX, qq. 40194, 40476.
77. Above, 6L(i); his evidence in PP. 1865 VI; 1875 XXIV, p. 98; 1878 XXVIII, p. 421.
78. PP. 1877 XXIX, pp. 496–8; 1884 XXXI(1) APP. pp. 203–5; 1887 XXIX, qq. 32626 ff., 33792 ff.; 1895 XLVI qq. 13278 ff.
79. Above, 2D; PP. 1867–8 XVI, q. 729; J. Venn, *Alumni Cantabrigienses*; PP. 1872 XXV, q. 7933; above, 6B(i); PP. 1872 XXV, qq. 851, 858; above, p. 238; *Who's Who* (1937); Bingham, op. cit., p. 111.
(1937); Bingham, op. cit., p. 111.
80. See G. T. Rimmington, 'English Rural School Boards', in History of Education Society, *Studies in the Local History of Education* (1977), pp. 34–45.
81. Protest organised by Brookfield and signed by forty-one inspectors: PP. 1864 IX 13, App. p. 50.
82. H. Johnson, *The "Sompting" Correlated Lessons* (undated); [E. Holmes] *A Village School* (printed privately and anonymously 1908); E. Holmes, *What is and what Might be* (1911); Fabian Society, *The Educational Muddle and the Way Out* (1901), p. 14.
83. A. H. D. Acland, *Memoir and Letters of Sir T. D. Acland* (1902), p. 279.

APPENDIX ONE

NOTES ON SOURCE MATERIALS

It is not intended that these notes should contain a comprehensive survey of sources. There is an excellent general survey in chapter VII of W. B. Stephens, *Sources for English Local History* (1973) which may be supplemented by R. J. Unwin and W. B. Stephens, *Yorkshire Schools and Schooldays: a Guide to Historical Sources and Their Uses* (1976). The Irish University Press's volume on *Education* (G. Sutherland and others, 1977) in the series 'Government and Society in Nineteenth Century Britain' is also useful. Whilst it is limited to those papers which form part of the Irish University Press's 'British Parliamentary Papers' series, the interpretative essays are helpful and the bibliographies comprehensive. The comments which follow seek only to supplement these works and to call attention to some of the special problems of investigating the nature of voluntary schooling.

Accurate statistics on nineteenth-century voluntary schools are hard to come by. Those collected by voluntary groups or individual polemicists were usually intended to further some cause and are consequently open to suspicion. Even the Educational Census of 1851, regarded by both contemporaries and modern students of the subject as the most reliable source on which to base estimates of voluntary provision, was dismissed by both Lingen and the Registrar General as too partial and imperfect to be useful.[1] The statistics in the *Reports* of the Education Department are incomplete since they refer only to grant-aided schools; whilst the survival of school records has been too much a matter of accident to justify the assumption that what still exists can be treated as a valid sample. Nor can material from one school be equated precisely with similar material from another; even such apparently straightforward evidence as that of accounts or attendance registers contains pitfalls. As the Education Department's auditor complained in 1866,[2] school fees were often retained by the teacher as part of his remuneration and never recorded as income whilst some managers paid bills out of their own pockets and never entered them as expenditure. Even when registers were accurately kept, their format could produce strange results. The overall attendance pattern at Winston (4G(ii)) was very similar to that recorded in 1866–7 in a register from Stalbridge, Dorset,[3] but the weekly attendance percentage appears to be higher, simply because the Stalbridge register was a standard form which was only re-written quarterly whilst the teacher at Winston used an ordinary exercise book and cleared out the dead wood every four or five weeks when turning over the page. The amount of published material available for comparison is at present limited; hence at the moment a clinical rather than a statistical approach to the activities of voluntary schools seems more rewarding.

Official material The few documents which escaped the general destruction of early Education Department records (in PRO Ed. 9 . . ., Ed. 11 . . .) are an indication of what might have been available had they survived. School files exist, of course, for the latter part of the century; for earlier years the *Minutes and Reports of the Committee of Council on Education* must be the basis for any study. The early inspectors' reports are of particular value; they are of enormous length and detail. Owing to the circumstances of their appointment, no attempt was made to muzzle HM Inspectors' freedom of speech before the early 1850s; and until 1856 the Department published summaries of the reports on individual schools. On the whole the Anglicans wrote the most informative reports, partly because, unlike their undenominational colleagues, most of them had been actively involved in running schools before entering government service and therefore tended to have a better understanding of the problems they encountered; still more because they worked in smaller districts in which they could, and frequently did, involve themselves in the general educational activities of the area.

The *Reports of the factories and mines inspectorates* provide a useful supplement and, sometimes, corrective to those of the Education Department. Both devoted attention to schools, the factory inspectors because of their statutory duty to supervise half-time, the Commissioner for Mines (Tremenheere) because, having been kicked upstairs from the school's inspectorate in 1843 to pacify the British and Foreign School Society, he regarded himself as an educational expert.

In addition to annual publications, *Parliamentary papers on education* range from the reports of the great commissions to returns, e.g., 4C(iii), produced in answer to Parliamentary questions.

They are discussed in the Irish University Press's publication cited above. Here two points may be made: (i) The reports on secondary and scientific education are important for the study of elementary schools. They all contain evidence from experts like Moseley, Best and Norris, whilst the later volumes of the Taunton Report provide an indispensable survey of endowed elementary, as well as secondary, schools. (ii) In addition to the obvious need to identify witnesses' bias before accepting their evidence it is important to distinguish between evidence collected by assistant commissioners and their glosses upon it, since many of them were ignorant of conditions in elementary schools, e.g., Bryce's frequently quoted remark in the Taunton Report that the natural-history collection which he found in Bispham Endowed School would have been unthinkable in a grant-aided school.[4]

Before 1870 there were no local statutory bodies concerned with elementary education. After 1870 the records of those *school boards* which cooperated with local voluntary schools are useful.

A discussion of the archives of the *voluntary societies* was published in 1975 by J. Alexander ('Endangered Source Material for the History of Teacher Training in England and Wales' in History of Education Society, *Archives and the Historian of Education*, pp. 1–12) which includes a useful survey of some of the scattered records of diocesan boards. Other diocesan material is sometimes of value, e.g., records of visitations by those bishops who were interested in schools. A published example is E. P. Baker (ed.), *Bishop Wilberforce's Visitation Returns for the Archdeaconry of Oxford, 1854* (1954).

The *National Society's school files* are an unrivalled source of information about the motives and the problems of voluntary-school managers, consisting, as they largely do, of appeals for funds written to the society as to friends and equals and consequently with more candour than was always shown to possibly hostile government officials. British and Foreign records were destroyed in an air raid, so nothing comparable survives for undenominational schools. All the societies, however, published voluminous *annual reports* which contain useful accounts of the activities of their inspectors.

The *periodicals* published by the societies were more than mouthpieces of their policies. The National Society's *Monthly*

Paper, in particular, provided a forum for the discussion of educational problems large and small, e.g., the plight of a girl whose father would not allow her to wear a crinoline and who was refused apprenticeship on the grounds that, without it, she would be the school laughing-stock.[5] *Other periodicals* published for or by teachers were naturally concerned with questions of salaries and conditions of service, but also devoted a lot of space to discussion of teaching methods and school organisation which has an immediacy greater than that to be found in many contemporary manuals, e.g., 6C(ii).

The publications of the *Society of Arts* and of the *Association for the Promotion of Social Science* are worth attention. Paget's half-time experiment, for example (4J) was first described in a paper to the Social Science Association.

Two types of *text books* may be identified: school books and manuals for the use of teachers and trainee teachers. Until the middle 1850s reading books were essentially lesson books, intended to combine the teaching of reading with the conveyance of useful information. Pre-eminent amongst these were subsidised books of the Irish National Commissioners, widely bought because they were cheaper than any others. Subsequently, reading books became more specialised whilst manuals or readers in individual subjects were provided for the more advanced children. There are several collections of such text books, notably that in the library of the School of Education of the University of Leicester; and, once they have been identified, many may be found in the British Library. But identification is not always easy since many authors preferred not to admit to such works. The naturalist W. B. Tegetmeier, for instance, who taught at the Home and Colonial College, never included his immensely successful *Manual of Domestic Economy* when he listed his publications and it is not mentioned in his obituaries.

The second type of textbooks are manuals of school management. A number were written by principals or masters of method in training colleges to accompany their method courses. These are particularly illuminating on the minutiae of organization and curriculum; an outstanding example is John Gill (master of method at Cheltenham), *Introductory Text Book to Method and School Management.* Other books on method were written for more general audiences to introduce new ideas (as with Richard Dawes's works) or simply because the author regarded himself as an authority. Curiously enough, one of the very few modern reprints of non-political Victorian texts on education is of a rather inferior example of the last category: Jelinger Symons, *School Economy* (1971).

Whilst the writings of politicians and secularists have been extensively studied, the many publications of *school managers and school promoters* have been almost totally neglected, although they provide a third dimension to official papers and local records essential for a balanced estimate of the work of the voluntary schools. In the nineteenth century publication was quick and cheap. It was normal practice to print in pamphlet form sermons, lectures and letters to newspapers. Most of the persons mentioned in this book indulged themselves thus. The semi-autonomous position of the inspectorate permitted even HM Inspectors to publish – not merely innocuous sermons, e.g., H. W. C. Bellairs, *Work, the Law of God, the Lot of Man* (1852), but more explosive material. When Frederick Watkins found his reports censored in the Education Department he presented his findings in pamphlet form (*A Letter to the Archbishop of York on the State of Education in the Church Schools in Yorkshire* (1860)). Every educational crisis produced a flood of pamphlets (1839–40, 1846–8, 1861–4, 1868–70), but there was always a steady stream of publications on such topics as urban problems, rural needs, technical education, attendance and experimental work. A successful pamphlet was a means of attracting support, used systematically by, for example, William Rogers. Every time his schools needed a large sum of money he published another pamphlet. Some examples of pamphlets are listed in the bibliography (pp. 261–2).

Best's *Manual* (IK) was intended for his parishioners but the large number of clergy manuals published at a time when training for parochial work barely existed give useful indications of the Anglican concept of the elementary school. Examples are John Armitstead, *Parochial Papers* (1851–5) and Archdeacon John Sandford (father of Henry, HMI, and uncle of Sir Francis, of the Education Department), *Parochialia: or Church, School, and Parish* (1845).

Family papers may provide evidence in the same field; whilst they have been extensively used for studies of the politics of education, e.g., the Granville papers and the Harrowby papers, they have much to yield about the minutiae of school life, e.g.,

IA,B,C,E. In the case of papers deposited in a record office the catalogue will usually indicate whereabouts, in the collection, school material may be found. Two points should be noted: estates are not confined by county boundaries, e.g., the Radnor correspondence covers schools far outside Berkshire; and personal correspondence is frequently of interest. Ties of blood relationship, marriage and friendship bound many of the most active school patrons to each other* and their interest is often reflected in their correspondence. Late nineteenth- and early twentieth-century biographies of the 'life and letters' type may provide useful leads.

Individual school records, studied not simply in the context of statements in textbooks of educational history but in conjunction with the sources listed above, have much to add to our understanding of development. A casual reading of, for example, a batch of log books in a record office will immediately suggest that contemporary assertions, e.g., about the effects of the Revised Code, or modern constructs, e.g., of the process of social control, need modification.

The printed *annual reports* circulated by the more prosperous schools do not survive in large numbers. In some schools they were regularly pasted into the managers' minute book but otherwise they only exist if some recipient happened to keep his copy. However, annual meetings, public examinations and prizegivings were usually reported in the *local press*, from which it is frequently possible to construct an adequate history of a school without the help of its records.

There has been immense destruction of such records. They have disappeared in salvage drives, been thrown out as rubbish, carried off as the personal property of the last head teacher on the closure of a school or used as scrap paper.† Until recently some

*E.g., the individuals involved in the revival of the National Society in the late 1830s belonged to an extensive network of this kind: Manning, the Gladstones, the Wilberforce brothers (Robert and Samuel), the Harrowby family, the Lytteltons, C. B. Adderley, Stafford Northcote, T. D. Acland, Henry Hoare, William Rogers, etc. In an earlier generation they connected with Mrs Hippisley Tuckfield, authoress of *Education for the People* (1839) and the Wenlock family, school promoters in East Yorkshire. Later they produced Lord Sandon, Lady Frederick Cavendish (Lucy Lyttelton) and, surprisingly, A. H. D. Acland.

†A friend of the author once saw the margins of an early log book in use as cricket score sheets.

local authorities showed no interest in their preservation; but the situation has improved in the last ten years and county record offices are now acquiring an increasing amount of material.*

The records most commonly encountered are *minute books, accounts, registers and log books*. When regularly kept, minute books are very informative (3H, 4D, 5A) but the futility of the long-drawn-out controversy over the management clauses is shown by the number of instances, Anglican, Wesleyan and undenominational, in which there are long gaps when some individual manager took sole responsibility for running the school. On the whole, London committees and those run by Quakers seem to have been the most assiduous; and ladies' committees were muchmore assiduous than the men. Some problems of using registers and accounts have already been noted; the comparatively rare instances of a hyper-conscientious treasurer retaining every bill and every receipt, e.g., St Peter's, Chesil, Winchester[6] are very valuable.

Log books deserve a paragraph to themselves. Every student of educational history must applaud Articles 55–63 of the Revised Code which prescribed their use. Indeed they could serve more general historical purposes. They would be a mine of information for students of meteorology or for the study of general religious and social attitudes, e.g., the sour comment of a low-church teacher upon a local farmer's marriage to a papist.[7] They provide a record of the day-to-day running of thousands of schools, especially valuable in the early stages when daily entries were compulsory and when the head teacher was directly involved in the teaching of every pupil. Moreover they reveal teachers writing unaffectedly, without the self-conscious polish which many of them applied to their speeches and their contributions to periodicals. A few resented log books and filled their pages (until discouraged by HM Inspector) with OP (ordinary progress) or even NTR (nothing to report). Others made their entries dull or lively according to their own personalities. Many used log books as a means of self-expression, recording their hopes and fears, their struggles and successes; some unconsciously revealed what trials

*A complication for researchers seeking the records of an individual school is that if they were deposited before 1973 they remain in the archives of the county to which it then belonged, irrespective of its position after local-government reorganisation.

they themselves must have been to their employers and their pupils. As time went on, log-book entries inevitably became more formalised and mechanical; but though less interesting, they retain their value as records.

School photography first appeared in the 1860s. Thus an absentee patroness arranged in 1866 for the children of Sissinghurst School to be photographed so that she might keep up her knowledge of them.[8] School and class photographs portray the stance of the teacher, the state of health and nourishment of the pupils and, in respectable schools, the cut of their best clothes. Indoor photographs, inevitably (given the necessary length of exposure) artificially posed, are nevertheless useful records of *equipment and furniture* of which some examples are preserved in certain museums, notably in the University of Leeds Museum of Educational History (for a brief discussion of the topic see R. Pallister, 'Educational Capital in the Elementary School of the Mid-nineteenth Century' in *History of Education*, vol. 2, no. 2 (1973), pp. 147–58). Additional evidence may be sought in the engravings which accompany advice on buildings and methods in the manuals discussed above, and in commercial advertisements.

School buildings have been authoritatively studied by M. Seaborne, *The English School* (1971). The plans submitted with applications for State building grants escaped the general destruction of Education Department records and are now held by the appropriate county record office; they are worth attention. Large numbers of buildings now destroyed are recorded in photographs but many nineteenth-century schools still survive as church halls, commercial premises, or, modified and extended, serving their original purpose. The worst voluntary buildings, like the worst board-school buildings, are gone, pulled down or fallen down; but enough remains to throw light both on the layout considered appropriate for the schooling of the masses and on the assumptions of the founders. The opulence of Titus Salt's schools at Saltaire, the sober Cotswold dignity of Painswick National School, the rustic prettiness of many a village school built by the local Lady Bountiful show that urban school boards were not the only lavish spenders in this field; differences of expenditure were as great before as after 1870.

Notes

1. To Granville, 28/9/1853 (PRO 30/29, Box 23, Part 2).
2. PP. 1867 XXII, pp. xxxi–lvii.
3. Stalbridge Attendance Register (Dorset CRO).
4. PP. 1867–8 XXVIII, Part VIII, p. 692.
5. *Monthly Paper*, 1865, pp. 230, 246–7.
6. In Hampshire CRO, 1840–44.
7. Nympsfield CE Log Book, 25/2/1865 (Gloucestershire CRO).
8. See Log Book in Kent Archives.

APPENDIX TWO

SUMMARY OF MAINTENANCE GRANT REGULATIONS FOR ELEMENTARY SCHOOLS, 1846–99

1. *Minutes of 1846*
   A. *To Pupil-Teachers* – after satisfactory completion of each year's apprenticeship, Year 1, £10, rising by £2.10s. p.a. to year 5 £20.
   – after satisfactory completion of apprenticeship, on examination, Queen's Scholarships of £20 (2nd class) or £25 (1st class) at inspected Normal School ($\frac{2}{3}$ds for women).
   B. *To Stipendiary Monitors* – for 4 years – after satisfactory completion of each year – Year 1, £5, rising by £2.10s. p.a. to Year 4, £12.10s.
   C. Gratuities to *Teachers* for instruction of the above – for pupil-teachers, £5 for one; £9 for two; £12 for three; £3 additional for every other.
   – for stipendiary monitors, £2.10s. for one; £4.10s for two; £6 for three; £1.10s. additional for every other.
   D. *To Certificated Masters* – augmentation grant of from £15 to £30 (depending on class of certificate) provided managers pay salary of double the grant and provide a house rent free or the equivalent ($\frac{2}{3}$ for mistresses).
2. *1852* Grants to *Assistants* – Grants of £25 (male), £20 (female) to ex-pupil-teachers serving as assistants in inspected schools under certificated teachers.
3. *1853 Capitation Grant* – for schools in agricultural districts and unincorporated towns (under 5000 pop.) Annual grant to schools admissible under Minutes of 1846 for each scholar attending 192 days (reduced to 176; 88 in the case of half-timers) of:

No. of scholars in school	*Boys*	*Girls*
Under 50	6s.	5s.
50–100	5s.	4s.
Over 100	4s.	3s.

Provided i. Income of 14s. per boy, 12s. per girl
ii. Fees charged of between 1d. and 4d.
iii. Mixed schools under mistress excluded (modified, 1854).

4. *1853* Grants to *Registered Teachers* – All teachers, to qualify for pupil-teachers or capitation grant, henceforward to hold certificates or, if over 35, to pass Registration examination, showing 'sound, if humble attainment'.
5. *1854* Grants to *Infant Teachers* – after one year's training course and examination – augmentation grant, Class 1, as for Class 3 Certificate; Class 2, £8.
6. *1855* Grants to *Night School Teachers* – £5–£10 p.a. for night school teachers not otherwise receiving public money *provided* fees equal grant and school connected with day school.
7. *1856 Capitation Grant* extended to qualified schools in urban areas.
8. *1858* Cancellation of (2). Stipends of £25 (male), £20 (female) to probationer teachers for two years after passing certificate examination provided *either*: teacher of small rural school *or*: assistant to certificated teacher in large school.
9. *1859* Number of *pupil-teachers* limited to 4 pupil-teachers to one master or mistress.

ALL ABOVE REGULATIONS CANCELLED BY REVISED CODE

10. *1862 Revised Code* – Grants to schools under certificated teachers.
    A. On *Average Attendance* – 4s. per scholar, day school; 2s.6d., night school.
    B. On *examination of 3Rs* – (i) of scholars over 6 years old attending day school 200 sessions, 8s. (2s.8d. per pass in each subject).
    (ii) of scholars attending night school 24 sessions, 5s. (1s.8d. per subject).
    C. On *attendance* – every scholar under 6 years old, being present at inspection, attending 200 sessions, subject to HMI's report of suitability of instruction, 6s.6d.
    provided – parents are of labouring classes (Article 4).
    subject to reduction (Article 52):
    i. on recommendation of HMI

ii. if staff insufficient
iii. by excess over fees and subscriptions
iv. by excess over 15s per scholar on average attendance.

11. *1863* Grant reduced by amount of any annual *endowment* (Article 52d).
12. *1864* (11) cancelled in rural schools provided grant and endowment combined not in excess of 15s. per scholar.
13. *1865* (12) extended to all schools.
14. 1867 *Additional Grants*
    A. of 1s.4d. per pass (not exceeding £8 per school)
    provided i. staffing meets requirements of Code
    ii. number of passes in 3Rs exceeds 200% of average attendance of children over 6 years old.
    iii. one or more of 'higher subjects' on time-table in which 1/5th of number in average attendance over 6 years pass satisfactory examination.

    B. of 8s. on examination (for 1 year) of children already passed in Standard VI provided pass examination under A iii.
    C. of £10 for every male pupil-teacher entering training college with Class 1 pass; £5 for Class 2,
    of £8 for every male ex-pupil-teacher who at end of first year's training passes in 1st Division; £5 for 2nd Division.

[From this point the regulations become increasingly complex; only the major changes are listed below]

15. *1870* (Education Act) Grant to be reduced by excess over income from all other sources. (see 10Ciii, 13)
16. *1871* (10A,B,C and 14Aiii modified as follows):
    A. On *Average Attendance* – 6s. per scholar.
    B. On *examination* – (i) of 3Rs, of scholars attending 250 sessions, 12s. per scholar (4s. per subject).
    (ii) of 3s. per scholar on one or two *specific subjects* (listed) in Standard IV +.
    C. On *attendance* – every scholar 4–7 years old, attending 250 sessions, 8s.; 10s. if taught in separate department.
    D. (15) to apply when grant in excess of 15s. per scholar.
17. *1875* (16Bi) reduced to 3s. per subject. Grant of 4s. per scholar in average attendance aged 7+ and in Standard II+

on passes in two *class subjects*: grammar, geography, history, plain needlework [subsequently and frequently modified].

18. *1876* (Education Act) (16D) cancelled. Reduction to apply when grant in excess of 17s.6d. per scholar.
19. *1882*
    A. Grants to be calculated on proportion of number of passes to number presented.
    B. Standard VII (see 14B) formally constituted.
    C. *Merit grant* payable on report of inspection, of 1s. (fair), 2s. (good), 3s. (excellent) per scholar in average attendance.
    D. Grant for *class subjects* (of which one must be English) of 1s. or 2s.
    E. Grants of 4s. per scholar for *specific subjects* payable only to Standard V+.
    F. For course of 40 lessons in *practical cookery* to girls over 12 years, 4s. per scholar.
20. *1890* (16A,B,C, 19A,C,D cancelled)
    A. *Principal grant* of 12s.6d. or 14s. and 'discipline and organisation' grant of 1s. or 1s.6d. per scholar in average attendance payable on *report of inspection.*
    B. All scholars present liable to examination.
    C. *£10 grant* to schools with population under 500 in 2 mile radius.
21. *1891* (Education Act) Grant of *10s. per scholar* in lieu of fees to schools in which fees abolished or reduced; not to be included in calculation of 17s.6d. limit (18).
22. *1897* (Voluntary Schools Act)
    A. Grant of up to 5s per head on average attendance to necessitous schools.
    B. (18) repealed; no reduction of grant by excess over income.

SELECT BIBLIOGRAPHY

This bibliography is confined to books and pamphlets especially relevant to the theme of this book; and does not list articles cited in the notes or references in Appendix One.

CONTEMPORARY MATERIAL

GENERAL

Akroyd, E., *On Factory Education, and Its Extension*, 1858.
Armitstead, J., *On the Means Possessed by the Church for the Education of the People*, 1847;
Popular Education: Its Present Condition and Future Prospects Considered, 1856.
Baines, E., *Letters to . . . Lord John Russell on State Education*, 1846.
Bartley, G. C. T., *The Educational Condition and Requirements of One Square Mile in the East End of London* (2nd edn), 1870.
Briggs, A. (ed.), F. Adams, *History of the Elementary School Contest* and J. Morley, *The Struggle for National Education* (reprints), 1972.
B.[rotherton], E., *The Present State of Popular Education in Manchester and Salford*, 1864.
Fabian Society, *The Educational Muddle and the Way Out*, 1901.
Hadden, R. H. (ed.), *Reminiscences of William Rogers* (2nd edn), 1888.
Hutton, W. H. (ed.), *The autobiography of Robert Gregory, 1819–1911*, 1912.
Lyttelton, Lord, *Thoughts on National Education*, 1855.
Manning, H. E., *National Education*, 1838.
Morris, N. (ed.), Sir J. Kay-Shuttleworth, *Four Periods of Popular Education* (reprint), 1973.
National Education Union, *The Debate in Parliament during the Progress of the Education Bill*, 1870.
National Society, *The Church Education Directory*, 1853.
Richson, C., *Education in "Trade Schools" Necessary to Promote National Education*, 1853.
Sadler, M. and Edwards, J. W., *Public Elementary Education in England and Wales, 1870–1895: Special Reports on Educational Subjects*, 1897.
Sandford, H., *The Gradation of Schools*, 1869.
School Board Chronicle, *School Board and Attendance Committee Directory*, 1878.
Wilberforce, R. I., *On the Establishment of a National Board of Education*, 1839;
On the System of Inspection Best Adapted for National Education, 1840.
Yorke, G. A., *The School and the Workshop: Why Should They not Combine?*, 1856.
Zincke, F. B., *Why Must We Educate the Whole People? and What Prevents Our Doing It?*, 1850.

SCHOOLS AND SCHOOLING

Ashburton Lord, *Ashburton Prizes for the Teaching of Common Things* (2nd edn), 1854.

Austin, S., *Two Letters on Girls' Schools*, 1857.

British and Foreign School Society, *A Handbook to the Borough Road Schools*, 1854.

Burdett-Coutts, A. G., *Prizes for Common Things* (2nd edn), 1856.

Chester, H., *Hints on the Building and Management of Schools*, 1860.

Dawes, R., *Hints on an Improved and Self-paying System of National Education*, 1847;

Suggestive Hints towards Improved Secular Instruction, 1847;

The Teaching of Common Things, 1854.

Ellis, W., *On the Importance of Imparting a Knowledge of the Principles of Social Science to Children*, 1859.

Finchley National and Industrial Schools, *The Finchley Manuals of Industry: I Cooking.* II *Gardening.* III *Household Work.* IV *Plain Needlework*, 1852.

Flint, J., *Plain Hints for Organizing and Teaching a Church School*, 1856.

Hawtrey, S., *A Narrative-Essay on a Liberal Education*, 1868.

Hill, A. (ed.), *Essays upon Educational Subjects, Read at the Educational Conference*, 1857 (reprint), 1971.

[Holmes, E. G. A.], *A Village School* (privately printed), 1908.

Home and Colonial School Society, *Hints on the Establishment of Schools for Early Education*, (5th edn), 1851.

H.[ubbard] L. M., *Work for Ladies in Elementary Schools*, 1872.

Jenyns, L., *Memoir of the Rev. John Stevens Henslow*, 1862.

Johnson, H. Finlay, *The "Sompting" Correlated Lessons, N. D.* (1906).

Morley, C., *Studies in Board Schools*, 1897.

Moseley, H., *Trade Schools*, 1853.

Norris, J. P., *The Education of the People; Our Weak Points and Our Strength*, 1869.

Norris, W. F., *Elementary Schools*, 1904.

Salmon, D., *The Practical Parts of Lancaster's 'Improvements' and Bell's 'Experiment'*, 1932.

Sneyd-Kinnersley, E. M., *H.M.I.*, 1908.

Society of Arts, *Report of the Committee Appointed . . . to Inquire into Industrial Education*, 1853;

Catalogue of the Educational Exhibition, 1854.

Stow, D., *The Training System of Education*, 1836.

Templar, B., *Ten Years' Experience of the Manchester Free School*, 1866.

Thompson, Sir H., *National Schools: Hints on the Duty of Diocesan Inspection* (2nd edn), 1848.

Unwin, W. J., *The Primary School*, 1862.

LATER WORKS

GENERAL

Ball, N., *Her Majesty's Inspectorate, 1839–1849*, 1963.

Bingham, J. H., *The Period of the Sheffield School Board*, 1949.

Binns, H. B., *A Century of Education, 1808–1908*, 1908.
Blyth, E. K., *The Life of William Ellis* (2nd edn), 1892.
Bradley, J. L., *Chester College and the Training of Teachers*, 1975.
Burgess, H. J., *Enterprise in Education*, 1958.
Chadwick, O., *The Victorian Church*: Part 1, *1966*. Part 2, *1970*.
Clark, G. Kitson, *Churchmen and the Condition of England, 1832–1885*, 1973.
Cruickshank, M., *Church and State in English Education*, 1963.
Davies, A. M., *The Barnsley School Board, 1871–1903*, 1965.
Dunford, J. E., *Her Majesty's Inspectorate of Schools in England and Wales, 1860–1870*, 1980.
Eaglesham, E., *From School Board to Local Authority*, 1956.
Gordon, P., *The Victorian School Manager*, 1974.
History of Education Society *New Approaches to the Study of Popular Education*, 1979.
Hughes, T., *James Fraser, Second Bishop of Manchester*, 1887.
Hurt, J., *Education in Evolution*, 1971;
Elementary Schooling and the Working Classes 1860–1918, 1979.
Jones, M. G., *The Charity School Movement*, 1938;
Hannah More, 1952.
McCann, P. (ed.), *Popular Education and Socialisation in the Nineteenth Century*, 1977.
McClatchey, D., *Oxfordshire Clergy, 1777–1879*, 1960.
Murphy, J., *Church, State and Schools in Britain, 1800–1970*, 1971;
The Education Act 1870, 1972.
Paz, D. G., *The Politics of Working Class Education in Britain*, 1830–*50*, 1980.
Roper, H., *Administering the Elementary Education Acts, 1870–1885*, 1976.
Rubinstein, D., *School Attendance in London, 1870–1904*, 1969.
Selby, D., *Towards a Common System of National Education. Cardinal Manning and Educational Reform*, 1977.
Sturt, M., *The Education of the People*, 1967.
Sutherland, G., *Policy-Making in Elementary Education, 1870–1895*, 1973.
Tropp, A., *The School Teachers*, 1957.
Wardle, D., *Education and Society in Nineteenth Century Nottingham*, 1971.
West, E. G., *Education and the Industrial Revolution*, 1975.

SCHOOLS AND SCHOOLING

Bamford, T. W., *The Evolution of Rural Education, 1850–1964*, 1965.
Bramwell, R. D., *Elementary School Work, 1900–1925*, 1961.
Docking, J. W., *Victorian Schools and Scholars: Church of England Elementary Schools in Nineteenth Century Coventry*, 1967.
Gadd, E. W., *Victorian Logs, 1863–1877*, 1979.
Goldstrom, J., *The Social Content of Education, 1808–1870*, 1972.
Gosden, P. H. G. H., *How They were Taught*, 1969.
Horn, P., *Education in Rural England, 1800–1914*, 1978.
Johnson, M., *Derbyshire Village Schools in the Nineteenth Century*, 1971.
Layton, D., *Science for the People*, 1973.
Seaborne, M. and Isham, Sir G., *A Victorian Schoolmaster: J. J. Graves*, 1967.
Sellman, R. R., *Devon Village Schools in the Nineteenth Century*, 1967.
Silver, P. and H., *The Education of the Poor; the History of a National School*, 1974.

INDEX